Frozen Desire

Frozen Desire

the meaning of money

James Buchan

Farrar Straus Giroux / New York

Farrar, Straus and Giroux
19 Union Square West, New York 10003

Copyright © 1997 by James Buchan
All rights reserved
Printed in the United States of America
Published in the United Kingdom by Macmillan Ltd, London, 1997
First American edition, 1997

Library of Congress Cataloging-in-Publication Data
Buchan, James.
    Frozen desire : the meaning of money / James Buchan.
        p.   cm.
    ISBN 0-374-15909-2 (cloth : alk. paper)
    1. Money—History—Miscellanea. I. Title.
HG231.B79   1997
332.4—DC21   97-16107

IN MEMORIAM

CONRADI JOSTEN NOVESIENSIS

1912–1994

Contents

'Tis of great use to the sailor to know the length of his line, tho' he cannot with it fathom all the depths of the ocean. 'Tis well he knows that it is long enough to reach the bottom, at such places as are necessary to direct his voyage, and caution him against running upon shoals that may ruin him. Our business here is not to know all things, but those which concern our conduct. If we can find out those measures, whereby a rational creature, put in that state which man is in the world, may and ought to govern his opinions and actions depending thereon, we need not be troubled that some other things escape our knowledge.

Locke, *An Essay Concerning Human Understanding*

Frozen Desire

Introduction

*Le Ciel m'ayant permis de réussir à faire la pierre philosophale,
après avoir passé trente-sept ans à sa recherche, veillé au moins
quinze cents nuits, éprouvé des malheurs sans nombre et des pertes
irréparables, j'ai cru devoir offrir à la jeunesse, l'espérance de son
pays, le tableau déchirant de ma vie.*

Hermès Dévoilé, 1832

Having succeeded by Heaven's grace in making the philosopher's
stone, after thirty-seven years in the quest, at least fifteen hundred
nights without sleep, countless misfortunes and irreparable losses, I
have thought it my duty to offer young people, in whom our
country rests its hope, the shattering image of my life.

I first thought about money in 1978, in the city of Jeddah on the
Red Sea. I thought about banknotes, collected in bundles and held
by twine, and delivered to my hand, in an unsealed airmail envelope,
on the last Wednesday of each lunar month. I had had money
before, handled, spent, hoarded, won and lost money, but never in
such quantity or in so exotic and repellent a shape. I had come to
the city not to accumulate money but to evade it, or rather to delay
my induction into manhood; and yet here I was, sheathed in air-
conditioned sweat, signing for ten thousand Saudi Arabian riyals in
bills, the price of a month's labour, boredom and misery.

In those days I worked at a newspaper I'll call the *Saudi News*. It
was in a plywood building at the end of the airport runway, and the
newspaper and the building and the airport have since vanished; for
they were embarrassing physical reminders of an earlier epoch in
Saudi history, the years before 1973, before money. The quadrupling

of the dollar price of crude oil at the end of that year had detonated the world's trading system, and money was streaming into Saudi Arabia as once the silver of America into Spain. The burden of world history had passed to a few pale, fat men gliding like phantoms at noon towards their Lincoln Town Cars. The Muslim civilisations of Egypt and India, with their ancient architecture and civil sentiments, had become worthless. Europeans and Americans waited for days in the anterooms of dozing assistant deputy undersecretaries of state. The British, who had once set up and knocked down these princelings, wheedled and bribed with the best of them.

For two years, every day of the week except Thursday, I left home at three in the afternoon and crossed the silent blazing city to this ramshackle address. I worked till three in the morning, then went down, and inhaling the damp of early morning – it was never chill – threw a twist of paper to wake the Yemeni printer asleep on a mattress of newsprint. Occasionally, as I walked home, there was a fugitive breath of wind, or I found myself in a fabulous suburbs that had not existed the week before, raised like a volcanic island in the eruption of money. Stretched out on my sodden bed, as the air-conditioners began to beat, beat, beat in unison or the trucks ground like teeth at Palestine Circle, I thought that whatever I'd expected of life, it wasn't this. An hour or two later, the *Saudi News* was delivered and confirmed my existence, yet with inexplicable injuries: here a caption dropped, there King Khaled cropped to his nostrils, and inside, a story unravelled like an old sleeve to fill an aching void of white.

The room I worked in had two windows blocked by air-conditioners, four steel desks, four burst chairs and four manual typewriters, a telephone with one outside line, a glutinous carpet and a strip of fluorescent light. On that Wednesday night, the last of the lunar month, I sensed the room begin to shake and roar; the accountant glided in with his briefcase and flip-flops; a blizzard of Arabic greeting ('My darling,' 'My sweet'); and then the haul of envelopes from the briefcase, like fish pulled in on a hand-line.

This moment wanted to appear – and perhaps did appear to some of my friends in the room – as a moment of unity that abolished our identities as British or Yemeni or Indian or Egyptian and relabelled us as men, who labour and are paid. The banknotes, with portraits of King Abdul Aziz ibn Saud (who never had any money till Standard Oil of California gave him thirty-five thousand gold sovereigns in 1933) or King Faisal (who was murdered in 1975), were our common consolation for the nights of work and days without sleep, the indifference of our hosts, the misery of our women if we had them and of our solitude if we hadn't. And for the treadmill of heat.

Within the consolation of money was an exasperation. These banknotes inflamed our particular or national humiliations. For the Egyptian, it could not make good the demolition of a worldly Arab culture that had arisen in the metropolises of the Delta and flourished in the Arab nationalism of Abdul Nasser; nor soothe, for Nasser ed Din of Lucknow, the secret disappointment he'd felt at his Pilgrimage; while it reminded the Eritreans and Sudanese and the Somali head proof-reader with scars on his cheeks, that their grandfathers and grandmothers had been slaves. Their bearing towards me, communicated not in words but in reflexes, was tinged with shame and pity: that an Englishman, whose grandfathers had organised these sheikhs, sold them armoured cars and biplanes if they were good and, if they were bad, shipped them on destroyers to picturesque islets, should now take their pay. The riyals were consolation and exasperation, and intolerable but for one other secret they concealed: they were the means of escape. Not escape, in the sense that they could buy an airplane ticket to Sanaa or Djibouti, though they could, for nobody might leave the country without a visa from the Foreign Office beside its stinking lagoon, and that must itself by endorsed by the proprietor; but in a sense that contained a whole existence, away from this hell-hole: a corner shop one day in Murree or Dindigul, or a rental flat in Helwan, or a father's brother's daughter just turning sixteen. For a moment, those dreams of liberty vibrated in the roaring plywood room.

The moment dissipated. My friends picked up their money; gripped it at the twine between the middle and index finger of the right hand; flicked it over; and with the thumb counted the notes fanned by the counter-force of the flick. This action, both familiar and deft, occupied them for half a minute; but I left my money uncounted. That was for several reasons. I was not capable of such dexterity – I'd tried and taken instruction. I was indifferent to its sum, not just because a hundred-riyal note really would not be missed in a ten-thousand-riyal bundle; but also because I sensed that indifference, the vice and virtue of the British, was my chief protection in this gaol and linked me to our masters, who themselves never really believed in the prosperity that had fallen on them in a few days of October 1973, and could quite happily return to herding and growing dates and trading bullion and fleecing pilgrims. Nothing about the city had any permanence or conviction. F-15s gathered dust at the end of the runway amid a litter of surface-to-air missiles; Corvairs were abandoned on the Corniche still with their dealership stickers; palaces looked ready to tumble the day their wooden scaffolding came down: restless and indifferent expenditure, like the million dollars the Crown Prince had lost as a young man in half an hour at Monte Carlo. (In fact, the Saudis did squander their fortune, first in equipping the Iraqi armed forces and then, in 1991, in paying British and United States mercenaries to destroy them.)

What need had I of money? There was nothing I wanted to buy in the suq, except a camera with a long lens to photograph baboons (which I broke over somebody's head and didn't replace) and whisky, which came in in the holds of C-130 aircraft and cost two hundred and fifty riyals a bottle (about £40 in 1978 money, about £100 today). I had no interest in what people now call positional goods, for where were my witnesses, my publicity? Not this demoralised Babel or a dying generation in England, absorbed in a society that was manifestly on its last legs: the future, in the shape of Margaret Thatcher's handbag, was at that moment struggling to take form. And though my mind's eye filled with lawns and swimming pools, tended by placid women, cold horses, bank robbery, spectacular and maudlin acts of secret charity, inextricable frauds, my intellect told me those were merely metaphors of extinction or escape. I didn't care to provide for my old age, for I didn't think I'd have one. Anyway, I couldn't put out the money at interest, for interest was *haram* (anathema), and the banks paid their depositors just half a per cent of commission (while they lent their money abroad at eight, and earned fabulous profits and no doubt a fair stay in hell). I could not own real estate for rent, for that was denied to foreigners. I could not put the money at risk, for there was no stock market, jsut as there was no income tax or social security. (The next year, a group of Hadhrami merchants in the suq tried to corner the world's gold market; and for a month or two, the money price of gold rose steeply and my friends bought bars of it downtown, including one of ten kilograms, a handsome thing. As they bustled in each afternoon, they seemed inflated to abnormal size by their unrealised capital gains, and their sympathy for me became palpable, expressed in small acts of consideration or contempt. Then the corner collapsed, and my friends deflated and for three weeks of afternoons and nights, nobody spoke a word.) Each evening, after the edition, I'd carry my liquid person downtown, down cratered streets and over building sites to toy with electronics in the suq or eat dinner among inconsolable Lebanese at Keymak Glace: dreaming, as I think the tourist dreams, of some relation with the host country other than money purchase.

Yet I saw that money was a deep, almost unbreakable, social relation. The banknote I gave the Lebanese waiter was not a simple object, whose function could be deduced quite quickly, like a pencil or, once the control-knob has been found, a television. The engraved swirls and signs, even the King's portrait, did not suddenly reveal the note's purposes to someone who knew nothing of money. The banknote was an outcrop of some vast mountain of social arrangements, rather as the little peaks called *nunataks* that I later marvelled at in Antarctica, are the tips of Everests buried under miles of ice. It occurred to me that, in using money, I had submitted to the authority of a society of which I knew little, but in which I found as much to deplore as admire: subscribed, as it were, to the tottering triangles in the suq that were women or the tense scamper after Friday prayers when we all coralled into an open space downtown to witness a beheading. There was something sacramental about my pay: that I'd offered up to some higher organ my primary social relations, that it was to me and my friends as a flag is to a regiment or a crucifix to the Christians. I felt compelled. I was not a volunteer of Saudi Arabia or any society: I had been pressed. My wages came to me not to satisfy any need – mine were anyway private, affectionate, atrocious – but to make my needs universal: to incorporate me in the mainstream of men and things in which my work was not for me but for everybody; and to take what was special in me, my most secure and precious sense of myself, and make it general and banal. In short, I was to be civilised.

I read Adam Smith for the first time that year. I saw that of his three great, original and constituent orders of society, I belonged not with the landowner or capitalist, but with the labourer. I received labourer's wages, whose real value arose not in the money I received but – Smith again, forty pages later – in what could be got with them and that was nothing. I realised that I was a prisoner or a slave.

*

A man of twenty-three should occupy his thoughts with women. If they are abstracted from him, if they are so alien that he forgets even their anatomy, his mind has empty places which must be colonised. Of the young women I'd been attached to, I had two mementoes: a diamond bracelet that spelled the name of a famous racehorse with its hasp broken – I was anxious to return it and did – and the occasional letter which might have contained some crystalline narcotic: if so, it had been dissolved into the paper by the humidity, and therefore useless for sensation or commerce or patronage or any purpose, except to get me executed. After a while, these women seemed to me inexplicable, as if of a different medium, of water or sky.

In my cauldron of solitude and desire, I thought I should try to learn to think and, for the first time, down ways not chosen for me by teachers or professors or the set questions of newspapers and television. I thought there must be some reason why I was doing what I was doing. For a while, I decided I was learning a trade. But going into the press at three in the morning, crushing a ball of paper to throw at the printer in his Madras kilt, I sensed that I was the last man in the world to have learned hot-metal typesetting. No doubt I was also learning Arabic, a difficult language; but in reality, I was forgetting even the moderate amount I knew.

There were occasions those years when I felt a sort of relief, and most often in the desert at night or in the deep sea. On the escarpment behind the town, while trucks grunted around the hair-pins on the road up to Taif, I gaped at the squabbling baboons as the sun turned to ghee in the west; and as it dissolved in the sea, the animals would fall silent and sit, motionless, looking westward, as if they too were apt to melancholy. Or descending into deep water, stinging with sunburn from the long walk over the coral reef, I felt a calm come over me. The world was filled with colour and brilliancy, and merciful cold and silence, the inverse of the blinding monochrome tumult above. Coming up once, at the limit of my compressed air, I passed into a band of turbid water and realised there must be a sandstorm overhead. I could not see reef or water column. After a while, my watch showed I'd decompressed and I rose into hot hail and razor sand, and no sun or tide to indicate the shore. I had a choice: to float on my empty tanks till some hand scooped me up as one might a locust off a swimming pool – an attractive sort of death – or to cast the tanks adrift ($250) and go down, by the weight of my legs and belt, again and again, each foot of depth an agony of nitrogen and panic, again and again, until the reef shimmered in the murk, safe as a rockery, and pointed the way to shore.

So my purpose was not to die, it seemed, and not to learn a trade and Arabic nor to experience the dignity and sociability of labour. My purpose must have been to acquire money. What was this thing, this rectangle of watermarked paper, engraved by De La Rue in London but now stinking from some labourer's armpit, worthless in itself, but available for commerce or hoarding by consent (and not always even then, for *badu* taxi drivers would sometimes reject a clean note, merely because it felt obscurely wrong to them)? That was stronger than love of liberty or women, self-respect and despair; or rather that drew into itself a portion of all those sentiments? That was, it seemed, a self-evident and self-sufficient purpose for all the human existences I saw about me. A passage from Adam Smith depressed me for weeks: 'The principle which prompts to save, is the desire of bettering our condition, a desire which, though generally calm and dispassionate, comes with us from the womb, and never leaves us till we go into the grave. In the whole interval which separates those two moments, there is scarce perhaps a single instant in which any man is so perfectly and completely satisfied with his situation, as to be without any wish of alteration or improvement, of any kind. An augmentation of fortune is the means by which the greater part of men propose and wish to better their condition.'[1] It seemed to me that since I wasn't going to die, or not for a while, I should do something with the interval and would indeed try to better myself: not by saving, but by thinking. I would study this thing, make it my life, wrestle with it as Jacob with the angel.

I was not interested in the operation of money in society or the creation of social wealth. The science we now call economics seemed to me, from my reading and a study of the Saudi economy – admittedly primitive – modest in its aims. In reality, economics seemed to have fallen prey to the very social mechanisms it attempted to describe and authorise; and the various theories merely confirmed or denied the privileges or fantasies of social classes. Even so, I busied myself with economics, rather as one might learn the rules of baseball: as a social adornment, and to put people at their ease. Yet I could never penetrate beyond the first pages of Ricardo or Marshall without a sort of exasperation: that long before money had even been defined to my satisfaction, we had moved on to the profits of stock, as if all study of money were a mere distraction from its pursuit. I learned book-keeping, and for a moment the world came into focus, as if I had mastered philosophical German. In reality, to describe the world purely in terms of the replacement value in money of its institutions and inhabitants was itself at best ideology, at worst insanity.

I wanted to pierce the veil of money not to find some piece of metaphysics – value, utility or labour – which resides in the economists' money like yet another Russian doll, but the emotions and sensations that nestled there. I took as my motto a passage from Dickens, whom I was reading at that time, for his chaste and sober volumes could be cleared from the airport customs with as little delay as Adam Smith. It is where he describes an industrial process in *Hard Times*:

> So many hundred Hands in this Mill; so many hundred horse Steam Power. It is known, to the force of a single pound weight, what the engine will do; but, not all the calculators of the National Debt can tell me the capacity for good or evil, for love or hatred, for patriotism or discontent, for the decomposition of virtue into vice, or the reverse, at any single moment in the soul of one of these its quiet servants, with the composed faces and the regulated

actions. There is no mystery in it; there is an unfathomable mystery in the meanest of them, for ever.[2]

I thought I should try to penetrate that psychological mystery: to begin at the point at which economics leaves off: to work not with the statistics of CIF imports or the price of dates at inland markets but with the insights of imaginative literature and, for my own times, the symptomatic patter of bankers and thieves. I would study the mind as it responds to money, and vice versa, would collect and preserve those monetary epiphanies that others had experienced at higher latitudes and beside colder seas. As books arrived, and passed through the customs, and were read, my empty head began to rattle with the coins of literature: the single gulden Nikolai finds in his waistcoat pocket at Roulettenburg in *The Gambler;* the gold of Silas Marner in the firelight; Sir Thomas Bertram's gift of a thousand a year; the bonds presented to Josepha in a cornet of sugared almonds; the forged coupon in the Tolstoy story; the hail of silver in the Synoptic Gospels. Eventually I read the *Quixote*, which appeared at the crest of the first great money inflation of modern times, but gives up its meaning only reluctantly and only to the force of concentration. Where the world saw windmills, like Don Quixote I saw giants. Like him, I had my rusty armour, and pasteboard visor and bony steed: an education, which included some ancient and foreign languages, an acquaintance with classic literature, an uninstructed innocence, an unfathomable conceit, I thought my essay would be the swan song of that amateur and impressionistic learning that had flourished in the English schools as late as the 1970s.

I recognised at this early stage that there were pathological aspects to my enquiry; that my interest in money arose in disordered tracts of my biography; and that money represented for me, as no doubt for Dickens, something in my orphan history that did not bear thinking about: to do with margarine and funerals and dismantled rooms. I did not know, as I know now, that six siblings, whose income never exceeded £2,000 a year, had for some years spent £4,000 a year to preserve their family existence; and the end, when it came, was bound to be a smash. In retrospect, I believe I must still have been reverberating that first moment I descended the aircraft gangway into the mucilaginous Jeddah night. It occurred to me that, in occupying myself with money, I might restore my disordered childhood without the bother and expense of a psycho-analysis; for I was not sure that Freud, in his self-analysis, devoted sufficient time to money; or that the psycho-analytic fee, that pillar of the Freudian analysis, was quite so clinically self-evident as the founder made out.

In 1980, I picked fights with several influential men and was politely shown the way to the airport. I converted my bundles of riyals into sterling: they made, I guess, about thirty thousand pounds, or the equivalent in purchasing power of about seventy-five thousand in the money of 1997. Because I regarded money with suspicion, I changed it into property of one type or another; and that accorded with the spirit of an inflationary age. The money was, in its time, a mortgaged house in Lavender Hill, a slow racehorse, stock in the Dresdner Bank, an excessive number of eighteenth-century engravings of St Petersburg, an apartment in lower Manhattan, stock in supermarket corporations. At each transition, it shed chips off the side to stockbrokers, picture dealers, realtors, the Inland Revenue, the Customs and Excise, the IRS and the Federal Taxation Office, but always disintegrated into more money than at its previous dissolution. I travelled the world at this period, and assembled an obsessive collection of banknotes which I stored in the drawer of an old desk my mother had left me in her will: a highly symptomatic action, I recognise. There were Yemeni and Iranian riyals, Kuwaiti dinars, Iraqi dinars, West and East German marks, United States and Fijian and Maria Theresa dollars, zlotys, roubles, rupees, shekels, Ecuadorean sucres, Mexican and Chilean pesos, French and Swiss francs, English, Turkish and Egyptian pounds.

It was not a miser's collection, as in Balzac's neurotic catalogue in *Eugénie Grandet,* for they were daily, with a few exceptions, becoming useless as a hoard or medium of payment. I experimented once with a high Turkish bill, ten years old, which I presented at Istanbul airport in the belief it might still buy a packet of fags. It couldn't buy Chiclets. So much for the economists' store of value! I kept them because I sensed their value evaporating, their moneyness seeping into the old satinwood, till they were just coloured paper you couldn't even write on. And at some moment, I cannot remember when, looking at that confetti, I had a thought: I realised that moneyness was not a permanent attribute of those pieces of paper, but attended them for a period of their existence, rather as good fortune had attended me as a young man; in reality, attended them only so long as they were in motion. The banknotes shared that character with no other physical object, for a clock remains a clock and an automobile a vehicle even when they do not move. Further, I realised money must be visible, for a buried hoard is not money until it is exhumed; and must have an owner, for a banknote blowing in the street, like an Egyptian half pound I once saw on the Corniche of Alexandria, is not money until it is run after and picked up, as my companion ran after it and picked it up. Money becomes money only at the instant it incorporates a wish; and I saw that it was a treadmill, that it led us all on a mad bacchanal from which we could not break out and sit down.

At about that time, a change came over my life. The money from Jeddah began to breed, first slowly, then convulsively. While I slept, or was drunk, or made love, or smoked a Benson on the porch, my money worked; and, as far as I could tell, with smaller effort and for greater reward than I did. My future receded down a darkling enfilade of compound interest, as if two mirrors had been placed to face each other. I felt an unbearable regret: that that lightness which comes with empty pockets, the airy, tremulous sense of self which had been mine throughout my teens, the alienation from even the fabric of commercial society, its street corners and bullying office blocks and lighted shops – in short, my liberty – was now lost to me, possibly for ever. I felt disabled. It was as if my subject, while enabling this project by relieving me of care, were also mocking me.

In analysing the new situation, I thought perhaps there was some quality about my labour from 1978 to 1980; some particular virtue; which gave it uncommon power in commanding the labour of others. (I once accosted a man in the South Seas who was planting some taro root. That action of his, lasting fully twenty minutes of a rainy morning, was, he said, enough to keep his family in food and grog and cash for a year.) No doubt at the depths of every *rentier*'s existence, from duke to retiree, there is the faint shadow cast by some dead labour; but it is lost in the glitter of present possession. The notion that work stood at the heart of money – that it was congealed labour as Smith, Ricardo, Marx and Proudhon thought – seemed to me, in my idleness, quite ludicrous. Yet my enrichment had a benign psychological effect. In my childhood, the possessor of money might be virtuous or wicked, but he or she wore an authority that was thought to inhere in money riches: that is, that money precedes and guides a rich man like the deity, invisible to the rest of humanity, who stands beside the Greek warrior in battle. Since I knew I had little ability and no virtue, only some money, I was free to ignore the rich and pursue my project without their psychological invigilation.

In that, I was fortunate. For together with this disesteem of money – the inflation that had troubled the world since the price of Saudi crude oil quadrupled at the turn of 1974 – was a new and exaggerated esteem for money. In Britain, Germany, the states of Central Europe, Russia, Latin America – indeed everywhere I went, but particularly in Britain – money was quickly displacing all other psychological goals. Duty, religion, public service, liberty, equality, justice or aristocracy – all the cultural flesh that clothed the bones of money for those that possessed it – all became suspect: only money, it seemed, was to be trusted. In Britain, at least, that no doubt had to do with the frustrations of the young who had had it up to here with the senile prattle of a society they thought ripe for the boneyard. In Russia and Eastern Europe, money took on the character of emancipation and modernity more comprehensively than even the early paper money of the United States or the first issues of *assignats* in revolutionary Paris. Only money could measure success or failure, happiness or misery. Only money could reward or punish. States and governments must just stand back and money – which reconciles all clashes of human will – would see us right. Money was good.

Now, I had learned by then that money is our greatest invention, has done more to make our civilisation even than letters – for those must be translated, whereas money is the language that almost every human being speaks and understands; enabled the movement of people and ideas; given us world wars and monuments of architecture; transformed our notions of luxury or want. As a means, I saw that money was all but absolute: it could now realise every fantasy of creation or murder. And at that moment of extreme instrumentality, it was transforming once again: into an absolute end. Money was valued not for its power to convey wishes: rather it was the goal of all wishes. Money was enthroned as the God our Our Times.

I was in New York on the morning of October 19, 1987, and felt the foundation of that religion tremble. That morning, I concluded that a failure of money in two of its instrumental aspects – measure of value and means of payment – was not so much impossible as quite likely; and ever more so as money increased in abstraction, lost even the gossamer physicality of banknotes and became mere impulses in electronic ledgers, girdling the city at the speed of light, a million million dollars in motion every day. In London and New York, I met people who invested fortunes in financial enterprises they simply could not describe or explain. No doubt quite soon, a bank would discover it had lost its capital in those obscure speculations; other banks would fail in sympathy; there would be a depression in trade; trade wars; killing wars.*

I felt I was running out of time. In the British Library, to which I walked each day in Marxian poverty, I was haunted by a phantom rival: I feared that somewhere in that domed room, a stranger was reading the same books; and that one day my slips would come back to me marked 'Out to———' and they would be defeat and death to me, as the black flags at the Pole were to Scott, Wilson, Evans and Bowers. One Sunday, in Hampstead, I walked into a junk fair and saw, on a table among fake Bohemian glass and ratty trinkets, a set of currency notes in a cellophane wrapper. Behind the table was a small old woman. She seemed fragile, cunning, old-fashioned, cosseted, like a painted Easter egg in cotton wool. I sensed she must have been hard-used at one time, and had not lived much or changed her habits since that time. I looked at the glass and the W.I. badges and then, offhand-like, at the notes.

'How much are these?'

She looked at me. She was trying to establish their value in British money, which was not easy for her, because they had no value to her; and because she did not know of my obsession, did not know their value to me. She could not judge my willingness to buy, only my ability, and for that she must look to my appearance, which was not encouraging: I was wearing jeans and flip-flops and had not shaved. I was not used up by my investigation – No, ma'am! – but had become

---

* That sentence, appearing in a magazine the week before the collapse of Barings, gained me a quite unwarranted reputation as a prophet.

careless about my dress, no longer wore a suit north of Oxford Street, disliked giving occasion for any monetary predicate. I had abandoned financial speculation, and even spending money except in a new addiction to tobacco: the gold of the cigarette packet soothed and excited me more than ever the metal.

'It'll have to be twenty-five pounds. They're . . .'

I knew what they were. At that moment, I thought (though not necessarily in this order): how deep are the ironies of my topic that for these currency notes, which never ever bought anything, I am about to exchange something that'll buy this lady heat or light or *Kaffee und Kuchen*; and that I am now reversing the famous law that holds that bad money drives out good. The money in its wrapper on the table was not just bad, but the worst ever minted. I picked up the notes, and put them down again. The topmost was biscuit-coloured, watermarked, in good condition. Its face value was a hundred crowns. It was dated January 1, 1943, in Austrian German and signed by a Jakob Edelstein. Its reverse showed the sum and a warning in High German which read: Any person counterfeiting or copying these bills or handling forged bills will be severely punished. In a roundel was a nice portrait of Moses carrying the Ten Commandments.

I paid twenty pounds.

These notes which were signed by the Chief Elder of the Council of Jews in the concentration camp of Theresienstadt in Bohemia and issued as wages or dole, barely circulated, according to the historian of the town, and were used chiefly as counters in card games. Jakob Edelstein was murdered at Birkenau on July 20, 1944. The notes stood in the same relation to reality as the postcards certain deported prisoners sent from Poland: *The journey was exhausting but without incident.* The fraud and consolation that inheres in all money becomes, in these *Ghettokronen*, pure deceit, pure fantasy. People believed in them as we all believe in money, because without it we cannot live in the world, which presses in, becomes a prison at night clanking with long trains setting out for the north. As Byron kept a skull upon his desk, so I keep these notes in their cellophane wrapper – here, on the machine on which I'm writing this sentence – so that I do not forget the people of Theresienstadt and my eventual pauper's grave.

1

Mineral Stones

> Material objects have in themselves no power, but, since it is
> our practice to bestow power upon them . . .
>
> Proust, *Le Temps Retrouvé*

Money, which we hope to see and hold every day, is diabolically
hard to comprehend with words. Throughout history, men and
women have identified money with gold, silver, coins and banknotes, or applied to it attributes of weight or colour or feel that
belonged properly only to the money they happened to be using.
To many generations gold and silver appeared to be money in a
very particular sense: Ibn Khaldun, the medieval philosopher of
Muslim history, said God had given humanity those 'mineral stones'
as ideals to which all earthly treasure could aspire.[1] Yet in time
they were revealed as mere substances that derived their prestige
not from some inner secret in their metal but from their ancient use
as money.

When Stanley set out to find Livingstone in East Africa in 1871,
he took with him three types of money – wire, cloth and beads –
because, at the level of his consciousness where money and Africa
had their existence, those seemed to be what Africans would make
of the gold, silver and copper of Victorian London and post-bellum
New York. As it turned out, he did not use much of this money –
if that's what it was – lugged by two hundred porters half-way
across the continent, but had resort to another nineteenth-century
currency, the bullet.[2]

From our vantage, we can see that money is of no particular
substance and may be of no substance at all; that whatever money is,
it may be embodied in coins or shells, knives, salt, axes, skins, iron,

rice, mahogany, tobacco, cases of gin; in persons; in a word or gesture, paper, plastic, electronic impulses or the silver ingots raced through the streets on trays at sundown to make up accounts between the foreign banks in my mother's father's days in Hangkow. Over time, money has shed its qualities, as a suitcase caught in the door of a moving train scatters possessions, and the only attribute of a modern piece of money is its quantity, its oneness or fiveness or fiftyness: everything else about it is redundant or tasteless ornament. Adjectives of quality applied to money – good, bad, sound, cheap, dear, funny – are, nowadays, mere descriptions of quantity: they tell us only how much money there is about.

Over the ages, men and women have racked their brains to understand why things sell for such an amount of money and not for another. Philip VI of France declared that something was worth what he said it was worth, on account of his being the King.[3] The economists sought to pierce the forms of money and things bought for money and extract a permanent reality; but their theories of value turned into one of the great wild-goose chases in the history of thought; and their discoveries – Value! Labour! Utility! Marginal Utility! – were probably only synonyms of money. In truth, value can only be a mental attitude, sometimes shared by people, some-times not: Proust showed that in the first volume of Le Côté de Guermantes, where the sexual favour of an actress in a suburban lane is dear at twenty francs to one man, but has cost the man beside him more than a million.[4] As for utility, if that truly were the counterpart of money in the world, then, as Davanzati put it, men would pray to bellowing, not golden, calves. Dejected, the economists con-structed cumbersome functional definitions of money which could barely accommodate Gold Standard sterling; and were helpless when confronted, at the turn of the twentieth century, by leering objects that appeared to be forms of money, such as the immense stone rings displayed or transported by the Yap people of the Caroline Islands.

'It is a natural resource,' De Quincey wrote, 'that whatsoever we find it difficult to investigate as a result, we endeavour to follow as a growth. Failing analytically to probe its nature, historically we seek relief to our perplexities by tracing its origin.'[5] But there was no relief to be found in ancient history. Numismatists cannot agree about the origin of coinage, let alone money. Rebuffed as to money's form, content and origins, we are left merely with its effects, which are overpowering. It seems humanity inhabits a world of whose most important component it is wholly ignorant.

Yet almost all human beings have a vivid sense of what money is, for it arises in their innermost nature: their sense of Self as nurtured by possession. They recognise that modern moneys are disintegrating, often convulsively, and that the promise-to-pay on modern banknotes is just a dreary central banker's witticism: if you present the Bank of England with a five-pound note, it will give you a duplicate or its complement in base-metal change. Yet money itself has untroubled existence in their minds.

For just as a word describes more than its vowels and consonants, is a symbol of a particular existence in the world on which at least two people agree, and will convey a notion of that existence, without the bother of building it or transporting it to view; so money is not just its particular form but a symbol of something else in the world, something desirable. The difference between a word and a piece of money is that money has always and will always symbolise different things to different people: a banknote may describe to one person a drink in a pub, a fairground ride to another, to a third a diamond ring, an act of charity to a fourth, relief from prosecution to a fifth and, to a sixth, simply the sensations of comfort or security.

For money is incarnate desire. Money takes wishes, however vague or trivial or atrocious, and broadcasts them to the world, like the Mayday of a ship in difficulties. Unlike the Mayday, it appeals not to sensations of individual benevolence or common humanity (which the philosophers since Machiavelli have anyway attempted to deny); but offers a reward that is not in any sense fixed or finite – there is no objective or invariable value in money – but that every person is free to imagine in the realm of his own desires.

That process of wish and imagination, launched or completed a million times every second, is the engine of our civilisation. While barter seeks to match two wishes and annul them, money survives each sale or payment and must be deployed by its new holder or it ceases to be money. In thus mobilising wishes, money sets people and matter in motion, has made great cities, railroads, satellites in the heavens, phantom warehouses of computing power, systems of law and equity, gardens, immense and long-winded corporations, sanguinary wars, monuments of architecture, teeming populations. Edward Gibbon, writing in the eighteenth century, compared the spread of money with the spread of writing and used a sentence of which any writer would be proud:

> The value of money has been settled by general consent to express our wants and our property, as letters were invented to express our ideas; and both these institutions, by giving more active energy to the powers and passions of human nature, have contributed to multiply the objects they were designed to represent.

Money, to use an old-fashioned mechanical metaphor, has become a sort of railway shunting yard which is for ever receiving the wishes and dreams of countless people and despatching them to unimagined destinations.

Thus modern money's lack of content, however repugnant to the scientific, is the key to its employment. If a money has a use other than as money, as a cow and a hoe and a piece of gold have other uses, it cannot carry the impression of such uncountable and varied wishes: its boorish or ornamental nature will in time get in the way. Likewise if a money is felt to have a solemn purpose, such as the Maundy Money of the English monarch or the cases of gin given to the parents of a bride in the Nigeria of the 1920s. For the objects of human desire are limitless, or rather limited only by the imagination, which amounts to the same thing. Money has expanded over history to accommodate not only larger possession but ever bolder flights of imaginative desire. In the process, it unites society more effectively than tyranny or blood; for in taking money, you deliver yourself up to the other users of money, accept their freedom to choose, their frivolity and selfishness, their universal subjection to desire, their humanity. When Crusoe returns to the wreck and picks up his money, his creator lets all the air out of the story: the reader now knows that the island cannot be deserted.

In Cambodia in the 1970s, a group of revolutionaries of Maoist vintage abolished every symbol of civilian life, including cities and money. In 1979, the Vietnamese invaded their neighbour and scattered the Khmer Rouge. Money flowed back in like the tide up a creek. Someth May, who had survived abominable years in the Khmer Rouge labour camps, recorded the moment:

> Apart from foraging for rice there were three ways of making your living. Those who didn't want to leave the village, for fear of meeting the Khmer Rouge, worked in the market or made palm sugar or toddy. Then there were the fishermen, who went in groups for safety. And then there were the gold-diggers, who wandered round the outskirts of the village searching for corpses and graves. Most Cambodians had gold-capped teeth, so these men became known as millionaires. With astonishing speed – this all happened in a matter of three weeks – the gold-diggers had motorbikes, brand new Hondas which they had bought along the border. They had amazing watches, gold chains round their necks, shirts open to the waist, Thai cigarettes.
>
> Gold was the currency. It came in sheets. If you wanted to pay for something small you snipped a bit off with scissors. People didn't yet have scales. When they cut up the gold from the old regime they discovered for the first time that it was impure – there was a core of some kind of heavy metal powder. But the gold was just sucked out in the direction of Thailand.
>
> In its place came sarongs and jeans, cloth, proper milled rice, cosmetics, tinned foods, fruit, cigarettes and alcohol.
>
> Sisophon . . . was the centre of the gold economy, and everybody knew what he was doing. The tradesmen had balances in glass cases. The smugglers had their own balances. Even the Vietnamese had balances, so that they could settle the arguments which frequently broke out. The tradesmen held the gold in gas jets, heating it till it was red hot, then letting it cool. If it discoloured as it cooled it wasn't pure. All gold had to be cut before it was accepted, to make sure there was no core of base metal. The most elaborate bracelets were being chopped up in this way. There were little children who waited for the traders to go, then searched where they had been cutting the gold for the tiniest specks of dust. And the point was that all Cambodia's gold was leaving the country. It was being sucked out in Thailand, as if by an enormous vacuum cleaner.
>
> There were other currencies as well: there was an old kind of coinage which was called trough money, dating from pre-colonial

days and shaped like a toy pig-trough, some of it elaborately decorated; when it was sawn in half, the silver was absolutely white and pure. The traders were hammering them into different shapes, testing their malleability.

Then there were the jewel dealers, usually women. Not far from here, in Pailin, there was a sapphire mine and many Cambodians were expert in valuing jewels. The women had low cut blouses and nice big bosoms to distract the customers. The stalls were simple low tables, about a metre square. Nothing was on display. They paid for the jewels in gold or *baht*, Thai money.⁶

Here, money is not simply a commercial appearance. The actual delectation, utility, value or convenience of the objects bought for money – those gold chains, Hondas, jeans, fags – are, as Someth makes admirably clear, quite accidental. In his bewilderment and overwhelming relief, he recognises pretty women and sapphires as simply aspects of a metaphysical identity which is nothing less than the Self: the reality of the will, dominion over phenomena, and selection out of the eerie, silent, starving, black-pyjama-clad crowd.

Of such things is money made.

*

The most enduring theories of the origin of money, in the West, the Muslim world and China, found themselves on what Adam Smith called the division of labour. Sheikh Abu al-Fadl Jaafar al-Dimishqi, who wrote an Arabic treatise on commerce that can be dated after A.D. 860 and before A.D. 1174 from the coins he talks about, said money was invented by a super-race of early men, whom he calls in Arabic the *awail*, the first ones, to create a system of equivalences. Life is too short, he writes, for a man to master all the occupations of civil existence and therefore:

> In recognition of these difficulties, the *awail* sought something to which they could apply the price of everything, and lit first on what was near to hand: plants, animals or living property. Plants and living things they rejected because they were essentially unstable, and easily spoiled. From the minerals they chose the hard stones that could be smelted, but rejected iron, copper and lead; iron because it rusted, copper for the same reason, lead

because it turned black and quickly became soft, and too easily
changed its appearance. Likewise some rejected copper because it
became covered in verdigris; but others minted it as one mints the
dirham and made copper coinage for trade at retail. All men
concurred in preferring gold and silver because they were so easily
cast into shapes, hammered, smelted, refined and formed at will.
In addition, they shone prettily and had no unpleasant smell or
taste, could be buried in the earth without losing their integrity
and could take on their surface signs (*'alamat*) to protect them; and
these signs that protect them from fraud and counterfeiting are
stable. So they minted gold and silver and made them a means of
payment for everything. But they eventually saw that gold had the
most beautiful sheen, was the most hard-wearing and survived
long burial and repeated smelting.[7]

That view of money's invention, as spontaneous, careful and rational,
probably derives from classical antiquity. In the essay called *The
Politics*, which Aristotle composed about 330 B.C. or just at the
moment when the liberties he was celebrating were about to be
destroyed by Alexander the Great, Aristotle asked the question –
Why did humanity invent money? – and came up with the answer:
Men invented money, and then coinage, to make possible an
international division of labour:

> When the inhabitants of one country became more dependent on
> those of another, and they imported what they needed, and
> exported what they had too much of, money necessarily came
> into use. For the various necessaries of life are not easily carried
> about, and hence men agreed to employ in their dealings with
> one another something which was intrinsically useful and easy to
> handle in general life, for example, iron, silver, and the like. Of
> this the value was at first measured simply by size and weight, but
> in the process of time they put a stamp upon it, to save the trouble
> of weighing and to mark the value.[8]

Like his master, Plato, and like Dimishqi and Adam Smith later,
Aristotle assumed that men did things for good reason: there had to
be money, just as there had to be a state, because of the division of
tasks among men and women according to their different aptitudes.
Aristotle, of course, didn't know the history of money any better

than his successors. He knew no archaeology, but he knew logic, which he uses as the archaeologist uses his trowel: he gives logical reasons why money might have appeared useful to the men and women of earlier generations. Likewise Sima Qian, writing in China in the early first century B.C., argued that money had come into being 'long ago and far away' once commerce had been established between the country and the town.[9] All those writers assume a high degree of civility in early society: they project back their civilisations – Glasgow of the 1770s, the medieval Levant, fourth-century B.C. Athens, Han China – onto the remote past.

Money may be older than writing but we will never know: an archaeologist may think an object he finds is an old money, but he cannot know it is without an inscription to tell him so. Cuneiform inscriptions from Mesopotamia, dated to the third millennium B.C., record the weighing-out of barley for taxes, rents and compensations; the Chinese writing system, developed in the next millennium, uses the symbol of a cowrie shell in characters relating to the notions of treasure, giving and payment. The Old Testament has many references to payments of silver, for example the twenty shekels' weight for which Joseph was sold by his brothers to Midianite merchants.[10]

The earliest European written records make no mention of money. Great numbers of clay tablets unearthed at the beginning of this century in the Greek Peloponnese and in Crete, and inscribed with a script the archaeologists called Linear B, were partially deciphered in the 1950s by Michael Ventris and John Chadwick and revealed as inventories. Chadwick called them 'the account-books of a long-forgotten people': lists of women, children, tradesmen, rowers, troops, flocks of sheep and goats, grain, oil, spices, land leases and yields, tribute, ritual offerings, cloth, vessels, furniture, bronze, chariots, helmets.[11] But there was evidently no money. We have not, said Ventris, 'been able to identify payment in silver and gold for services rendered.'[12] There was no evidence 'of anything approaching currency. Every commodity is listed separately, and there is never any sign of equivalence between one unit and another.'[13] The tablets seem to reflect some sort of feudal system of land tenure and service, but we cannot be more precise.

In Homer, there does seem to be money of a sort. Classical

scholars agree – usually a dangerous thing, but perhaps not here – that the *Iliad* is a poem or song; that it was not written down at the moment of composition, like the verses Goethe scratched one evening with his diamond ring on the pane of a forester's hut; but evolved over time and was first given its physical form as late as five centuries after it first took shape in memory. In the *Iliad*, in whose crepuscular splendour we seem to see reflected the technical glory of the Greek Bronze Age, possessions and slaves are transferred according to a standard of quantity, cattle; but there is no passage where cattle are actually used for payment, as by the modern Masai: the Greeks always give something 'worth so many head of cattle' in exchange, not 'so many head of cattle.'

In a passage of Book VI of the *Iliad*, a Greek warrior (Diomedes) makes a fool of a Trojan (Glaucus) by exchanging armour worth nine oxen for armour worth a hundred. The passage has always enchanted the economists, for it makes the distant past seem just like the present, which many find comforting: in reality, the passage records an epoch-making shift in mental attitudes. When the two warriors meet on the battlefield, they resolve not to fight, because of an ancient friendship of their grandfathers. Instead, Diomedes proposes that they swap armour, not for profit or subsistence or out of Adam Smith's 'propensity in human nature . . . to truck, barter and exchange,'[14] but to commemorate and honour that ancient friendship. It is an act of piety. Their purpose is to perpetuate their mutual obligation – which one does by exchanging presents – not to dissolve it – which one does by payment. (You may want to return to the bookshop where you bought this book, but you don't *have to*. If, however, you were given it by the sales clerk, you are obliged to him, and should return.)

There follows this comment:

> But Zeus the son of Cronos must have robbed Glaucus of his wits, for he exchanged with Diomedes golden armour for bronze, a hundred oxen's worth for the value of nine.[15]

In other words, Glaucus was robbed. Poor Glaucus, a man of the heroic age, cannot think in monetary categories. His desire is for friendship: it is conveyed by the gift of his most precious possession – his armour, his manliness – and the receipt of that of Diomedes.

How many cattle either possession might, ideally, buy is beside the point of that heroic reciprocal sacrifice; or rather Glaucus gains prestige from his generosity. The sensation of advantage that underlies all sale and barter transactions – the secret belief that one has got something more delightful than one gave – without which the Self cannot come whole from the transaction – is alien to him. And it is not Diomedes (who may have suggested the swap in heroic good faith) but the first of the gods, Zeus, who is the voice of economic urbanity: as the greatest literary critic of antiquity, the person or persons called Longinus, noted, the *Iliad* makes men of gods and gods of men.[16]

The ancient Greeks liked to attribute the providential or bizarre to the gods as the Muslims today still do to God. But I suspect the Zeus of the Glaucus and Diomedes story is the god of all stories, the author; and that particular author comes quite late in the composition of the poem as we have it now. The exchange of armour does not sit at ease in the *Iliad*. The chief story of the poem has no monetary or commercial aspect: it is about vengeance, not trade. It is, as Homer helpfully tells us in the first line of the poem, about Achilles' anger. And why is Achilles angry? Because Agamemnon, the leader of the Greek expedition to Troy, has confiscated a piece of property, a favourite captive. The issue is not resolved through money. It is not resolved at all, except by death.

For money cannot coexist with an epic picture of the world: if there had been money, then the girl Briseis could have been priced, and Achilles could have been compensated. By Book IX, the Greeks are offering Achilles not just Briseis but seven other girls, but still he will not relent: the hero Ajax criticises him for becoming so worked up 'about a girl, a single girl.'[17] But for Achilles there is no such thing as an exchange: Briseis, or rather his own pride or rage that she embodies – his *menin*, the very first word of the poem – is unique in quality, not measurable in quantity.

The world Odysseus sails through after leaving Troy is a different world from the world of the *Iliad*: reality always looks transformed after battle. Presents are exchanged in the *Odyssey*, but in a manner that is almost compulsory, and with a book-keeper's eye on value. Such gift exchanges are more than half-way to sales. I suspect that's why Longinus admired the *Iliad* beyond all expressions of the human spirit but called the *Odyssey* a 'comedy of domestic manners.'[18]

The picture becomes clearer at the beginning of classical times in the work of Herodotus, known to antiquity as the Father of History. The first book of Herodotus' *Histories* is about money and it surprises me that the ages have ignored it. For it is precisely what you would expect. Herodotus was born (in or around 490 B.C.) and lived on the east coast of the Aegean, where the Mediterranean world met the land empires of Asia, and where, as far as we can tell, the first things that have survived that we can call coins were struck late in the seventh century B.C. Those coins, which were discovered in the foundations of the Temple of Artemis in Ephesus and are of a gold and silver alloy called electrum, panned from the river Pactolus, are probably the parents and pattern for all the world's coined money except that of pre-nineteenth-century China. (The first coin-like objects we have from China, though made at roughly the same era, are quite different things: they are bronze pieces in the shapes of spades and knives.) Thus literary history and archaeological supposition meet on the Aegean coast of Asia, like tunnel-builders in the Alps.

Herodotus was a traveller, and the word 'histories,' which he gave us – and means for us the story of human beings in society – meant for him merely inquiries or investigations. He is among the first people in Europe who can travel out of choice and at leisure. He is not a soldier, refugee, merchant, pilgrim or beggar: he seems to have travelled simply – as he says of the philosopher and lawgiver Solon – 'to have a look round.'[19] What makes such antique tourism possible is money. Reading the first book of the *Histories*, one has a strange feeling, as somebody said about the Lydian and other early coins in the British Museum, 'of assisting at the very birth' of money.

Herodotus might not have known he was writing about money, any more than Balzac and Dickens knew they were writing about money twenty-two centuries later; but they all were. Embedded in the first book of the *Histories* are the exploded fragments of an immense monetary anthropology: references to coins, value, robbery, gift, prostitution, gold, slavery, mines, oracles, payment of mercenary soldiers, the purchase of women and finally the sort of peaceful commerce Aristotle and Adam Smith would have recognised. Sometimes, Herodotus writes down reports that are so strange that one cannot reconstruct their meaning:

> Lower-class girls in Lydia prostitute themselves without exception to collect money for their dowries, and continue the practice until they marry.[20]

His master theme is the rivalry between Europe and Asia, which gave to history both the Trojan War of the epics and the over-whelming experience of his own lifetime: the Persian invasions of Greece and their defeat at Salamis and Plataea. Herodotus locates the origin of the quarrel, like Homer, in the theft of a girl, and repeated counter-thefts; but the heroic age seems old-fashioned to the age of money. The heroic story is stuffed into a prosaic framework and then mocked: there is even that sentiment, so beloved of the high court judges of my childhood, that women are only raped if they want to be. The story then proceeds to the Lydians, the people sitting on the join between the Mediterranean and Asian worlds, and culminates in this passage:

> Apart from the fact they prostitute their daughters, the Lydian way of life is not unlike our own. The Lydians were the first people we know of to use a gold and silver coinage and to engage in retail trade.[21]

The Lydian origin for coinage is supported, incidentally, in a fragment of the philosopher Xenophanes of Colophon.[22] Croesus, King of Lydia, is commemorated by Herodotus' account of the 'enormous quantities of gold' he sent to the oracle of Apollo at Delphi and by the proverb 'rich as Croesus,' which has passed without interruption into modern speech: Locke was later to argue that it was the invention of money that created such inequalities of possession.[23]

What the first coins were *for* we cannot say. Nor can we say how, out of Herodotus' farrago of war, rape, robbery, trade, gifts, ornament, worship, fines, mercenary wages, tribute and damages for injury, money emerges as the champion means of communicating needs and wishes. I'm sure if we did we would reveal the pre-occupations of our age as clearly as Aristotle and Adam Smith with their emphasis on commerce or, in our century, the anthropologists with their gift rituals. There may be meaning in Lydia's location. There Barbarian meets Greek, and it is generally unwise to take leave of strangers with any obligation outstanding: money is preferable to gifts in such dealings. Those strangers might include mercenary soldiers or skilled foreign craftsmen. The key point is that trust in money can act as a substitute for trust in people. Gradually, as we shall see, it will displace trust in all human relations except those of the inner family.

Money probably kept pace with the growth of positive law, presenting itself as a substitute for vengeance, in the way that the appalling train of counter-murders in the *Oresteia* is broken before the human judges on the Areopagus. In classical Athens, money is becoming the preferred form of tribute: the most famous buildings of antiquity, the Parthenon, Erechtheon and the Propylaeon on the Acropolis of Athens, commemorate the diversion by Pericles of the tribute paid by island allies for the upkeep of the Athenian fleet. By classical times, men and women have an entity that allows them to convey many wishes with justice and without violence: without, as it were, the embarrassment of Glaucus or the destructive rage of Achilles. Yet the society most admired in ancient Greece, Sparta, went to great lengths to restrict the operations of money: Xenophon reports that Lycurgus, the legendary law-giver of Sparta, banned the use of coin to free-born Spartans: presumably, he feared that money, in mobilising individual wishes, would detonate the tight-knit military organisation of the state.[24] That contest between moneyless and moneyed forms of social organisation fascinated the eighteenth century: Sir James Steuart called the Spartan system 'the wedge' and the Athenian and modern 'the watch', one solid and compact, the other delicate, complex and constantly in need of adjustment.[25] Indeed, that contest was an aspect of the rivalry between the United States and the Soviet Union known as the Cold War.

Yet even in Athens, there were deep misgivings about money. By Aristotle's time, banking had become established at Athens. We learn, by way of Demosthenes' legal speeches – the Athenians were as litigious as modern New Yorkers – of such bankers as Pasion and his successor, Phormio, of money-changers and loan-sharks. Both men were former slaves: and their immense fortunes, though the subject of comment and object of envy, are tainted with the pariah. Wealth is still embodied in land and liberty in citizenship: there is nothing wrong with having no money. Something of that lies behind Aristotle's attitude to money, even though it is phrased in the language of natural law. I must point out that Aristotle is not an economist: his interest in *Oikonomia* (the management of the household) attaches to its living members not their inert possessions. He comes at money from two angles: by way of politics (the best constitution for the state) and ethics (the science of right conduct). He is most emphatically not interested in the nature and causes of the wealth of nations.

At the heart of Aristotle's thought is a belief in a natural purpose to all things. A shoe can be used for wear and also can be sold for money or food, but the last is not its proper or primary purpose: in technical terms, its use-value has precedence over its exchange-value. Money is no different: its primary purpose or use is to gain the necessities of life; but it can also be used for getting more money through trade or lending. Modern political economy recognises that dual nature of money, under the terms 'currency' and 'capital', and generally applauds it: Locke argued that since men *had* invented money, they *must have* consented to inequalities of fortune and to possession without need. In contrast, Aristotle thinks in terms only of natural need and for that reason distrusts money. For while the necessaries of life are limited by nature and definition – one can only eat so much, be under one roof at any one time – there is no limit to the pursuit of money, *because there is no limit to human desire.* You can wish the world.

The problem had long been dramatised for antiquity in the story of Midas, King of Phrygia. In the story, money is transformed from means to end and this is not only an offence to the gods – what we call unnatural – but a source of human misery: both elements, by the way, are captured in Poussin's great picture of the late 1620s now in New York: Midas' back, as he frantically washes the gold from his hair into the Pactulus, exudes a brutish degradation. Aristotle invokes the story to illustrate why money cannot be wealth.

How can that be wealth of which a man may have a great abundance and yet perish with hunger, like Midas in the fable, whose insatiable prayer turned everything that we set before him into gold?[26]

I cannot exaggerate the importance of that thought. Here, at the dawn of money, men already recognise its deepest meaning: that money, because it has the potential to fulfill any mortal purpose and convey any mortal desire, becomes the absolute purpose and the object of the most intense desire it can convey. Schopenhauer saw that as inevitable: 'Men are often criticised in that money is the chief object of their wishes and is preferred above all else, but it is natural, even unavoidable. For money is an inexhaustible Proteus, ever ready to change itself into the present object of our changeable wishes and manifold needs. Other goods can satisfy only *one* wish and *one* need. Food is good only for the hungry, wine for the healthy, medicine for the sick, fur for winter, sexual love [*Weiber*] for the young, etc. They are all *goods for a particular purpose*; that is, only relatively good. Money alone is the absolute good: for it confronts not just *one* concrete need, but Need *itself* in abstract.' Schopenhauer went on to give money its best definition: money is human happiness in abstract: *die menschliche Glückseligkeit* in abstracto.[27]

But the antique philosophers were repelled by that conclusion. Plato, though he accepted there must be money in the state – indeed that it was a key to the sharing of skills in the community – saw it must eventually destroy that state. His solution was to outlaw it for his Spartan super-caste of warrior-defenders, the Guardians: the *Republic* is the first of a long series of moneyless Utopias that pass by way of Sir Thomas More to the fantasies of science fiction; and by way of the Franciscans and the Shakers and Robert Owen and Proudhon's bank to the atrocities of the Khmer Rouge. Aristotle thought that the accumulation of money not only was unnatural but would subvert the state by capturing all other arts:

> The quality of courage, for example, is not intended to make wealth, but to inspire confidence [in others]; neither is this the aim of the general's or of the physician's art; but the one aims at victory and the other at health. Nevertheless, some men turn every quality or art into a means of getting wealth; this they conceive to be the end, and to the promotion of the end they think all things must contribute.[28]

The modern or economists' belief, that the pursuit of money creates the general's and physician's art, would have seemed to Aristotle perverse beyond description: for it confuses his ends and means. The economists, with their notion of a quasi-divine or natural order of which money is the instrument – Adam Smith's invisible hand, the efficient-markets doctrine – are here diametrically opposed to the ancients. For even Diogenes and the Epicureans, though they were interested in the individual rather than the state, saw the emotions provoked by money and its use as barriers to wisdom and happiness.

Aristotle's hostility to money as capital is recorded in a famous passage in the *Politics*. The passage is as controversial as it is hard to understand; but it is among the most influential group of sentences ever written: it haunted Aquinas and the Middle Ages, was familiar in some version to Shakespeare and Marx, was the basis of Proudhon's philosophy. It is the rallying cry and point of honour of all those who dislike or distrust capitalism. Wealth arising from exchange or retailing (what we term profit)

> is justly censured; for it is unnatural, and a mode by which men gain from one another. The most hated sort, and with the greatest reason, is interest, for it makes a gain out of money itself, and not from that for which money was devised. For money came into being for the sake of exchange, but interest makes the money itself greater. And that's the reason why the term 'interest' [*tokos*], which means the birth of money from money, is applied to the breeding of money because the offspring resembles the parent. That's why it's the most unnatural way of enriching yourself.[29]

It is clear that this passage, whatever it means, is not economic (modern sense) in intention, but ethical. Interest (*obolastiki*, which has the connotations of small loans or loan-sharking) is condemned not because it does not make wealth, but for something in the way that it does make wealth. The argument proceeds through pun or etymology: another Greek word for interest is *tokos* or offspring. The language is the language of sexual tabu, and one expects a mythical embodiment, an Oedipus to balance our Midas. Aristotle is saying that lending or usury, in using money to gain money rather than necessities, is a perversion of both human and monetary nature.

Dante was later to develop the thought when he bracketed usurers with sodomites in hell.[30]

It need hardly be said that this passage, for which Shakespeare's *Merchant of Venice* is a commentary, was not much selected by the economists for quotation. Later generations found it bizarre, while our times will not tolerate a commercial lecture from a philosopher who defended (however unsatisfactorily) the institution of slavery on grounds of natural law. For money – and perhaps, who knows, Aristotle sensed it – cannot function and reproduce except in conditions of technically free wishes. It is money that emancipates the slave and serf, opens society to women, delivers children from the authority of their parents, makes Greek and Barbarian alike: indeed, one might almost say that liberty as a modern idea is represented by money. I suspect that is the meaning of an even more abstruse passage in the *Nicomachean Ethics*, which we must now, with reluctance, address:

> It was for this that men invented money, which serves as it were as a middle term, for it measures all things, and shows where there is surplus or deficit: such as how many shoes are equal to a house or so much food. As a builder is to a shoemaker, so are shoes to a house or a quantity of food (for without it, there can be no exchange or association); and it can't be unless they are equal.
>
> It is necessary that all things should be measured by one thing, as was said before. This thing is in truth need, which is what keeps everything together (for if men need nothing or their needs change, there will be no exchange or it'll be different). Money has come to be the conventional substitute for need, which is why it is called CUSTOMARY THING (*nomisma*), because it exists not by nature but by custom, and can be altered or annulled at will.[31]

The passage appears in a discussion of justice in the world: for exchanges to be fair, they must match need, for which money is an artificial measure. The difficult sentence that has offended the economists – to the extent that Schumpeter said Aristotle was no economist – is the sentence that begins: *As a builder is to a shoemaker* . . . For it is a principle of money that it is quite indifferent to the person of the buyer and seller: in the developed money economy, all distinctions of character, station, sex, age, strength and colour of the payer are dissolved. Yet I think its meaning can be unravelled and Aristotle was no economist only in the sense that Plato was no tennis player.

Aristotle reached by logic the notion that builder and shoemaker were equal before money – were equalised by money as men as money equalised their labour and products – but was horrified by the next stage of the argument: that men were equal before society and the law. For such a conclusion would demolish his world of slave and free, Greek and Barbarian. And indeed, Aristotle's world is going to hell: Alexander is at the gates of Athens, and he will unite the whole world in one empire and take coined money as far as Spain and India, and be himself reborn as a Greco-barbarian deity. Aristotle's ethics are as nostalgic as the gentleman culture of the planter class in the ante-bellum American South or the ideologies of the old Communist Party of the Soviet Union: to the age of money, which cannot tolerate any commercial discrimination, let alone slavery, they sound like the rankest hypocrisy.[32]

Money is normative. So pervasive is its influence on our lives that it makes less moneyed ages incomprehensible, consigning them to barbarism or folklore. Yet history is not inevitable: antiquity did not aspire to our present condition and might have generated a quite different present. Meanwhile, money has helped multiply things and people, and subtracted other living creatures, animals and plants – that is, quantities – but not made progress – a matter of quality. Masterpieces of thought, poetry and drama, sculpture and architecture are rare in all cultures except the ancient Greek, where they are like pests: to speak of progress in literature, philosophy or the plastic arts from them to us is to talk nonsense. Even Rome, a less attractive civilisation, produced unexampled monuments in law, public works, civil administration and soldiering. As late as the sixteenth century, Montaigne was haunted by the parsimony of the republican Romans and their astonishing achievements.

It does appear that Greek civilisation conspired in its own destruction: that its great invention, coined money, undermined its other monuments of art and intellect. That was certainly the conclusion of Longinus. His treatise, which is in Greek so difficult that even so good a scholar as Gibbon nearly gave up on it, is known on its surviving manuscripts as *Peri Hypsous* or *De Sublimitate* (*On the Sublime*). It begins as a conventional manual of rhetoric and then transforms into the purest gold. In it one senses a great civilisation turning to dust, the death of learning and the extinction of liberty; and on that scanty evidence, the scholars have dated it to imperial Rome. Towards the end of the manuscript, Longinus speculates why the world he loves has disintegrated, and comes up with the only answer possible: *he gar philochrematia*, it is love of money.[33]

S £ ¥ S £ ¥ S £ ¥ S £ ¥ S £ ¥ S £ ¥ S £ ¥ S £ ¥ S £ ¥ S £ ¥ S £ ¥ S £ ¥ S £ ¥ S £ ¥ S £ ¥ S £ ¥ S £ ¥ S £ ¥

Thirty Pieces of Silver

Benedictus qui venit in nomine auri et argenti[1]

Blessed is he that cometh in the name of gold and silver.

Christians believe that Jesus Christ was a man, subject to human grief and mortality, and yet also an omnipotent God. In the breadth of his power, Jesus could have chosen to be a human being of any description, stature, degree, condition; and yet he chose to be poor. Jesus' poverty is an important attribute: the most important (after his divinity) to some of the early Church Fathers, to St Francis of Assisi and his followers in Umbria in the thirteenth century and to the English poet Christopher Harvey in the seventeenth:

> It was thy Choice, whilst thou on Earth didst stay,
> And hadst not whereupon thy Head to lay.[2]

To the modern mind, both poverty and divinity have lost conviction; but for several centuries, from about the reign of the Roman emperor Constantine until Columbus' voyages of discovery, the biography of Jesus fascinated the Europeans and they took it with them wherever they went. Throughout the Middle Ages, Jesus is forever appearing to the saints not just as God but as pauper: muffled, in the nightmare of Peter the Banker in sixth-century Alexandria, in a cloak Peter had that day tossed in a fit of fury at a beggar. St Francis ordered his followers 'not to handle or receive money and coins, or cause them to be received; and have no more use or thought for money and coins than for stones.'[3] The implications of Christian poverty are very profound: for if the poor are the image of salvation, then the daily struggle to ward off poverty – the whole worldly existence of accumulation and provision – is merely a side-show to the true drama of life. In time, of course, that side-show will become so elaborate and various that it will gain its own self-evident authority and displace the other attractions of existence.

Within Jesus' theology, we are concerned solely with his attitude to money and the unworldly note it introduces into human activity, which still has not quite died away: so unworldly that I, for my part, sometimes wonder whether Jesus could have been all man. The doctrine barely has predecessors, among the philosophers and prophets, and its successors set off in another direction. The teaching of the Koran, which the Muslims hold to be the word of God recited by the Prophet Mohammed, is expressed in the most homely commercial language (if the word 'homely' can be used about the Meccan Arabic of the seventh century. There is no blasphemy there: Allah can use any language he chooses, and he chose that one.) The Muslims do have difficulty with the productivity of money – if that indeed is what is meant by the word *riba'* in the Koran – but they are at home in the world of money to an extent Christians can never be and still be Christians. The Koran looks with favour on private property, the inequalities made possible by money, and commerce in general: Muslims may even trade on the Pilgrimage to Mecca.[4] By paying the annual alms tax (*zakat*) the Muslim 'cleanses' or 'purifies' the fortune that remains to him. Thus the manners of Muslim wholesale merchants in modern Egypt or Iran, with their mixture of piety and margin, which seem so hypocritical to the Christian, are, in fact, not so at all: those men believe they are doing not merely well but right. The great theologian Ghazali, in his *Renewal of the Religious Sciences* of the turn of the twelfth century, quoted the Koran, traditions of the Prophet and sayings of wise men of the past to argue that honest trade was preferable to self-denying piety; for the sincere merchant, as Ibn Jazid al-Nahai is said to have said, 'fights the jihad with the devil in his weights and measures and his transactions.' The Caliph 'Umar is said to have said, 'Death can come upon me nowhere more pleasantly than where I am engaged in business in the market, buying and selling on behalf of my family.'[5] The Sufi or dervish tradition, which glorifies mendicancy and gives such lustre to Iranian literature, is actually a Christian influence.

In contrast, there is a cussedness about Jesus' statements on money, and an irrational hastiness about his conduct in money matters, that were stumbling blocks to his contemporaries and, to the eighteenth century, quaint impediments to progress as measured and made possible by money; while to our age the Gospels, like Aristotle's philosophy, seem mere antique protests at pecuniary habits of thought as they penetrate the most intimate corners of society. And yet, returning to the Gospels I read as a child, with their demoralising mixture of the strange and the intensely familiar, I am struck again by the obstinacy of Jesus' monetary theology: how it resists the dull pressure of events and the sameness of human thought and aspiration. But that, I recognise, is ideology.

The Gospels glitter with money, and it is possible, without great effort, to identify which coins Jesus had in mind on each occasion he spoke about money. Those coins, whether Roman, Greek, Phoenician or Jewish, survive in one or two exemplars, for it's hard to destroy the precious metals. Some were accidentally lost or buried in hoards in times of trouble; others overstamped or welded into jewelry for girls and women; or converted into other coins or cups or plate; so that the thirty Tyrian tetradrachms which were the price of Jesus' life have certainly come down the generations to us, if not in form at least in essence; and somewhere, in some museum or collector's cabinet or dealer's stock, dispersed in a necklace or cuff-links, still blaze with their ancient deicide.

Money is used in the Gospels not in the reflexive fashion of today: each use requires a decision. From both circumstance and choice, Jesus and his disciples don't have much to do with money[6] and when they handle money, it is never casually. Indeed, when money does enter the Gospels, there is always a certain tension or quickening of the narrative: as if the evangelist were saying, Now, just listen to what he had to say to this! For it is as if Jesus recognises money as a competitive authority: that in embodying happiness and reward in tangible, earthly form, money is more persuasively heaven than Heaven.

In fact, the coins in the Gospels represent several competing authorities. The most domineering is that of the Roman Empire, which had taken control of Judaea and Samaria sixty-three years before the year traditionally held to be the year Jesus was born. The Roman general Gnaeus Pompey captured the Temple Mount in Jerusalem and, according to the turncoat Jewish historian Flavius

Josephus, entered the Holy of Holies and saw (but did not touch) two thousand talents of 'sacred' or tribute money.[7] (A talent is an exceptionally imprecise measure of weight, equivalent here to about 25 kilograms.) Another is the Jewish state, submerged for the moment under Roman rule but somehow eternal, and clustered round the Second Temple, which embodies the personality and privilege of Jewishness. Both authorities presume to levy taxes from the inhabitants of Palestine, but only in their own moneys; and in the tribute coins, the Roman denarius and the shekel or substitute shekel, there is a sort of opposition, as if they were constantly threatening to clash and explode like two pieces of plutonium. They eventually do so. The Roman procurators Pontius Pilate and then, about A.D. 66 and spectacularly, Gessius Florus attempt to get their hands on the temple treasure.[8] The Jews revolt, and mint from the treasure a haunting series of coins. The Romans retaliate and bring down a cataclysm on the Jews from which they sense they have never recovered. Nobody knows whether the Second Temple had been destroyed by the time Matthew, the name given to our chief source, came to be written down or whether it lowers over Matthew's tales of money as prophecy or history.

The chief Roman money is called in the Greek Gospels *denarion*, which is denarius in Latin, penny in the English of the Authorised or King James Version of the Bible and, in the inflationary Revised Version, shilling. It is a little silver coin that had been first minted about two hundred years before Jesus and passed into Palestine either as payment for Jewish produce or labour or as wages for the Roman garrison. According to Matthew, who may be the disciple described as a customs officer in Chapter 9 and certainly has a good grasp of money matters, it was pay for a day's unskilled labour.[9] It survived the collapse of the Roman Empire, and, when money was revived in Europe in the seventh and eighth centuries A.D., for about five hundred years was the only European coin: until, indeed, the expansion of commerce in the thirteenth century caused the cities of northern Italy to mint heavier coins of fine silver – *grossi* or 'big ones' – and golden florins, ducats or sequins and genovines. In England, *d* was the abbreviation for a penny until 1971; *denaro* is the usual Italian word for money; and dinars are still coined or printed for use in Kuwait and Iraq and the smaller states of the Persian Gulf.

The denarius is important because it is, in Jesus' telling phrase in Matthew, *to nomisma tou knesou*, the money in which the Roman poll-tax is paid.[10] It is, as it were, the star under which he was born in Bethlehem, where − according to another evangelist, Luke − his earthly parents had gone for registration for tax purposes. It is the embodiment of Roman sovereignty. To pay or withhold it is to express an opinion on the legitimacy of that sovereignty: indeed, simply to handle the coin is to acquiesce in the Roman Empire. One of the examples in the British Museum, minted in the town in France that is now called Lyon, shows the head of the Emperor Tiberius, facing right and wearing a wreath of laurel, with the inscription

TI CAESAR DIVI AUG F AUGUSTUS

while the other, or reverse, side has a female figure seated and holding a sceptre and flowers, with the abbreviation

PONTIF MAXIM

Translated out of inscriptionary Latin, it reads: *Tiberius Caesar Augustus, son of the divine Augustus, and high priest.* But to the Jews, for whom there is only one God, merely to portray the emperor was wrong, let alone to deify him. 'Thou shalt not make unto thee any graven image,' says the God of Exodus, 'or any likeness of any thing that is in heaven above, or that is in the earth beneath.'[11] As a collection of words and pictures, this coin simply could not have been more offensive to Jewish sensibilities. The Jews who collected this hateful money on contract for the Romans, men such as the disciple Matthew before his call, are regarded in the rabbinic literature as turncoats and are in the same category of sinfulness as prostitutes. In the gospels, these 'publicans' are always bracketed with sinners.

Matters come to a head soon after Jesus enters Jerusalem in triumph. On the third day of the Passover festival, the religious puritans known as the Pharisees and the monarchist Herodians ask him whether Jews should pay the Roman head-tax. It is an insurrectionary question, and Jesus' answer is diplomatic in the extreme: it is also one of the most important statements ever made about money. Jesus calls for a denarius and asks:

Whose is this image and superscription?

They say unto him, Caesar's. Then saith he unto them, Render therefore unto Caesar the things which are Caesar's; and unto God the things that are God's.[12]

At first sight, that all appears naïve to the point of stupidity. In no sense can Tiberius be said to own the denarius in question, any more than the Queen of England owns the British banknotes or the heirs of George Washington the billions of dollar bills in circulation. Self-interested claims that princes owned their nation's moneys were demolished by Nicholas Oresme and Ibn Khaldun in the Middle Ages. In fact, it is a highly sophisticated answer. Jesus first distinguishes between two realities, the political and what we'd now call economic – the kingdoms of Caesar and money – and the eternal – the kingdom of God. Then he answers the underlying or hypocritical question: No, there will be no armed revolt or even passive resistance to Rome: the tax and the coins themselves are simply temporary and indifferent expedients which will soon be abolished because the kingdom of God is at hand.

It was a successful answer. The Pharisees and Herodians were impressed and, according to Matthew, left him in peace for the last few days of his life. But it was a fatal answer. For as the kingdom of heaven was postponed, year after year, century after century, Christians interpreted Jesus' statement to mean quite the opposite. For his statement, intended presumably as an ascetic or revolutionary negation of the world of money, can just as easily be its affirmation. With that statement, Jesus dug his doctrinal grave. For he seemed to be authorising the creation of two separate and co-ordinate kingdoms, religion and what is now called the economy. To the Muslims, such a separation was (and is) nonsensical; but it was an opportunity that Europe and America seized with both hands. Between one revenue official, Matthew, and another, Adam Smith, the Christian doctrine is turned on its head.

The chief other money is Jewish money, by which I do not mean money made by Jews but rather available for Jewish purposes. Religion and custom enjoined on Jewish men the payment of half a shekel a year for the maintenance of the temple operation: the practice seems to have begun after the return from Babylonian exile

and harked back to a prescription of Moses in Exodus.[13] The tribute
was generally paid at the time of the most important festival, that of
Passover. The problem was that the various Jewish puppet rulers
hadn't the credit or the authority to mint anything but copper coins,
which were hardly suited to the temple tribute. The equivalent in
Greek money, and the word Matthew uses, was the *didrachma* – the
double drachma – but that itself was a rare coin. It seems therefore
to have been the practice for two men to combine and pay with the
relatively current four-drachma coin – the tetradrachm or stater –
minted by the Phoenician city of Tyre or some other Asian city
such as Antioch. (The British Museum examples of the Tyrian
tetradrachm have a portrait of the city deity, Heracles-Melquart, and
look far from ideal from a Jewish point of view; but no doubt they
were better than the hateful denarii.) It will be clear from the above
that the whole situation was immensely complicated and money-
changers would be heavily in demand.

Let us follow the course of monetary events in Matthew, which
is the sort of systematic account one would expect from an official
of the revenue. In Chapter 17, Jesus and the disciples are again in
the north, at Capernaum on the Sea of Galilee, where Matthew the
disciple had farmed the taxes before his call. Passover is at hand and
the temple tribute-collectors approach Peter:

Doth not your master pay tribute?

To which Peter answers, Yes, and goes inside to Jesus, no doubt to
get the money. The question may have been quite straightforward,
a simple rattling of the tin; but Matthew doesn't present it so. The
evangelist seems to take it to mean: does Jesus intend to provoke a
schism?

And when he was come into the house, Jesus prevented him,
saying, What thinkest thou, Simon? of whom do the kings of the
earth take custom or tribute? of their own children, or of strangers?
Peter saith unto him, Of Strangers. Jesus saith unto him, Then
are the children free.[14]

Again, a worldly dilemma is translated to the eternal, where it loses
all urgency and even sense. Yet, as ever, Jesus wants nothing to do
with overt political action and there follows a miracle. It is one of

only two miracles in Matthew that are not clearly labelled as such.[15] Its legendary quality does not inspire great confidence; but let us take the text as it has come down to us.

> Notwithstanding, lest we should offend them, go thou to the sea, and cast an hook, and take up the fish that first cometh up; and when thou hast opened his mouth, thou shalt find a piece of money: that take, and give unto them for me and thee.[16]

The coin in question, for which the word is 'stater', is a tetradrachm, and was minted either in heaven or in Tyre. The temple tax has been paid by God. There is no question of Jesus himself submitting, through the medium of money, to the official cult or defying it. The schism has been avoided.

In Chapter 21, Jesus enters Jerusalem in triumph, goes straight to the temple and, in an act of outrageous petulance, overturns the money-changers' tables. It is possible that they were overcharging the pious, as some interpreters have surmised, but then I imagine Matthew or the other gospels would have told us so. It seems much more likely that the service they were providing and where they were providing it, though useful and legitimate, were in some way abhorrent to Jesus. With the bankers out of the way, Jesus preaches in the court by day, though he leaves the city, no doubt on advice about his safety, at nightfall.

The first half of Chapter 26 deals with the events of the fourth day of the festival. It is dramatic in form. It opens with the secret meeting of the elders and High Priests at the house of Caiaphas

> And consulted that they might take Jesus by subtilty and kill him[17]

and then cuts, in a fashion more familiar from films than literature, to the house of Simon the Leper in Bethany, where Jesus is having dinner. It is not clear whether this is a simultaneous event or a recollection.

> There came unto him a woman having an alabaster box of very precious ointment, and poured it on his head, as he sat at meat.[18]

The disciples, who see the ointment as a sort of liquid money, are aghast, 'for this ointment might have been sold for much, and given to the poor.'[19] Jesus, who seems in these passages to be oppressed to the depths of his nature at the prospect of his ordeal, also finds a quality within the ointment but it is certainly not money. Nor is it charity in its modern sense of pecuniary bounty to the poor. It is charity in the sense of love in the face of death:

> For ye have the poor always with you; but me ye have not always. For in that she hath poured this ointment on my body, she did it for my burial. Verily I say unto you, Wheresoever this gospel shall be preached in the whole world, there shall also this, that this woman hath done, be told for a memorial of her.[20]

Matthew cuts back to Jerusalem, the High Priests and the kingdom of money. He now introduces the most famous money in theology, the *triakonta argyria*, the thirty pieces of silver.

> Then one of the twelve, called Judas Iscariot, went unto the chief priests, and said unto them, What will ye give me, and I will deliver him unto you? And they covenanted with him for thirty pieces of silver. And from that time he sought opportunity to betray him.[21]

These famous coins have a triple existence, Jewish, Christian and, as it were, universal. At the Jewish level, they are tetradrachms out of the temple treasury, thirty of them, of the type that Peter drew out of the mouth of the fish at Capernaum; that Pontius Pilate had, according to Josephus, tried to confiscate for a water project and thus provoked the unrest for which Jesus was a scapegoat; that financed the revolt in A.D. 66 and were denounced, again according to Josephus, by the Roman general Titus, in his speech to the insurgents in the smoking temple ruins.

> And what is our chief favour of all, we gave you leave to gather that tribute which is paid to God . . . till at length you became richer than ourselves . . . and you made preparations for war against us with our own money.[22]

He demanded the Jews henceforth pay their tribute as war reparations to the Temple of Jupiter on the Capitoline Hill in Rome.[23] These coins therefore embody the independence of the Jews extinguished by Titus in A.D. 70.

For the Christians, these coins are minted out of the centuries of prophecy and prove that Jesus was the Messiah; for as the German philosopher Friedrich von Schelling said in the eighteenth century, the life of Jesus 'had been written long before his birth.' The coins originate not so much from the temple treasury as from a prophecy of Zechariah, at the time of the building of the Second Temple: a passage so corrupt or deranged that in the Authorised Version, at least, it seems to make no sense at all. (Matthew wrongly attributes it to Jeremiah.)

> And I said unto them, if ye think good, give me my price; and if not, forbear. So they weighed for my price thirty pieces of silver.
> And the Lord said unto me, Cast it unto the potter: a goodly price that I was prised at of them. And I took the thirty pieces of silver, and cast them to the potter in the house of the Lord.[24]

Underlying that passage is one yet older, a fragment of the law of Moses no less. Exodus 21:32 stipulates that the compensation for an injured slave is thirty shekels of silver. (Here a shekel is a measure of weight since there was no coinage in the time of Moses.) It is nearly impossible to disentangle what those ancient prophecies and pre-scriptions meant to Matthew and his auditors, but it seems to have something to do with value. There is a dramatic or ironical contrast between the slave and the Messiah, between what the High Priests thought Christ was worth and how the Christians valued him.

The coins have another layer of meaning. You may read what I have to say here as theology or literary criticism depending on who you think is the author of the story: God or the person or persons called Matthew. At Capernaum, Jesus was reluctant to pay the temple tribute *because he foresaw what use it would be put to*. Jesus saw, in a sort of monetary epiphany, his own agonising and shameful death. The puzzle is unravelled piece by piece: the strange miracle of the fish and the coin, the cleansing of the temple and the overturning of the money-changers' tables, the box of ointment, the thirty pieces of silver. Jesus will inevitably appear irrational, petulant or sentimental unless we recognise that he saw, in money, the agent and symbol of his death. Which, after some hesitation and in regret, he embraces.

In many representations of the Last Supper, the thirty pieces are portrayed as the instrument that breaks the magic circle of Jesus and the Twelve; for unlike Peter's timidity or Thomas' doubts, they pierce the ring while Jesus is still alive in all his authority. In one such fresco I have seen, I cannot remember where, the purse of coins that Judas holds beneath the table is stamped with a black devil like a tarantula; while another demon is incinerating Judas' chair leg. The writer William Hazlitt the elder, who lived at the turn of the nineteenth century, recalled an occasion when he and his friends played a conversational game: Whom would you most like to see from the past? They ranged over historical worthies until, right at the end, Charles Lamb said, 'I would fain see the face of him who, having dipped his hand in the same dish with the Son of Man, could afterwards betray him.' All were agreed that not even Leonardo da Vinci, in his famous Last Supper in Milan, had managed adequately to portray Judas Iscariot.[25]

They didn't know that one artist did attempt such a portrait. The picture I have in mind is the one numbered A15 in the first volume of the famous *A Corpus of Rembrandt Paintings*, published by the Stichting Foundation Rembrandt Research Project in The Hague in 1982. It is a smallish oak panel, measuring 79 cm × 102.3 cm and, according to the learned Dutch scholars, 'certainly authentic' since it is documented as no other early work by this artist.[26] It is generally called *Judas, Repentant, Returning the Pieces of Silver* and was probably painted in 1629: the same time as the Poussin Midas we talked about in the previous chapter and that, as we shall see, is no sort of coincidence.

From the moment it was painted, the picture was seen as something very special, inaugurating not just the painting of the Dutch Republic as an independent and self-conscious profession but an entirely new world of thoughts and conduct, what we would call modernity. Constantijn Huygens, the great contemporary historian of Dutch painting, saw the picture in 1630 and, in a Latin manuscript in the Royal Library in The Hague[27] recorded an almost overwhelming excitement:

> With the painting of the repentant Judas bringing back to the High Priest the pieces of silver that were the price of Our Innocent Lord, I will illustrate what is true of all his work. Let all Italy come, and all that has come down of what is fine and worthy

of admiration from earliest antiquity: the posture and gestures of
this one despairing Judas, leaving aside so many other stupendous
figures [brought together] in a single painting, of this one Judas I
say who, out of his mind and wailing, implores forgiveness yet
holds no hope of it, or has at least no trace of hope upon his
countenance; that haggard face, the hair torn from the head, the
rent clothing, the forearms drawn in and the hands clasped tight
together, stopping the flow of blood [*ad sanguinem* could be 'till
they bleed']; flung blindly to his knees on the ground in an access
of emotion, the pitiable horror of that totally twisted body – *that*
I set against all the taste and refinement [*omni elegantiae*] of the
past, and I just wish that the brainless imbeciles could see it, those
people who contend – a contention we have argued against
elsewhere – that nowadays nothing is being done or said that has
not been said before or that classical antiquity has not already seen
achieved. I assert, in fact, that Protogenes, Apelles and Parrhasius
[archetypical Old Masters of antiquity] could never have imagined
– nor, even if they came back to earth, would they ever be able
to imagine – the separate features and universal ideas (and I am
embarrassed to say this) that a mere youth, a Dutchman, a miller,
beardless, has brought together and expressed in the figure of a
single man. Truly, friend Rembrandt, honour is yours: the
bringing of Troy, of all Asia Minor to Italy [that is, by Aeneas,
who in Virgil's *Aeneid* escaped from blazing Troy and, after much
wandering, founded the city of Rome] was nothing compared to
what this Dutchman has done, in carrying off for the Dutch the
honour of Greece and Italy though he's barely stepped out of his
native town.

Behind that glowing patriotic outburst is the conviction that
Rembrandt had come to grips not only with Matthew but with the
essence or label of modernity, which, it is already clear to the Dutch
(and, to a lesser extent the Spanish and English), is money.

The arrangement of the picture is unique for its age; and though
literary description of pictures is like the moving of heavy furniture,
laborious and slow when the glance is easy and quick, I will try to
describe this one from its photograph. In the centre of a wood-
planked floor, and of the picture, is not a human or saintly figure
but some money: large coins of silver, exactly thirty of them. What

coins they are I am not completely sure. They are silver dollars, certainly, torn out of the mountain at Potosí in the High Andes, though whether minted at Mexico or Lima or, more likely, overstruck as *leeuwendaalder* ('Lion dollars') in the Netherlands for trade with the East, I cannot tell. What is important is their number: already, under the influence of commerce and science, thirty is gaining some precision as a number, and enumeration is displacing appreciation as the pre-eminent mental attitude. (The great tulip speculation is just six years away.)

Above all, Rembrandt recognises their power. They are like grenades tossed into a crowded shelter, scattering the human figures, the High Priest and the man wearing the Polish sable *kolpak*, into the shadows. (Sketches and X-rays reveal that Judas first confronted an enthroned High Priest at left: presumably thoughts such as those I've suggested above caused Rembrandt to paint him out.) Of the human beings only Judas can tolerate the propinquity of the coins, but at an unspeakable cost. He has ceased to be human. He has been reduced in his shame to the condition of a dog. He whimpers to be put out of his misery. The detail is shattering. Tiny brush-drips show blood on his head, neck and ear. Flecks of white suggest tears on his closed eyelids, foam on his lips, teeth.

What Rembrandt has understood, and portrayed as nobody before or since, is the strangeness of money: that it breaks the chain of desire and effect. Money provokes people to act, for the sake of payment, in a fashion that, if they knew how the action would turn out, they would not contemplate. Rembrandt seizes the moment when the veil of money is torn asunder and wish and consequence come explosively together: Judas realises that he has assassinated the Son of Man. It is a moment of drama unequalled in painting and the encomium of Constantijn Huygens has always seemed to me excessively lukewarm, reserved and half-hearted. For in this flash of recognition, the miller's boy, the Dutchman, saw into the marrow of history: that the divine in man is dead beyond all resurrection; that there is nothing left to us but a few coins on a dusty floor and our bestial natures; and that in every monetary transaction, wholesale and retail, Christ is re-crucified.

★

Some five centuries after the death of Christ, Bishop Jacob of Saroug (451–521), a Syrian Monophysite, had a vision of the devil which he preached as a homily. His Satan is a cheerful sort of fellow, who has suffered a setback in Christ's redemption of humanity; but he is not disheartened, and he doesn't quit. He has a wonder weapon up his sleeve, which he calls in Syriac *rebitha*, and which we would call interest or usury or even capitalism. Priests and monks will, he thinks, be drawn to it and it will be their undoing. 'I do not mind,' says the devil, 'if the priest uses the interest he draws from his money to buy an axe with which to smash the temples of my idols. The love of gold is a greater idol than any image of a god . . . It is worth as much to me as all those idols put together! They have cast down the idols, but they will never cast down the coins that we shall put in their place.'[28]

3

An Idea of Order in Borgo Sansepolcro

Jérusalem l'ennuie.
Zola[1]

Jerusalem's a bore.

Coined money, the greatest legacy of antiquity, survived the collapse of the Roman Empire. Only in Britain, which lost the protection of Roman legions in A.D. 410 did money fall into disuse and then only for the purposes of trade. (It is a perversity of history that Britain, the country in which monetary habits of thought are most deeply entrenched, is yet the only place to have used money for a long period and then given it up.) Roman coins were still used as gifts and jewelry and for the assessing and possibly payment of damages: the laws of the Salic Franks, codified in Gaul in the sixth century, set Roman money values on every sort of injury down to the loss of a finger: as we have seen in the *Iliad*, money can exist in a sort of ideal form even when it isn't used for payment.

Archaeology is a random science, and one should not draw conclusions from a single site; but the early seventh-century Frankish gold *tremisses* (a third of a solidus) found in the ship burial at Sutton Hoo in Suffolk − 37 of them, with three blanks and two ingots beside the remains of a very beautiful purse of gold and Afghan garnets − are too marvellous to ignore. The numismatist Philip Grierson brilliantly surmised that they were wages to pay 40 ghostly crewmen, the captain and the pilot: parallels can be found in the little coin placed in the mouth of the dead in antiquity or the 'Hell Money' burned today at Chinese New Year.[2] The difference here is that money has lost its quotidian function and yet survives to discharge the ideal or supernatural wishes of kings, and perhaps only of kings. (The English monarch still does not handle money, except a special issue known as Maundy Money.) As for the earthly business of kingship, payments to military supporters are increasingly made in land: the forms of feudal organisation begin to take shape.

In the course of the next century, trade and political authority revive to the point that rulers and ecclesiastics, inspired by the faint memory of Roman civility, mint silver coins, a little smaller than a U.S. cent, that they call denarii. By the beginning of the next century, the eighth after Christ, a money standard based on weights of silver has become entrenched all over Western Europe. The equations

12 pennies, *deniers, denarii, Pfennige* = one shilling, *sou, soldo, Schilling*

and

20 shillings etc. = one pound, *livre, lira, Pfund*

are not challenged until the political revolutions of the late eighteenth century and will survive until decimalisation of the English and Scots coinages in 1971. I don't suppose it occurred to the British government of that year, which wanted nothing more ambitious than a little mild debasement to buy social peace, that it was abolishing an institution more ancient than the British nation, parliament or monarchy.

By fitful and hesitant steps, marked by false starts and gradual failures, silver coins begin to appear and circulate beyond the old frontiers of the Roman Empire of the West: in Bavaria, Bohemia and Saxony in the tenth century; then Denmark, Norway, Hungary, Poland, Baltic Russia and the Ukraine, Sweden, Scotland and Ireland; and, in the end, the Americas. Those coinages often attend the establishment of the Christian religion and a monarchical state: indeed, in restrospect, those institutions seem inseparable. In the literature of many places and times, there is a moment in which money has still not quite lost its strangeness, as here, from the thirteenth-century saga of the Faroe Islanders:

> Then Leif stepped over to Thrand, and took the purse and carried it farther out in the hut, where there was some light, and poured the silver out on to his shield, turned it over with his hand and

said that Karl should look at the silver. They looked it over a while. Then Karl asked Leif how the silver looked to him. He answers: 'I think that every single bad coin in the northern Islands has found its way here. . . . I am not willing to accept this money on the King's behalf.'[3]

That is the Western tradition of money. Meanwhile, the Muslims – the inheritors of Constantine's Roman Empire of the East – mint gold dinars (the *denarius aureus* of the Byzantine Empire) and silver dirhams, which pass into Spain and Africa, Russia and the Baltic and all over Europe. In 1266, Pope Clement IV rebukes the Bishop of Maguelonne in southern France for minting coins with the legends 'There is no god but Allah' and 'Mohammed is his Prophet': such imitation money is, it seems, 'displeasing to God and unprofessional in a bishop.'[4] In the East, the Muslim money eventually collides with the Chinese, which has long passed from spade and knife money to strings of cast bronze coins with a square hole in the centre and, from about the eleventh century, paper representations of them. The Islamic and Chinese traditions of money are eventually engulfed by the Western in the colonial period, as are the so-called exotic or primitive moneys including the peripatetic money cowrie of Asia, Africa and North America.

It is a quality of money that it does not divulge its history in use. *Pecunia non olet*, money doesn't stink, was a commonplace derived from commentaries on Suetonius' life of the Emperor Vespasian. Yet in the medieval hoards, or in works of literature from the Middle Ages, there are coins that seem to have passed across the known world. Dimishqi was transfixed by the strangeness of a Hindu coin he handled one day in the suq of Tripoli in what is now Lebanon.[5] Ibrahim ben Ya'qub, a Jewish traveller from Tortosa in northern Spain, found central Asian coins in the market of Mainz, on the Rhine, in 965: they had been minted in Samarkand two generations earlier.[6] Francesco Balducci Pegolotti, an officer of the Bardi banking house in Florence, who wrote an account of commercial practices on the eve of the Black Death, said merchants carried Italian linens to Urgench on the Aral Sea, sold them for bars of silver (*sommi*), which they took with them to China, exchanged the ingots for paper money at the border and used that to buy silks for the home market.[7] Marco Polo's account of the Chinese paper money, from the generation before, may not have been at first hand but it is particular and very plausible.

None of those moneys was as beautiful as the coins of the Greek cities – very few things are – but they were much more abundant. In the second half of the thirteenth century in England, in the reign of Edward I, there was, according to the numismatic historian Peter Spufford, more silver money (admittedly all in pennies) than at any time until the time of Pitt the Younger: between 1294 and 1298, Edward shipped abroad 120 tonnes of pennies to pay troops and allies in the Low Countries.[8] In the face of this inundation, the price of the use of money – what we now call the rate of interest – began to decline. Interest rose and fell and rose and fell in the course of the Middle Ages, but its long-run tendency, at least to commercial borrowers, was downward, and the fall in the thirteenth century was more steep even than that of the nineteenth. Unsurprisingly, coins are by far the most abundant artefact to have survived from the High Middle Ages.

Of course, the availability of money in Europe depended on the supply of silver and, a little later, gold; and the mines of the Harz Mountains and Freiberg in Saxony, the Tirol, Bohemia and Hungary were exhausted progressively more quickly as the skills of the miners increased. There was a permanent drain of money to the East to pay for the luxuries Europe had craved since the time of Christ, to finance the Crusades and to prop up the rickety Crusader kingdoms in Palestine. In times of trouble, money was buried or converted into plate or otherwise withdrawn from use. But such shortages of metal money – *strettezze* in the commercial Italian of the period – merely spurred ingenious merchants to devise surrogate moneys; and they had the wit to see that what they needed to reproduce was not money's substance (that is, metal) but its effects (payment). By the end of the fifteenth century, when the shortage of bullion for money was driving men over the oceans or into alchemical work-shops, Europe had the makings of a modern monetary regime: a hierarchy of gold, silver and copper or other base-metal coins; various kinds of surrogate money such as bills of exchange, local cheques, traveller's cheques, marketable securities and certificates of deposit; public credit, including, in Italy, municipal bonds and annuities; private banks; and a book-keeping system that has altered very little in the ensuing half-millennium. So much for the backward and monkish Middle Ages.

It is important not to be carried away by what we read. There is an unbreakable connection between money and written records; and the written evidence, from the worlds of court, church and counting-house, tells us nothing of how ordinary people used money. It is probable that even at the end of the fifteenth century, money in England, for example, was largely confined to London and the sea-ports except at harvest-time. Yet in the final version of *The Vision of Piers Plowman*, composed by William Langland in the 1390s, in Chaucer and in the carols of the fifteenth century, there is a familiarity with money and confidence in what it can do: *Gramercy my purse!* (that is: thanks be to my money!) is a common refrain in which the blasphemy is so faint as to be almost extinguished. François Villon, implicated in a spectacular burglary of 500 gold écus in Paris in 1456, uses money as a fund of scurrilous metaphor:

> *N'espargnez homme, je vous prie!*
> *Car vielles n'ont ne cours ne estre,*
> *Ne que monnoye qu'on descrie.*[9]

[Screw any man you find, for Heaven's sake, for you'll get old, and old women are like devalued money: they aren't legal tender.]

Mentally, the world has been changed out of all recognition. In Europe during this period, as later in Japan, the Americas and Africa, the use of money is beginning to transform relationships of both space and time: and so radically that it seems as if reality has been given a twist, rather as, in the early history of the Muslims, prayer was re-oriented from Jerusalem to Mecca. This change of *qibla* – to borrow the useful Arabic term – we cannot date with any precision, but there seems to be a period of accelerated change around the end of the twelfth century, when Richard I was King of England and St Francis was at Assisi: indeed, Richard's ransom and St Francis' elective poverty seem in retrospect to be fanfares for the triumph of money. Among the famous frescoes in the vault above the saint's tomb in the lower church at Assisi, known as the *quattro vele*, or four sails, is one of Christ espousing St Francis to a ragged but amiable

Lady Poverty: in so impersonating money, if only in its negative, Christianity at last awakes to its challenge.

In 1237, the bankrupt Latin government of Constantinople mortgaged Christ's crown of thorns to a syndicate of Venetian and Genoese merchants for a loan of 13,134 bezants, or iperperi (coins of African gold, known in Greek as *hyperpyroi*, or 'exceedingly pure,' which had replaced the debased solidus of Constantine). The relic was despatched to Venice but was redeemed by that pious monarch, Louis IX of France. On August 18, 1239, it was borne in triumph through the streets of Paris, the King himself leading the procession, barefoot and in his shirt. To house the crown and other relics, St Louis built the famous chapel in Paris known as the Sainte-Chapelle at a cost of 20,000 marks.

It is a characteristic of money to set matter in motion, and thus reveal to history the changed fortunes of men and states. The transfer of a crown from Byzantium to Paris in the thirteenth century seems, in retrospect, very much the proper thing to have happened. We don't know what value St Louis discerned in the crown: salvation, or something precious, regal and inert like a jewel, or a source of pilgrims' pennies on the Ile de la Cité: all three, no doubt, but in proportions we simply cannot reconstruct. Gibbon, describing the event with the double impatience of Protestant England and the eighteenth century, saw the relic as mere capitalised superstition. We can be sure that for the Venetian intermediaries it was merely a collateral security, so many Venetian lire in the form of a crown of thorns. The essence of the crown – that it was of thorns, not of gold – turns out to have been an illusion: it is of gold, after all. An entire doctrine begins to turn to powder.[10]

★

We apply the word 'feudalism,' loosely enough, to a set of social arrangements which bind human beings with ties of reciprocal service without using money. Indeed, the feudal systems of Europe and Asia appear to be reconstructions of relations in societies where both money and the central power have fallen into decay. In Japan, feudalism survived alongside a regulated money economy until the arrival of the Americans in the nineteenth century.

In its European form, a vassal kneels before his master, puts his hands between his master's hands and vows to provide complete and unremitting service; in return, he can theoretically expect protection and care, though it might just as easily be the most naked exploitation. The services demanded or discharged are political or honourable, as it were, rather than economic: indeed, anyone thinking in terms of profit and loss or asset and liability will have difficulty making sense of the feudal world: Adam Smith simply could not *understand* the Scots Highlands of his childhood. 'It is not thirty years ago,' wrote Smith with a shudder of relief and bafflement, 'since Mr Cameron of Lochiel, a gentleman of Lochabar ... whose rent [income from tenants] never exceeded five hundred pounds a year, carried, in 1745, eight hundred of his own people into the rebellion.'[11]

Feudal services have none of the precision of a sale or purchase for money: they might be as specific as a spring campaign or as vague as loyalty of you and yours until death. Money, which extinguishes the sensation of obligation – you may wish to return to the bookshop where you bought this book, but you do not *have to* – would appear to be fatal to this world of enduring interconnections; and that is indeed what happened. Money gnawed at the foundations of feudalism in Europe from the end of the twelfth century, Japan from the seventeenth, and the Arabian sheikhdoms from the twentieth.

Imagine a landscape: a meadow sloping steeply down to a stream, a mill with a watersplash, a locked chapel, a stand of oaks. (I have in mind a place in the Lot-et-Garonne district of France.) You will see in this landscape values both economic, in its actual and potential crops of fruits, grain, timber and money, and aesthetic, in its resemblance to a painting or a touristic brochure or a literary fantasy of rusticity. What you will not feel is the medieval sense of the place's uniqueness. For to the Middle Ages, the valley near Caylus I am talking about had no exchange equivalent, was inextricably bound up with its lord and tenants, could be improved or ruined but not sold and bought, for it existed in a sort of spiritual mortmain, still, inalienable, come to rest. (Indeed, if it was owned by the church, say the Abbaye de Beaulieu-en-Rouergue nearby, it was held in actual mortmain in a realm beyond the reach of money or exchange. It was the final and perfect embodiment of property as the earthly counterpart and sample of God's realm in heaven, eternal and inalienable – or at least until a Mirabeau or Napoleon Bonaparte comes along.)

The same can be said about the human beings who inhabit this landscape, tending hogs in the oak wood or bent double under bales of timber. They are not free, but they are also not the subject of market dealings: as yet, the labour of men cannot be detached and sold separately, like a lamb's fleece, nor, as far as we can tell, can a woman's sex. Even the lord is not free in any modern sense: he, too, is attached to the land, which, as Marx noted in wonder in his notebook in Paris in 1844, inherits him rather than he it. Eight generations of the Sacchi family worked on the plate of Milan cathedral.[12] Possessions are extensions of the personality: swords; beds and chairs carry names as glorious as those of suburban villas today. Even women and children – at least in the lord's rights to dispose them in marriage or wardship – fall within the vassal's personal duty. The so-called *droit de cuissage* or *ius primae noctis* may be a mere fantasy of prostitution projected back into a moneyless relation, but it is within the logic of European feudalism: that the system of rights and services embraced even the most intimate of a woman's attributes.[13] I find it significant that when women finally do re-enter European literature at the end of the twelfth century, for example at the court of Eleanor of Aquitaine at Poitiers, it is in a hallucinatory reversal of legal and customary reality: it is now the man who is plunged into the most abject subjection to his all-powerful lady; and such is still sometimes the basis of courtship in the Muslim world.

What is life like in such a society? Without money to defer wishes, human beings are delivered up to nature. Time is not money, as in our age, but the seasons. Fruits must be eaten or exchanged before they spoil; animals must be slaughtered and served up. Courts rotate around productive estates and Eleanor is reunited with her murderous sons. Wealth is displayed not so much in possession as in consumption: think of the feasts of Beowulf and the *Shahnameh* and Thomas Becket or, in our times, the Saudi princes in their nostalgic desert camping expeditions. The value of an object apparently derives not from monetary desire for it or from its ability to generate money, but from something interior or ideal: something is said to have a 'just price,' which is the return that permits its producer to maintain his station in a timeless society. Society is rigid:

it is hard to gain or lose wealth except through warfare or marriage, or alter in status except through spectacular acts of cowardice, villainy or courage, as when Eleanor was ambushed and the young Guillaume le Maréchal fought for her 'like a wild boar against dogs. . . . Valiant and courteous lady that she was, she bestowed upon him horses, arms, money [*deners*] and rich garments' and launched him on a brilliant career at the Plantagenet courts.[14] The chief metaphor for society is of a body whose each limb performs a special task: the blood that feeds them all, which was to become the metaphor of the age of money, had yet to be discovered.

As silver money flows out from the mines of Saxony, and the Italian cities begin to strike the large silver coins known as *grossi, gros* and groats, the feudal system begins to totter: though it survives in parts of France till the late eighteenth century and in Germany and Russia to the nineteenth. It seems that from about the 1180s, and with a certain amount of back-sliding, landlords increasingly demand rents in money rather than fruits or service. Many other social functions, including military service, are priced and absolved in money. In the self-sufficient world of the lord and vassal, an alien element – money and the central power – enters.

For Georg Simmel, the greatest German philosopher of money, writing in about 1900, that was the magic moment of human emancipation. The following passage is at the heart of his thought:

> The . . . level, where the person is actually excluded from the product and the demands no longer extend to him, is reached with the replacement of payment in kind by money payment. For this reason, it has been regarded, to some extent, as a *magna carta* of personal freedom in the domain of civil law. . . . The lord of the manor who can demand a quantity of beer or poultry or honey from a serf thereby determines the activity of the latter in a certain direction. But the moment he imposes merely a money levy the peasant is free, in so far as he can decide whether to keep bees or cattle or anything else.[15]

We might add that the lord is freed from his wholesome and rustic diet: he ceases to be the creation of his tenants. In other words, the indiscriminate satisfaction incorporated in money emancipates its users from the innumerable restrictions of what they can do or get.

By the eighteenth century, such matters had become so self-evident that Adam Smith spoke of the money economy as 'the obvious and simple system of natural liberty.' Yet even within the world of money, the tenant is still liable to his lord if he fails in his money payments. His bondage has been transferred to money, which embodies not only his liberty but his subjection to another human being. Final liberation comes, Simmel believed, when all the payments in a foreseeable future are rolled into one payment, a process known as capitalisation. It is only at that moment, when the tenant buys his plot for its capitalised income, that he is free. Those who cannot free themselves lose even the threadbare protection of feudal reciprocity. Eventually, in England for example, they may be evicted from common land by the process known as enclosure. Why shouldn't landlords, wrote a minister of the church in Leicestershire in 1653, 'have liberty to lay down the Arable land for grasse, when pasturage is more profitable than tillage.'[16] That ominous pairing of liberty and money profit, the foundation of the society of the West, has it origins in the twelfth century.

The land itself begins to change. The sloping meadow and the mill are no longer primarily sources of produce – of corn, hay, rye, barley, meat, wool, plums, walnuts and flour – but of money. Forests are no longer pre-eminently places for hunting – a matter then, as now, as much to do with power and display as with the table – but the site of a money crop called timber. The place is no longer regarded as unique, for how can it be so, if it submits to calculation and comparison in the market of wishes? It is this view of nature as submitting to the monetary calculus that revolted St Francis of Assisi, who set up against it a mystical system of moneyless connections, of brother Wind and sister Water.

Now that the crop is in money, it can be transferred over great distances, and the lord need no longer live on his land: he can, through money, live independently of his people and possessions. From this period, we date the slow agglomeration of capital cities, as centres of administration, consumption and luxury. The nobility and higher clergy build themselves inns and *hôtels* in Paris and London and Southwark. Great fortunes can exist at anonymous addresses: a merchant in a room can dream himself a king on the potential of the cash and securities in his chest, which wealth, if it

were in real property and men, would *oblige* him to be king. The
so-called *rentier*, who lives in cities off distant sources of income he
has no power or desire to control, comes padding onto the European
stage. The luxury trades expand to absorb the bourgeois desire for
impotent display. We see that domestication, refinement and dis-
armament of luxury through which, according to Sombart, women
begin to exercise influence. The eighteenth century, which had
none of our illusions about the productive character of capital cities,
understood their hedonism perfectly. *On a plus de désirs*, Montesquieu wrote, *plus de besoins, plus de fantaisies, quand on est ensemble.*[17]
Cities, as Plato told us and we had forgotten, are creations of money.

   Property begins to disintegrate into its two components, title and
use, *usus juris* and *usus facti*, as Gregory IX expressed in the famous
bull of September 28, 1230 that demolished the Franciscan Rule,
Quo elongati. The counterpart and rival of mortmain is the mortgage,
which attempts to tease out from property its monetary essence and
set it to work. From at least the end of the twelfth century, cartloads
of ecclesiastical treasure are put into circulation as working capital,
not simply by theft but also by mortgage: as far as I can tell, the
Third Crusade was almost entirely financed by payments on mortgage with rich abbeys playing the banker. (They coined plate to
make the payments.) So begins the ruin of the *petite noblesse*, a class
that forever is getting into trouble when money becomes the
favourite conveyance of wishes. In the cities of Italy, men now see
that it is no longer right (in the sense of profitable) to hold a fortune
in coin, let alone in plate. Whatever the church has to say, there is
something inherently productive within land, treasure and money:
that thing is what we call capital. In 1268, the merchant Ranieri
Zeno, who was also Doge of Venice, died leaving just 3,388 lire in
coin, or under 7 per cent of his fortune: the rest was at work as
sleeping equity in partnerships, negotiable city bonds and real estate.
It is a thoroughly modern investment portfolio.[18]

   In this process of disencumbering capital from treasure, right also
had to be teased out of wrong. The usury doctrine was more than a
mere technical hindrance. The Middle Ages did not use arguments
of expediency: the authority of scripture and Aristotle's theory of
natural justice must accommodate new commercial practice, for
they were complete systems, all or nothing. In tinkering with the

usury doctrine, and disentangling legal profit or participatory risk or compensation from the general ban – *lucrum, fictum, damnum, interesse, donum, remuneratio, premium; dono, guadagno; frais, finance; interest, consideration, gratuity* all become separate from *usura* – the merchants and Schoolmen perforated a system that was supposed to be watertight and allowed new ways of thinking, to do with experience and expediency and subjective value and self-regulating markets, to flood in. Money itself will in time assume the cast-off moral authority and give its possessors, as in Calvin's Geneva, that sense of election immortalised in Proust's Françoise: 'riches were for her, so to speak, a necessary condition of virtue, failing which virtue itself would lack both merit and charm. She distinguished so little between them that she had come in time to invest each with the other's attributes, to expect some material comfort from virtue, to discover something edifying in riches.'[19] Once time can be bought and sold through interest, there comes a new urgency to temporal existence: by the turn of the sixteenth century, according to Simmel, the church clocks in Germany are striking the quarter-hour. Time, once a calendar of agricultural events, cycles of birth, nubility and death and the unfolding of God's will, begins to tick away in units of money: in hourly rates and per diems, weekly wages, monthly salaries, half-yearly dividends, annual raises or bonuses, superannuation pensions, perpetual stock and, eventually, in that redemptive eternity the economists call 'the long run.'

Political relations are re-established on a monetary foundation. From the end of the twelfth century, the money fief – *fiefs-rentes* or *feoda de bursa* – begins to engross feudal ties and reciprocal service eventually gives way to employment for pay. Knights and castellans receive payments of money like a modern civil servant: their reward is no longer hereditary, and the link between service, family and place begins to break. Money taxes are levied from the peasantry in a much more systematic fashion than earlier efforts, such as the English Danegelds of the tenth century: the novelty of those taxes survives into modern consciousness through the story of Robin Hood and the exactions of Richard's brother, John.

Rulers find that by having money they can maintain standing armies without giving away their realms in perpetuity. Knightly troops are replaced by collections of mercenaries, who introduce a new brutality into warfare: not because they are paid in money but, I suspect, because they aren't or not enough and have to make up their wages in theft and rapine. Their camps, littered with whores and looted church treasure, are harbingers of a money society no less than the *libri segreti* of the Medici or the traffic in papal indulgences. The knights, shorn of the weapons of war, which are now the privilege of the owners of money wealth – *point d'argent, point de suisse*, No money, no soldiers! – take refuge in tournaments of chivalry and love.

For the English poet William Langland in the fourteenth century, money, in the person of Lady Meed or *mede ye mayde*, has turned society upside down, converting direct relations – between man and Christ, labourer and master, king and commons – into indirect relations. (Knowing no algebra, Langland uses the scientific language he does know, which is Latin grammar.)

> relatifs indirect   reccheth thei neuere
> of the course of the case   so they cacche suluer

[Indirect relatives care nothing about the *case*, so long as they can get money.]

He dreamed that *mede ye mayde* would be banished and Love would usher in a golden age. He told Richard II:

> And ich dar legge my lyf   that loue wol lene the suluer
> To wage thyne, and help wynne   that thow wilnest after,
> More than al thy marchauns   other thy mytrede bisshopes,
> Other lumbardes of lukes   that lyuen by lone as Iewes[20]

[I'll bet my life that Love will provide you with more money to carry out your will than all your merchants or mitred bishops or the Lombards of Lucca that live like Jews from lending.]

He would have had many takers for his bet. For by the late Middle Ages almost everything is priced in money: territories, an imprisoned king, the Holy Roman Empire itself bought by the Fuggers for Charles V, ecclesiastical offices, even salvation in the next world. *Blessed are they which have money; for theirs is the Roman Curia.*[21]

The Middle Ages also had practical questions about money: Whose is the money? What is it for? The questions became peculiarly acute with the defaults and debasements in England and France to finance their long war in the fourteenth century: Edward III defaulted on his Italian loans while his adversary used the mints as a form of taxation: the silver substituted by alloy became an additional revenue or seignorage. These monetary debasements were disastrous to those living on incomes fixed in money, such as absentee landlords and *rentiers*, but a boon to those who could pay their debts in the debased coin, such as the poor and above all the crown: these *grandes alliances* have been at it ever since. Oresme, writing in the middle of the fourteenth century, sets out the terms of this super-secular struggle with admirable clarity; but, in truth, there is no common psychological ground between the adversaries. As a bishop and a landlord, Oresme comes down decisively on the side of hard money: money, he says, is not the property of the prince but of the community which uses it; and he argues, threateningly, that princes that abuse their money will lose their kingdoms.[22]

It is fascinating to behold. Just at the moment when princes, through their control of money, gain the upper hand over their feudatories, so they fall prey to the bankers, who, murdered or mulcted or bankrupted by monarchs, will lend to them only at rates that incorporate those rather substantial risks. The advanced cities of Italy, such as Genoa and Florence, had already alienated themselves to their bankers, a process made manifest in Florence by the Medici dictatorship; while Machiavelli thought the creditors of Genoa, collected in the House of St George, should have taken over the whole city.[23] When in the 1520s the French crown is finally in a position to borrow through annuities, those have to be secured on the city of Paris. The absolutism of the *ancien régime* conceals an abject dependence on the purses of the bourgeois. The revolutions of the seventeenth and eighteenth centuries are already present in embryo.

Marx, worrying away at the nature of money in long vigils in the Rue Vaneau in Paris in the spring of 1844, was deeply sceptical about the liberty embodied in the use of money. For him, the rootless lord, insubordinate vassal and emancipated serf are now subject to a set of autonomous and superhuman relations, the rule of money: 'The medieval proverb *nulle terre sans seigneur* [there is no land without its master] is thereby replaced by that other proverb, *l'argent n'a pas de maître* [Money knows no master] which suggests the complete domination of living man by dead matter.'[24] He saw money as the successor of medieval religion, as an amalgam of human fear and desire estranged from its originator and granted dominion over him: truly, a mortgaged crown of thorns. He sought to restore not religion, but humanity. He revived the medieval notion of the just price, appealing not to a divine standard, but to a human: the real value of anything was the volume of human effort and misery that had gone into its making.

Marx, unfortunately, was no saint, and it is given only to saints to see into the nature of money: to look past its bland exterior, its obstinate refusal to divulge its history in transaction, and unlock from it a merciless nature. Towards the end of the fifteenth century, St Francis of Paola attempted to restore the corrupted Franciscan teaching in a regime of extreme austerity and a total renunciation of money. Travelling through Naples, he was offered a bag of gold for his expenses by King Ferdinand I. He refused it because, he said, it was the price of the blood of the King's subjects. 'To prove it, he took one of the gold pieces and broke it in two, whereupon several drops of blood fell from the money.'[25]

★

The road to Borgo Sansepolcro rises up from the motorway through fields of flowering hawthorn. I took that road, at the age of nineteen, in the Lazzi bus from Santa Maria Novella in Florence, and sensed, through the tinted glass and wreaths of tobacco smoke, that I was embarked on a great adventure. I was travelling, as many people do, to see the famous Misericordia madonna of Piero della Francesca, which everything in my life to that moment had been celebrating: a monument to piety, beauty, chivalry, technique and Italy. I came down the hill with another idea, as if each journey contains, at its termination, the origin of a new one. Turning away from my first goal – for you cannot look at a picture for ever – I saw, under the arcade of the town hall, another monument, ugly as sin, and erected in 1878 by the business people of Sansepolcro.

To Luca Pacioli
Friend and Adviser

of Leonardo da Vinci
and Leon Battista Alberti
Who first gave to Algebra
The Language and Structure of a Science
And Discovered
How to Apply it to Geometry
Invented Double-Entry book-keeping
Wrote Works of Mathematics that gave Foundations and
Invariable Forms
To Future Thought:
To their Great Townsman
The People of Sansepolcro
On the initiative of its Municipal Society
Ashamed of 370 Years of Neglect
Erected
This Monument in 1878

There is a portrait said to be of Luca by Piero as St Peter Martyr in an altarpiece of the Brera in Milan.[26] I have not seen it. But I did see another thought to be of Luca, by a different artist, two months later in the Naples picture gallery. It was then called *A Demonstration in Mathematics* and was attributed to Jacopo de' Barbari, a painter active in Milan in the 1490s. It shows a burly friar in a grey Franciscan habit, pointing with a wand to a construction drawn in chalk on a slate, labelled on the side with the word EUCLIDES. To his left is a gorgeously dressed young man, once thought to be Duke Guidobaldo of Urbino but just as probably a self-portrait of the artist. To Luca's right, suspended in air, is an object that takes the breath away. It is a crystal polyhedron. It shimmers, drenched in light and yet impenetrable in its mathematical perfection. It seems to be made of some unearthly material, brighter and more translucent than diamond. All its twenty-six faces – eighteen squares and eight equilateral triangles – are simultaneously visible. Some of the faces reflect images of buildings, standing no doubt beyond an open window outside the picture frame.

It is as if the painter thought there was something miraculous about his subject, and many people from Thomas Gresham to Goethe, were later to agree. Across the interval of time, Luca does indeed seem admirable not simply as an overlooked hero of a celebrated age but even, as Goethe thought, one of its greatest. If his master, Piero della Francesca, and his friends, Leonardo da Vinci and L. B. Alberti, still astonish us with their notions of a mathematical order underlying phenomena – think of the Arezzo frescoes, Leonardo's sketch-books or Alberti's Tempio Malatestiana in Rimini – Luca identifies that order with money. His last work, incidentally, which includes Leonardo's drawing for the icosahexahedron, is entitled, not immodestly, *Divina Proportione*.

Luca never claimed to have invented double-entry book-keeping: indeed, he says he is merely reproducing the practices of the Venetian merchant houses where he served after completing his apprenticeship with Piero.[27] One need only read a paragraph of his treatise to see that we are dealing with a mature and tested system: the municipal accounts of the sea-port of Genoa, for example, are in double-entry even in the 1340s, which has led some scholars to detect an overseas, Islamic or even Indian, origin for the method. It was Luca's achievement to recognise, as many people still do not today, that such a body of technique is a worthy object of philosophy; and to print it clearly in the vernacular.

Fra Luca Pacioli or Paciolo or Paciolus was born, probably at Borgo Sansepolcro, between the years 1445 and 1450: that is, when Villon was studying in France and Henry VI was King of England. He was apprenticed to Piero – whom he describes as *el Monarcha ali tempi nostri dela pictura*, the King of painting in our times – possibly worked on the famous frescoes in the church of San Francesco at Arezzo, read in the ducal library at Urbino. 'When scarcely twenty years of age,' he moved to Venice as tutor to the three sons of the merchant Antonio de Rompiasi. In 1470, or thereabouts, he wrote a treatise on mathematics that he dedicated to the Rompiasi boys; and went abroad with them on business for, as he writes, 'on account of this merchant I travelled in ships carrying goods.'[28] At some point, he had met Alberti and lived with him in Rome in the early 1470s. He also, at some point, became a Franciscan friar and taught mathematics at Perugia, twelve miles from Assisi, at least until 1480. He seems to have been in occasional dispute with his order, possibly – and this is merely my guess – for activity in business, and was ordered back to his teaching post in 1486.

In 1494, he had printed at Paganini in Venice his *Summa de*

Arithmetica, Geometria Proportioni et Proportionalità under the name of Fra Luca di Burgo – that is, Brother Luke from Borgo Sansepolcro. It has five sections, of which the third is a treatise on book-keeping called *Particularis de Computis et Scripturis*. One of the most widely read books of the Renaissance, the *Summa* survives in 99 copies, of which at least one can be called up in an hour at the British Library. The book-keeping treatise was reprinted separately in 1504, again by Paganini, as *La Scuola Perfetta dei Mercatanti*, and passed by way of translation, imitation and paraphrase into Dutch, French and English in the next two generations. In 1546, Sir Thomas Gresham opened his journal, which is preserved in the Mercers' Company in the City of London, in exactly the fashion prescribed by Luca in his treatise:

> + LAUS DEO 1546
> . 26. Apryll.
> In the name of God Amen
> This present boke Shalbe the
> Jornall called + apperteyning to me Thomas Gresham
> of London mercer for therin to wryte with my own hande
> or els with the hand of my prentys Thomas Bradshawe
> all my hoole trayne and doynges [29]

Meanwhile, as the fame of the book resounded around northern Italy, Luca was invited to teach mathematics at Milan, where he met Leonardo, then at work on a bronze equestrian statue of Duke Lodovico and the fresco *Last Supper*. They probably worked together on the *Divina Proportione*, which is illustrated with woodcuts after Leonardo of the letters of the alphabet and the geometrical forms, including the polyhedron of the Naples portrait, which was no doubt painted at that time. A French invasion drove the court from Milan, and Luca seems to have wandered about princely and academic Italy, coming to rest as prior of a convent in Borgo Sansepolcro, where he had a reputation for laxness. In his will, written in 1511, Luca quotes a bull of Pope Julius II – his friend Giuliano della Rovere – giving him the right to dispose of 'up to three hundred large golden ducats.'[30] So much for Franciscan poverty in the High Renaissance.

To be able to keep books in double-entry is to have a machine for calculating the world. Understanding the technique is the work of a few days – practising it no doubt requires longer – but one feels one has mastered an ancient and far-flung language: one seems to see better into the nature of things. That soon reveals itself to be illusion. In reality, all one is seeing is a coded money value for all objects and occupations. Yet its influence on our thought has been almost without parallel. Our conversation is replete with assets and liabilities, depreciations, profits and loss, balance-sheets: all echoes of Luca's system. Above all, Luca laid the foundation of the modern conception of profit, not as some vague increase in possession, as in antiquity, but as something hard, even crystalline, mathematical and open to empirical test *at any time whatever* through an interlocking system of books.

Goethe, the last person successfully to inhabit the worlds of business and poetry, was entranced by double-entry. In *Wilhelm Meister*, a character calls it one of the 'loveliest inventions of the human spirit' and a reliable, daily measure of accumulating happiness.[31] Stephen Monteage, an English merchant writing in 1682, used the language of alchemy: 'This way of accounting which we Treat of, carries with it its own Proof; And here lies the Supreme Excellency and Usefulness of this mystery.'[32] Werner Sombart, wildly enthusiastic even on a bad day, was duly ravished:

> Double-entry book-keeping was born from the same spirit that gave rise to the systems of Galileo and Newton and the teachings of modern physics and chemistry. It uses the same methods as they to organise phenomena into an artificial system: indeed, it is the first cosmology on the basis of mechanical thought.[33]

He went on to detect the influence of double-entry in the theories of gravity and the conservation of energy and even of the circulation of the blood, itself the chief metaphor of the profession known as economics.

Modern practitioners of double-entry accounting affect a comprehensive tedium of manner as if to conceal the atrocious intellectual technology of which they are secret masters and mistresses. We would be wise to imitate them and, amid the Sombartian intoxication, to keep our heads. For we might just easily say that the duality of double-entry, which regulates both the accuracy and the completeness of the account, gave rise to Hegel's famous notion of the duality of historical events; and through Hegel to Marx's satirical masterpiece, *The Eighteenth Brumaire of Louis Bonaparte*. Luca's purpose, I imagine, and that of the Venetian houses who devised or perfected the system he publishes, was to protect their property against fraud, loss and damage now that their businesses had expanded beyond their families and households, and lending and borrowing scattered possessions out of sight and hand; and, through a comprehensive system, to measure the money-worth of one activity against another. 'You will always know,' says Luca, 'whether your affairs are going well or badly . . . and what needs remedying.'[34] It was not, I imagine, to invent capitalism.

You begin, says Luca, with the name of God. Your first journal should be marked with a cross, as Gresham's journal is and even some eighteenth-century sets of accounts that I have seen. Luca is a religious (of some sort, at least) and the world of business is still subordinate to religion: 'The end and object of every businessman is to make a lawful and satisfactory profit so that he may sustain himself. Therefore he should begin with the name of God.'[35] After making an inventory of all his possessions, moveable and immove-able, his money, and jewels and plate and bed-linen and chests, he should open three books: a memorandum (which is a diary of business events, which his wife may write in if he is absent on business), a private journal (which takes the daily entries of debit and credit based on the inventory) and finally the ledger, in which the main accounts are struck. Luca permits some latitude as to how the accounts are kept, but insists on one indispensable condition: that every journal and ledger entry must be made twice, as a *debit* on the left-hand side and a *credit* on the right-hand side. That means that at any moment a trial balance can be struck, which will reveal error, incompleteness or fraud; and the entries accumulated and cast off through a profit-and-loss account to give a notion of worth without the need for repeated inventory-taking:

> The Profit and Loss account shall be closed in this way. If the loss exceeds the profit (May God protect each of us who is truly a good Christian from such an eventuality), then credit the account in the usual manner. 'Credit Profit and Loss on such-and-such a day, debit Capital for loss sustained in this account . . .'[36]

Here is, without doubt, a rational framework for the pursuit of 'sustenance' and Sombart is no doubt correct to accord it a place in the capitalist pantheon:

> One cannot even imagine capitalism without double-entry book-keeping: they are as intimately related as form and content. There is a legitimate doubt whether capitalism created double-entry as a tool in its realisation or whether double-entry bred capitalism out of its inner spirit.[37]

Yet those Hegelian abstractions fall mournfully on the Anglo-Saxon ear; and Sombart was surely misguided in thinking that capital, which we define as property capable of generating profit, did not exist as a notion before Fra Luca's treatise (or, rather, the accounts of the Genoese *massari* and other pioneers of double-entry in the century before). Capital and profit existed in the antique mind: it is merely that in, say, the Roman manuals of estate management, or Cicero's forensic speeches, they are not defined with any precision. Indeed, what seemed in antiquity to be profit would sometimes be what we now call loss. Meanwhile, as the British economist-accountant Basil Yamey reminds us, institutions unconcerned with profit – monasteries, hospitals and municipalities – were among the early Italian users of *partita doppia*. The implication that the merchant houses that did not use double-entry – the Bardi and Peruzzi and Medici in Florence and the Fugger in Germany – were simply muddling through is quite daft. Against Sombart's German idealism, Yamey sets the British common sense of Defoe:

> Tho' the exactest book-keeping cannot be said to make a tradesman Thrive, or that he shall stand the longer in his business, because his profit and loss does not depend on his books, or the goodness of his debts depend upon the debtors accounts being well posted; yet this must be said, that the well keeping of his books may be the occasion of his trade being carried on with the more ease and pleasure, and the more satisfaction, by having numberless quarrels . . . prevented and avoided.[38]

The treatise is best understood as a symptom, rather than a cause. It reveals how property, which we have observed in this chapter slowly separating itself from the individual personality, has taken on, at least in the sophisticated merchant communities of northern Italy, a life and character of its own. In the conduct of the ledger, the businessman is actually the creditor or debtor of his own possessions! He must account *per* and *a* to those jewels and cash and Riga furs and Cremona linens and Palermo sugars and Toledo swords. In Van Eyck's famous *Arnolfini Marriage* of 1434 in the English National Gallery, the Bruges merchant Giovanni Arnolfini seems to disappear into his fur hat and cloak, and his wife into spendthrift yards of green silk. They look like royal children dressed up for a party: unformed personalities engulfed by their possessions.

Sombart thought double-entry abolished quality: that is, submerged the question Of what sort? in the question How much? 'One must no longer think of ships or shiploads, flour or cotton, but exclusively in terms of quantities, of increasing and diminishing amounts of value,' by which last word he means money.[39] The world is dissolved into numbers, and the undissolved residue – values that cannot be expressed in money – will ultimately be denied existence: *quod non est in libris, non est in mundo* (nothing exists unless it is in the books). That is an exaggeration. Luca insists on precise description of assets, not merely their enumeration and pricing. Even in the Arnolfini portrait, the painter is fascinated by the texture of the clothes and bed-hangings, even the fur of the lap-dog: they may be the pre-display trade samples of a far-flung business empire, but they are not mere congealed money.

In time, reality will be reduced to numbers by way of the financial markets. In the great speculations of the seventeenth and eighteenth centuries, tracts of the natural world are condensed into arbitrary money-values and traded feverishly for a while. Yet always some residual sense of quality – the fragility of a tulip or the dampness of a Louisiana swamp – at last breaks through mere quantity and the bubble collapses. Business people will find themselves frustrated by the characterlessness of money fortunes: and, wishing to display character, will convert their money into unrentable monuments. The Medici, for example, withdrew willingly from the banking business. Of course, rates of return on banking capital were falling, because there was more competition, but Lorenzo the Magnificent no doubt saw in Michelangelo's sketches for his library staircase qualities that defied calculation. In time, though, even works of

piety and art will submit to mobilisation by money. Whole altar-
pieces will be ripped out of Italian churches and taken to England,
and then to the United States, in return for money. Nowadays, a
work of art's chief predicate – what it is – is its auction-value. I have
found the funerals of friends less harrowing than the auctioning of
their property: a unique and loveable nature, already contracted to
its inert possessions, is broken into money and dispersed for all time.

Sombart's most interesting thought is this. The double-entry
account is not merely objective and rational and public, in the sense
of being comprehensible to others: it is also mechanical.[40] Once
started, and Luca is quite firm about this, it proceeds in a predictable
and specific fashion. The accounts become compulsory. Though
mere sheafs of figures, they acquire a dominion over the individual
who casts them up or has them cast up: 'Next to being prepared for
death, with respect to Heaven and his soul,' wrote Defoe, 'a
tradesman shall be always in a state of preparation for death, with
respect to his books.'[41] Nations, too, fall under their spell. The crude
accumulation of money by princes is displaced, eventually, by
national accounts with a left-hand page and a right-hand page.
Accounting quantities – for example, the surplus or deficit on
foreign trade or percentage increases in domestic product – become
shining goals of national aspiration.

All that lies in the lap of time. For the moment, in this beautiful
town, warmed by the genius of Italy like sunshine through a shirt,
let us celebrate a moment where history itself comes in by one gate
and leaves by another; and, while bidding farewell to Christian piety
and sexual chivalry in Piero's picture, welcome Luca's paean to
order and mathematics:

> Sixth   Debit Featherbeds. Credit Capital for so much in feathers.
> Record number of beds, description as per Inventory, and
> value in
> Lire   Grossi   Picioli[42]

4

A Disease of the Heart

Y yo estava atento y trabajava de saber si avía oro.
Columbus in the Bahamas[1]

And I took great care and effort to find out if there was
gold.

In the library of the University of Salamanca in Spain there is an old
document in Spanish so precious that an Italian translation was
entitled *lettera rarissima*, the rarest of letters. It is a copy of a despatch
written on the north coast of the island of Jamaica, addressed to The
Most Serene, High and Potent Princes, the King and Queen,
Ferdinand and Isabella of Spain, and dated July 7, 1503. A letter
addressed from the same place on the same day carries a curious
monogram, a mixture of Greek and Latin, that has been taken to
mean 'he who carries Christ with him': in other words, the Genoese
merchant-navigator known to Spain as Cristóbal Colón and to the
English-speaking world as Christopher Columbus.

The writings of Columbus have survived in abundance, but in
degenerate form: as manuscript copies or Italian and Latin translations
or paraphrases in the famous *History of the Indies* composed in the
next generation by the Dominican friar Bartolomé de Las Casas.
The letter in Salamanca is not in Columbus' own hand. Yet to read
it is as if to have written it: to see again the scalding beach and the
two worm-eaten hulks drawn up and roofed with straw for shade,
know hunger and thirst and a surly mutinous crew, and to dole out
European treasure – blue beads, combs, knives, hawks' bells and
fish-hooks – not for gold but for cassava. The letter is sealed and
handed to Diego Méndez de Segura, a young squire from one of

the vessels, who has bartered his helmet and cloak and one of his two shirts for a dug-out canoe. The 'enterprise of the Indies,' which began in triumph when Rodrigo de Triana sighted the Bahamas from the mast of the *Pinta* late on Thursday, October 11, 1492, and with it dreams of gold, salvation, commerce and empire, is ending in fiasco.

With another Christian and six Indians, Diego sets off against the current towards the Spanish settlement of Santo Domingo, on the island they have named Española. On the evening of the fifth day, Diego and the survivors make landfall at Cape Tiburon on the extreme south-west of Española. Years later, Diego remembered the journey as the capital event of his life. In the will and testament he dictated in Valladolid on June 6, 1536, he asked there to be carved on his tombstone a hollowed tree and the letters C-A-N-O-A 'for such a thing I navigated three hundred leagues.'[2]

The reputation of these men has sunk to a level lower than even in their lifetimes: it is as if, in their violence and avarice and religion, they inaugurate those elements in the United States and Latin America that those civilisations would prefer to forget. The cities and states and corporations named after them – all those Columbuses, Columbias and Colombias – now seem embarrassed by their names. The great monuments of the fourth centenary, crowned by the vast catafalque of Columbus in the cathedral of Seville of 1898, are ridiculed, at the fifth, by sceptical or mealy-mouthed biographies. That by Felipe Fernández-Armesto of 1991 – to choose one from a handful – declares Diego was bragging about a puny crossing easily made by small craft today; while the letter he was carrying was a mixture of delusion and outright lies.

The world is mapped, both actually and in the mind. Each sea voyage is a ferry-crossing, in which the islands that rise and fall so maddeningly on the horizon are all named, and appear to be inhabited. It is hard to imagine oneself a mariner setting out on a journey without knowing where he is going, how, when, even why. It is hard to reconstruct the mental attitude of faith.

For myself, I cannot read Diego's testament or the *lettera rarissima* without the most profound emotion. For in the letter, Columbus distils all the horror and regret of his devastated life. As he recounts the stations of his career for his royal taskmasters, alternately lucid and deranged, childlike, credulous, half-educated, pedantic, Columbus is plunged into self-pity or stabbed by a passionate self-regard. He does not know if Diego and the Indians will win through or even if the authorities in Santo Domingo, which had cast him into irons three years before, will send rescue. (In fact, it will take Diego eleven months to buy a boat and send it down to Jamaica.) Columbus fears he will die; and dying be delivered up to his greatest fears, poverty and hell. Indeed, he has never been able to distinguish the two any more than he can distinguish between money and salvation: 'Gold is a most excellent thing. It constitutes treasure. Whoever has it can do what he likes in the world and even manage to get souls into Paradise. The gentlemen of the districts of Veragua have gold buried with them when they die; or so it's said.'[3]

Columbus' nineteenth-century editor, Martín Fernández de Navarrete, took him to mean that riches could expunge sin through prayers and pious foundations and the like.[4] In fact, it was a two-way process. The enterprise of the Indies was financed by Genoese bankers with an advance of 1.14m maravedis* secured on the future sale of indulgences in Estremadura. It is Paradise that is also very excellent, for it will even get a body to Jamaica.

Half-way into the letter, Columbus begins to rave. He has seen the lands of the Massagetae, whose horses are bridled in gold. In Veragua, the modern Panama and Costa Rica, he had had word of the mines of Solomon, with which he would rebuild Jerusalem and convert the Emperor of China.[5] South of the island he'd named Trinidad, he had sailed into a gulf fed by sweet waters, which proved that he was approaching the Garden of Eden, the *Paraíso Terrenal*.[6] And for what?

> Speaking of myself, little profit have I gained from twenty years of duty, during which I have served with so great labour and peril, for today I have no roof over my head in Castile: if I wish to sleep or eat, I have no place to which to go, except an inn or tavern, and most often I can't even pay the bill.[7] ... I entered your

---

* Originally a gold dinar of the Almoravid rulers of North Africa and Spain in the twelfth century, imitated by the Christian kings of Castile and León, it was reissued in the thirteenth century as a silver groat and was, by Columbus' time, a debased money of account.

service at the age of twenty-eight years, and now my hair is quite grey, and I am an invalid. . . . Of worldly goods, I have not even a blanca [a coin of copper-silver alloy] for the offertory; in matters of the spirit, I have here in the Indies become careless of the prescribed forms of religion. . . . My soul will be forgotten if it leaves my body in this place. Weep for me, whoever has charity, truth and justice. I did not sail upon this voyage to gain honour and wealth. . . . I humbly pray Your Highnesses that if it please God to bring me forth from this place, that you will be pleased to permit me to go to Rome and to other places of pilgrimage.[8]

The rescue vessel arrived in June 1504. Back in Castile, Isabella had died, and Columbus spent his wasting breath in petitioning her widower for his sons' inheritance. He died on May 20, 1506.

We do not know what Columbus was searching for when he set out on his first voyage west from Palos, near Seville, on August 3, 1492. The preface to the captain's log of the first voyage, as copied by Las Casas and now in the Biblioteca Nacional in Madrid,[9] gives an idea of how Columbus understood his mission. Since their Royal Highnesses had completed the war with the Moors, and raised their royal standard on the towers of the Alfambra (Alhambra in Granada), and expelled the Jews from their realms, they had thought to commission him, Cristóbal Colón, to travel to the Indies, by a westward route, to visit their princes and peoples and convert them to the holy faith, and provided him with a fleet and the titles of Don and Great Admiral of the Ocean Sea and Viceroy and Governor of 'all the islands and mainland which I discovered and gained in perpetuity.' There is to him no tension between those spiritual, strategic and feudal aims: he will take the Granada campaign to the west, and thus outflank the Muslims pressing in on Europe, restore the links of Christendom to its sources in Palestine, beat up on the Jews and establish latter-day Crusader seignories all over Asia.

Columbus' is not a modern mind. He set sail not for the Caribbean, the Gulf of Paria and the mouths of the Orinoco, Haiti, Cuba, Jamaica, Trinidad, Honduras and Panama, but into old maps decorated with real places (Catayo, Cipangu – China, Japan) and beautiful suppositions such as the Garden of Eden. His picture of the East was built up of layer upon layer of medieval geology. Persuaded by his reading, he drastically underestimated the circumference of the world: *the world*, he wrote to Their Highnesses, *is small*.[10] Columbus insisted he'd found – and made his men swear to it – the Asiatic mainland, as later he became convinced he'd approached the *Paraíso Terrenal*. What he really sought, of course, was money, and in that lies his modernity. In the log of the first voyage, the word for gold occurs so often that it might be a part of speech. The first question Columbus asked in the New World was that quoted at the head of this chapter: Look at this, have you any of it here?

We have seen already how, from the close of the twelfth century and for all the interruptions and dislocations of the fourteenth, money had come to pre-occupy great layers of European society. The expansion of trade in the fifteenth century was not fully matched by an expansion in metal money. The scarcity of gold caused its price in other goods to rise: in the words of Pierre Vilar, 'those who had gold were able to buy more and more commodities.'[11] In the years of Columbus' childhood and youth, a sort of money-hunger took hold of Europe, sending the Portuguese to Senegal in search of the sources of African gold and ever further south till, in 1488, Bartholomeu Dias rounded the Cape of Good Hope and entered the Indian Ocean. With the eastward sea-routes to the Indies under Portuguese control, Columbus' Spanish customers were obliged to look to the westward.

From our vantage, atop a world where money is largely insubstantial, and in which at the last count a million million dollars passes between the U.S. banks by wire each day, we would naturally ask: why did Columbus, as later Cortés and Pizarro, wade through seas of brine and blood to find metal money? After all, as we have seen, the merchants of Columbus' native city had been using paper bills for three centuries (or, for comparison, quite as long as we have used Bank of England notes). Yet we must distinguish between small worlds and large. The forms of money reveal the institutions of the societies in which they circulate and we would imagine that the one is permitted to increase in vulnerability as the other gains in robustness: rather as, for example, women sunbathe naked in public parks only in well-policed societies. In a modern city that is under siege, it is the institutional moneys – credit cards, cheques, banknotes, coins – that go under first, leaving the hard moneys of gold, sustenance and ammunition. If Columbus had said, as John Law was to say two centuries later in France, we do not need to mine and murder, let us form an Indies corporation capitalised with banknotes, we must assume a population ready to submit to a social authority in which it has confidence. That may be an autocratic government, which can none the less persuade its subjects to accept light coins at face value, as occurred in Europe in the seventeenth century, or paper pictures of coins, as in Ming China; a public bank such as the Bank of Amsterdam that is trusted to keep deposits and make accurate transfers; and finally a central bank which embodies a democratic society in its monetary relations. We have merely to state these conditions to recognise that they simply did not obtain in the Spain of Columbus' lifetime.

In the Americas, gold and silver were in abundance but they were not, as far as we can tell, *money*, in the sense that they were used generally for payment: they were used for decoration, adornment or as emblems of royal authority. What Columbus does is turn this store of ornamental metal into money. On landing on Española, Columbus and his men first separate the people from their jewelry:

> So it was found that one sailor got gold weighing two and a half *castellanos* in exchange for a strap while others got other things worth much more for much less. For new blancas they'd give everything they had. [A *castellano* is a measure of weight for the precious metals, equivalent to one-fiftieth of a mark or 4.6 grams. The blanca is the coin of every day.][12]

According to Pierre Chaunu's estimate, the Spanish needed just two or three years to acquire gold ornaments that had taken the natives a thousand years to assemble.[13] The Spanish then forced them to pan the rivers, and then attempted to mine the hills at their sources. Two generations later, they discover a great mountain of silver, six miles round the base, at Potosí in the high Bolivian Andes, and by the last quarter of the century are shipping back each year hundreds of thousands of pesos to Seville (though much falls prey to English privateers): Potosí itself becomes proverbial for its grandeur, extravagance and quotidian violence. The money minted from the American silver at Potosí, Lima and Mexico, and at mints in Spain, the famous Spanish dollar or piece of eight reals or piastre or peso, becomes the world's trading currency par excellence which will survive, in a few isolated pockets, right up to our lifetimes: for I remember, in the town of Axum in Ethiopia in 1972, watching a man in jodhpurs buy a shawl out of a purse of Maria Theresa silver dollars.

What happens when a great civilisation that uses money meets one that does not? They smash each other to smithereens. The horror of the *lettera rarissima* is fully realised in events. Having sucked the gold out of the Caribbean, Columbus and his successors extinguished almost all the human life. The labour forced on the natives shattered not only their customary subsistence but also their morale, and many simply suicided. By the 1520s, when the Spanish turned their attention to Mexico, the islands of Cuba, Española, Puerto Rico and Jamaica were, according to Las Casas, depopulated. On the mainland, Bernal Díaz, an old soldier who had served with Cortés in the conquest of Mexico, would not sleep on a bed on his farm in Guatemala (unless there happened to be gentlemen staying); but paced with his wounds under the wet stars; and each time he closed his eyes he saw his companions dragged up the pyramids, and then their quaking hearts in the pyre-light; and men and horses crashing off the causeway.[14] The disciples of Bartolomé de Las Casas were in despair at the condition of the Indians, which seemed a poor exchange even for the introduction of God's incomparable grace to a hemisphere.

In his *Essais*, first printed in 1580, Montaigne teetered on the brink of a momentous thought. From his reading of the *History of the Indies* by Cortés' chaplain, Francisco López de Gómara, he contemplated a hemisphere in which gold was assembled for parade. Because gold was precious but money not in use, the gold of the Americas was quite motionless:

> Imagine that our kings had heaped up all the gold they'd been able to find over centuries and kept it immobile.[15]

Columbus and his successors saw the money in this gold. They set the gold and silver in motion, which caused the brittle empires of both the Americas and Spain to crack as comprehensively as the feudal arrangements of Europe. Their emotions were not merely that 'disease of the heart, that infirmity, that we have, my companions and I, and that we cure with gold,' as Cortés told the

Mexican ambassadors at Vera Cruz in 1519,[16] but also helplessness: marooned, as later H. M. Stanley, in a continent without money, they could not imagine how they could conduct their business without violence. The force of the smash derives from the polarities of ornament and money. In Peru, the Spaniards compelled Atahualpa to fill a room with two million pesos of gold and then garotted him. The Indians retaliated with their own sense of what gold was:

> The Indians having gotten him in their power, melted Two Pound of Gold and one of them pouring it down his Throat, said, Oh Baldivia, thou hast a very great and greedy Desire after Gold, we have us'd all possible means to satisfie thee, but could not; now by good hap we have thought upon a Way. Here is gold, drink thy Fill; for here's enough to content even the most Covetous.[17]

One mine capitalist in Potosí, seeing the hill-side ablaze with portable wind-furnaces and the Indian indentured labourers emerging from the freezing pits, thought the silver *es más sangre que metal* (is more blood than metal).[18] Arzáns' great history of the city, composed in the early eighteenth century, is a catalogue of gang warfare, robbery and rape, of men who walk the streets in four coats to repel the point of a sword, of rich town houses torn down and their inner walls spewing ancient corpses. Men murder women, women murder men, both murder children and are murdered in their turn: O memorable City, theatre of the most piteous tragedies without an end![19]

As the century progressed, thoughtful people detected a change come over metropolitan Spain, first slowly and then in a convulsion. Prosperity, which had seemed to subsist in the possession of the precious metals, had simply passed Spain by. The country had become, in a famous formulation of the time, the Indies of the foreigner, hopelessly poverty-stricken, exploited by neighbours, weak, indebted and waste: it was as if the silver were a contagious disease, like the pox men thought Columbus had brought back, and no less destructive.[20] The Potosí silver came in through Cadiz and Seville and passed rapidly out through the ports of the Cantabrian and Mediterranean coasts, in return for low-grade foreign goods at ever higher prices and rising workmen's wages; or it was squandered on the armies bogged down in the Netherlands mud trying to suppress the Dutch revolt. By the turn of the seventeenth century, prices at Seville were probably some four times what they had been when Columbus sailed westwards. Don Gerónymo de Uztáriz, secretary in the Council of the Indies, later estimated that some five thousand million dollars had come into Spain from the Americas since 1492, of which, by 1724, only about one hundred million remained in the coinage and household and church plate.[21] Even now, in the great golden *retablo* of Seville cathedral, and the baroque churches of Mexico, Peru and Ecuador, one sees the vestiges of a desperate psychological endeavour: to sterilise the American metals of their money content and direct the ornamental residue to the spiritual sensations of wonder and faith. That, essentially, is the baroque in religious architecture. As for the remainder, it passed into France, the Netherlands, England and the Baltic. Most of the silver probably came to rest in India, where it provided timely finance for the sea trade opened by Vasco da Gama in 1497. A necklace I bought my wife in the suq of Sanaa in Yemen, made by a Jewish silversmith in 1913 out of very old Indian rupees, was almost certainly dragged in sweat and blood out of the *cerro* of Potosí.

The catastrophe in Spain gave birth to a sub-category of baroque literature, known as the *arbitrismo*, which worried at the condition of the country rather as books and television programmes have picked at the 'decline of Britain' in the past thirty years. Inflation, which Oresme had seen as the consequence of improper princely tampering with the coin and caused Dante to crow at Philippe le Bel's untimely death,[22] now seemed elemental and uncontrollable, arising in the very nature of money, or that infirmity of the heart that Cortés spoke of or the vengeance of God. In certain writers, there is a sense that something new and strange has come into the world, for which history is insufficient explanation. For Martín González de Cellorigo in Valladolid, even scholastic logic is helpless:

> Consequently, if there is no gold or silver money in Spain, it is because she possesses so much of it; and the cause of her poverty is her wealth. This means that two mutually contradictory propositions are true – propositions which, while they cannot formally

be reconciled, must both be considered to be correct in our Spain.[23]

The theologian Tomás de Mercado, in a passage of great brilliance in his treatise on the legitimacy of business of 1569, identified the problem not at its capital source, which was Potosí, where horses, it was said, were shod in silver; but at a tributary, the steps of the cathedral of Seville, where cargoes were assembled for the Indies.

> I have seen a situation in which velvet is selling in Granada for 28 or 29 reals, and a fool from the *gradas* then comes along and starts to buy so recklessly for the cargo of a caravel that in a fortnight he has sent the price up to 35 or 36 reals. So the merchants and weavers of course keep it at this high price, and sell the velvet at this price to the people of the city.[24]

That is based on observation: but it contains the germ of a quantity theory of money to which Jean Bodin in France and Bernardo Davanzati in Florence were also groping, and is orthodoxy today: that as money increases, prices increase. Other writers looked into the psychology of the Spaniards:

> The scarcity of things in *Spain* proceeds ... from the neglect of Husbandry, Trades, Business and Commerce; the People, even the meanest of them, being so excessive proud, that they can't be content with what Lot Nature has given them, but aspire to something greater, loathing those Employments which are not agreeable to their affect'd Grandeur.[25]

In the first generation of the eighteenth century, an Irish banker in Paris, Richard Cantillon, carefully disentangled the commercial and psychological roots of the disaster:

> When the excessive abundance of money from the Mines has diminished the inhabitants of a State, accustomed those who remain to a too large expenditure, raised the produce of the land and the labour of workmen to excessive prices, ruined the manufactures of the State by the use of foreign productions on the part of Landlords and mine workers, the money produced by the Mines will necessarily go abroad to pay for imports; this will gradually impoverish the State and render it in some sort depend-

ent on the Foreigner, to whom it is obliged to send money every year as it is drawn from the Mines. The great circulation of Money, which was general at the beginning, ceases: poverty and misery follow and the labour of the Mines appears to be only to the advantage of those employed upon them and the Foreigners who profit thereby.

This is approximately what has happened to Spain since the discovery of the Indies.[26]

If that weren't insight enough for one day, Cantillon continues a few pages later:

When a State has arrived at the highest point of wealth (I assume always that the comparative wealth of States consists primarily in the respective quantities of money which they possess) it will inevitably fall into poverty by the ordinary course of things. The too great abundance of money, which so long as it lasts forms the power of States, draws them back imperceptibly but naturally into poverty. Thus it would seem that when a State expands by trade and the abundance of money raises the price of Land and Labour, the Prince or the Legislator ought to withdraw money from circulation, keep it for emergencies, and try to retard its circulation by every means except compulsion and bad faith, so as to forestall the too great dearness of its articles and prevent the drawbacks of luxury.[27]

What a mind! In that passage, Cantillon foreshadows not only the dialectical materialism of Marx but the open-market operations of the modern central bank.

But in Potosí, once the capital of the Indies, where the mountain had been nearly worked out by the 1730s, the historian of the city saw only the implacable conjunction of silver and the stars:

Everything is finished, all is affliction and anguish, weeping and sighing. Without doubt this has been one of the greatest downfalls ever to overtake one of the world's peoples: to see such vanity, such incomparable wealth turn to powder, to become nothing.[28]

It was Columbus, come full circle.

We, who have lived through an even greater inflation of money, where prices rose *ten-fold* in just thirty years, would be inclined to

search that era for something that corresponded to our own
experience: not just of rising prices, disrupted trade and national
enfeeblement, but of a brutal disorientation, a loosening of social
bonds and a thorough muddle as to what constitutes a value; and
also a certain disintegration of reality, or at least a weakening of
confidence in the objectivity of appearances and the conviction of
social postures. For these correspondences, we would look not at
lists of prices at different markets, as Earl J. Hamilton did with such
diligence, or at Vilar's *arbitristas*, or even the Spanish chronicles but
in the great masterpieces of literature.

> In a town of La Mancha, which I don't want to name, not long
> ago there lived one of those gentlemen who always have a lance
> on the rack, an ancient shield, a skinny hack and a greyhound for
> coursing.[29]

To read that sentence at the opening of a long novel is to feel an
overpowering relief: that at last, in this journey into the secret
history of money, we have a companion in whom we can repose
the utmost confidence, a Virgil to our Dante. Money, like the
liberty of a time-served prisoner, carries perils as well as opportunities; and as all property and rank are mobilised and personal
relations reform themselves into what Carlyle later called the 'cash
nexus,' there are many who are left stranded. Nobles and peasants,
even whole nations, subside into romantic decline or fall victim to
monetary delusions. To such people and societies we give the name
Quixotic.[30] In the adventures of the Knight of the Doleful Countenance, we at last have a hero who confronts the world of money in
all its fluidity and relativity, not on its own terms,

> He asked him if he had any money on him, and Don Quixote
> replied that he hadn't a penny on him, for he'd never read in the
> histories of the knights-errant of anyone who had.[31]

but on his. Like Columbus, he hasn't got a blanca; unlike Columbus
he doesn't care. He mounts his steed, which has more quarters than
a real, and sets out to do battle not just with the world of capital –
configured in the famous windmills – but with money itself. In the
process, Don Quixote inaugurates in prose, which is the language of
commerce, the novel of the modern West, whose very greatest

exemplars – *Great Expectations, Crime and Punishment, The Wings of the Dove* – re-stage that combat to the death of money and romance.

> There are authors who say that the first adventure he had was that of the pass of Lapice. Others say it was the windmills. But what I have been able to verify in this matter and what I have found written in the annals of La Mancha, is that he rode all that day, and that at nightfall his horse and he were weary and dying of hunger. Looking in every direction to see if he could descry any castle or shepherd's hut where he could take shelter and satisfy his hunger and need, he saw, not far from the road on which he was travelling, an inn, which seemed to him like a star to guide him to the gates, if not to the palace, of his redemption. So he hurried on, and reached it just as night was falling.
>
> Now there were standing at the door of the inn two young women, working girls [*mozas del partido*] as they are called, who were on their way to Seville with some carriers who happened to have taken up their quarters at the inn that evening. As everything that our adventurer thought, saw or imagined was shaped to the pattern of his reading, as soon as he saw the inn he convinced himself that it was a castle with its four towers and pinnacles of shining silver, complete with a drawbridge, a deep moat and all those appurtenances with which such castles are depicted. So he approached the inn, which to his mind was a castle, and when still a short distance away reined Rocinante in, expecting some dwarf to mount the battlements and sound a trumpet to announce that a knight was approaching the fortress. But when he saw that there was some delay, and that Rocinante was in a hurry to get to the stable, he went up to the inn door and, seeing the two loose women standing there, took them for two fair maidens or gracious ladies taking the air at the castle gate.[32]

At this, the knight's first adventure, the field of the confrontation is described so carefully that it astonishes me that critics have not made more of it.

For what is it that distinguishes a castle, with its four turrets and pinnacles of shining silver, from a flea-bitten inn? What distinguishes a pair of whores from two gracious ladies taking the air at the castle gate? It is, of course, money. The innkeeper and the whore must be paid, the castellan and the lady not. Money is the impenetrable veil that separates the feudal heroes from the modern world, and the true source of the Don's own delusion.

It is Cervantes' great originality as an artist to look out at his world and imagine it – really imagine it – without its most important component. The story then follows its own narrative inertia, leading the Don into rage, violence, madness and death: for money is for the feudal survivors as the Reconquest was for the Muslims of Granada, convert or die! The Don's delusion is not tragic, in the sense that the delusions of the Greek heroes – Euripides' Pentheus, for example – are tragic, but intensely comic: for in the age of money, where all values are and can only be relative and inconstant, there can be no tragedy, as there can be no epic. And yet there are passages that are stranger than anything else in prose literature:

> What seems to you to be a barber's basin appears to me to be Mambrino's helmet, and to another as something else. It shows a rare foresight in the sage who is on my side to make what is really and truly Mambrino's helmet seem to everyone a basin. For, as it is of such great value, the whole world would persecute me in order to get it from me. However, as they see that it is nothing more than a barber's basin, they do not trouble about it, as was evident in the case of the wretch who tried to destroy it and left it behind him on the ground; for I promise you that if he had recognised it he would never have left it there.[33]

Might not the Don have a point? Might not the delusion lie as much on the money side? Cervantes died in 1615, 'old, a soldier, a gentleman, and poor.' Nine years later, in the village church of Egmond Binnen in the Netherlands, Isaac le Maire bragged on his tombstone that he had *lost* a million and a half guilders in bear operations against the stock of the Dutch East India Company.[34] And in the next decade, the Dutch fell prey to a delusion of money in comparison with which Mambrino's helmet seems a mere trick of the light. But we will deal with that in its place.

★

On July 22, 1598, two years after the English fleet sacked Cadiz and brought home two rich Indies merchantmen as prizes, there was recorded in the Stationer's Register in London a play that is, in its way, as profound a meditation on money as the *Quixote*. It is the story of a merchant of Venice, named Antonio, and his friend Bassanio, who needs cash so that he can pursue his courtship of a country heiress, Portia. Because Antonio's capital is all laid out in ships and their cargoes, he hasn't got the money and agrees to stand surety for a loan to Bassanio from a Jewish money-lender named Shylock. Shylock, who has suffered great rudeness from Antonio in business, demands as security for the loan not Antonio's property but his very life.

It is clear from even the most rustic or amateur performance that *The Merchant of Venice* derives its drama from a series of formal contests between antinomies. These single combats, as it were – Gentile and Jew, woman and man, country and town, young and old, hatred and love, friendship and advantage, mercy and justice – do not at first sight seem to be fought out on the field of money; and, indeed, in certain beautiful passages in the verse – such as 'In such a night . . .' in Act V, Scene i – we seem to have passed into a moneyless antiquity. Yet parallel to these contests are monetary polarities so evident that one is tempted to look to them for the chief drama: Antonio and Shylock, real property and moveable property, usury and participatory risk, lead and gold. Both sets of contests are epitomised in the contest of the gold, silver and lead caskets from which, under the terms of her father's will, Portia's suitors must choose: and here, as in the *Quixote*, appearance is set against reality, gold and silver against lead. Yet the conclusion is different. Eventually, the chief contests resolve themselves in a single capital reality, which is heterosexual passion. Portia and Bassanio, Nerissa and Gratiano, Jessica and Lorenzo quit the stage not for business but for the bedroom: the last words of the play are lewd in the extreme. The great discoveries of the later Middle Ages, sex and money, are decisively put in order. 'The breed for barren metal,'[35] a phrase Shakespeare took from Aristotle, gives way to the breed of fertile women. In this gallant version of history, love not money is the veritable, transitory reality. It is a vision of such authority that it survives, with diminishing conviction, in Jane Austen and Henry James and in a million romantic pot-boilers today: only sexual love between young people can shatter the prison bars of the monetary order and reveal the world as it is.

Portia, Antonio and Shylock are all rich, but their riches distinguish their views of the world. Portia is 'richly left': she has inherited a fortune, no doubt from a merchant forebear ten times more villainous and crude than Shylock, but her family has followed the investment scheme laid down in antiquity. Plato's *Republic* opens in the sea-port of Athens, the Piraeus, where a merchant specifically states that it is better to inherit money than to earn it, for thereby one holds it the more lightly. Portia lives in the country, on the antique model: Cicero, in a beautiful passage in his *On Duties* or *Offices*, as it was known in Shakespeare's time, proposes that merchants 'should make their way from the port to a country estate, just as they have often made it from the sea into port.'[36] Portia's riches are not for accumulation but for disbursement in pursuit of happiness, in hospitality, love and charity.

Ranged beside her womanly personality – which is, by the way, one of the loveliest in all fiction – are three males who aspire more to her condition than to her bed. In Bassanio and Antonio, the process of monetary transformation – Cicero's debarkation and rustication – is not yet complete. In Bassanio, we have a man of a type who will become familiar in succeeding ages: the dandy. His assets are his blood and his handsome face, and those will support a substantial burden of financial debt. Antonio is a merchant, but he deals not in money but in things, and those things, for the author at least, have a hard and quite ravishing materiality:

> Which touching but my gentle vessel's side
> Would scatter all her spices on the stream,
> Enrobe the roaring waters with my silks;
> And, in a word, but even now worth this,
> And now worth nothing?[37]

In those five lines, Shakespeare sketches an aesthetic of the wholesale trade; while he gives to Antonio business practices – a readiness to lend without interest or stand surety for a friend – that arise in notions of commercial honour that are already hopelessly old-fashioned on the Rialto.

Shylock is a merchant in business not for beauty or honour or even Friar Pacioli's *sustenance* but for money. To present the contrast of purpose at its crudest, let me quote Marx — who knew the play well — when he makes an uncharacteristic resort to algebra. In Marx's pre-capitalist or what we might call Antonian commercial circuit (C-M-C), the commodity is the object and money merely the intermediary. In the second, capitalist or Shylockian circuit (M-C-M), money is the object and the commodity the means.[38] With Shylock, prosperity consists only in money. In fact, money is his personality: he hates Antonio with such passion because, by lending gratis, the Christian brings down the rate of interest in Venice — that is, *devalues* money.[39] When his daughter elopes with Lorenzo and takes her father's money with her, Shylock reveals the hopeless confusion of his values: *My daughter! O my ducats! Oh my daughter!*[40] It is not that he fears some abstract dishonour which might impair his credit on the Rialto. He simply cannot distinguish his living and inert possessions, any more than old Grandet in Balzac's novel or George Eliot's Silas Marner in that tremendous moment in the firelight where the little girl's hair gleams like his stolen gold. Jessica herself seems to our age to behave very badly, not in defying her father's authority (which we approve) but in stealing his money: but Shakespeare's audience would probably have thought the reverse. And she cares not at all for the money, frittering away eighty ducats in one night at Genoa. She knows what is valuable as clearly as Bassanio, when he chooses the leaden not the golden casket, or Antonio, when he stands surety, or Portia in the final act.

Having drawn up this account, I must now, like a conscientious auditor faced with some dodgy invoices, qualify it. All of the heroes and heroines of the play, not excluding Portia, see through the physical manifestations of wealth into a core of money. Bassanio's blood is as much money as Portia's golden hair and Antonio's argosies and Shylock's ducats. Even Christianity, supposedly the pearl of great price, has its proxy markets in hogs and bacon.[41] The great scene in which Bassanio and Portia come to their understanding is played out in the language of money. Bassanio comes 'by note' (that is, presents his bill of exchange); and Portia wishes herself

ten thousand times

More *rich*;

that only to stand high in your *account*,
I might in virtues, beauties, *livings*, friends,
exceed *account*; but the full *sum* of me
is *sum* of something; which to *term in gross*
is an *unlesson'd* girl, *unschool'd*, *unpractis'd* . . .[42]

I have italicised what I sense are terms of commerce; but I think they are to be spoken not facetiously, but playfully. When set against the sensations of love and friendship, those of business are pretty small stuff. Jessica, incidentally, is 'dear bought' by Lorenzo and their love is 'unthrift.'

Meanwhile, Shylock undergoes a transformation. For Shakespeare is the great dramatist of process: one shouldn't mistake Shylock for the rigid monetary types of the Elizabethan and Jacobean drama, those Overreaches, Mammons, Lucres, Gripes, Hornets, Bloodhounds and so on. Nor is he a mere Marxian cypher that symbolises the birth of the money mentality. For though we know, from history rather than from Marx, that Shylock ought to triumph, just as money, as the most mobile value, must capture all other values, whether they be Antonio's argosies or Bassanio's noble blood or Portia's country estates or even Nerissa's 'ring' (fanny), he doesn't and it doesn't. Shylock is no Smithian paragon, calculating and super-rational: in the course of the play, he abandons money for its predecessor, vengeance. At precisely the moment when he must succeed, Shylock falls prey to that violence that money was invented to replace. I cannot stress the point too fully. The pound of flesh is not a collateral security, like the mortgaged crown of thorns, for it cannot be sequestrated and turned into money. It simply does not belong in the world of money. Instead, it is an insane and primitive forfeit, a sort of *Wergild* turned on its head, in which money does not compensate an insult to the body but the other way round: not blood-money but money-blood. Shylock breaks the most elementary rule in the money book: that the person of the payer matters. That money, in the miraculous words of St Francis of Paola, bleeds.

In the great confrontation of the last act between Portia and Shylock, it is not just between woman and man, youth and age, charity and the letter of the law, real property and money, giving and possession, beauty and ugliness, or love and hatred (which love must be seen to win, else we can't live in the world). It is between reason and unreason. And the beauty of it all is that Shylock knows he is not acting rationally – that is, for money – and revels in his unreason in full court:

> You'll ask me, why I rather choose to have
> A weight of carrion flesh than to receive
> Three thousand ducats: I'll not answer that:
> but say it is my humour: is it answer'd?[43]

Shylock is more opposed to the capitalist spirit than the others. In contrast, Antonio sees in the neutrality of money – its indifference to the person of its payer – the very basis of modernity:

> Since that the trade and profit of the city
> Consisteth in all nations.[44]

No doubt, Antonio had done business at Antwerp and seen the inscription at the new Bourse: *Ad usum mercatorum cuiusque gentis ac linguae.* (For the use of merchants of whatever nation or language.)

Such is the progress of ideas, which rescues the play from programme and type; but, alas, at the cost of a certain disharmony. Were we not beguiled by Portia's beauty and lovely words, we'd find the quality of mercy pretty strained and the trial – if that's what it is – absurd and inequitable: we are suddenly told that, despite the 'all nations' theory, Shylock is an alien and does not have any civic rights. Had Portia been a modern jurist, and not a medieval casuist *en travestie*, she might have said, as later Lord Nottingham in his path-breaking judgement in *Thornbrough* v. *Baker* in 1676: 'for in natural Justice and Equity, the principal Right of the Mortgagee is to the *Money*, and his Right to the Pound of Flesh is only as Security for the *Money*.' But such a judgement could only be handed down in the case of a true collateral security, such as the landed estate in *Thornbrough* v. *Baker*.

Lord Nottingham thought of property as merely congealed money: henceforth in England, creditors must regard their security not as fields and woods and brick but as so many pounds sterling incarnate in those forms only because thus they can't abscond. On that foundation, great systems of equity have arisen.[45] Such a solution was invisible or repugnant to Shakespeare; and *The Merchant of Venice* resolves its inconsistencies, like a million million lovers' quarrels, in bed.

I say resolve, but the drama is not quite resolved; for even in this long criticism, I have not begun to exhaust the meaning of *The Merchant of Venice*. As the curtain descends, a character remains who has but a cold bed to go to: Antonio. He stands four-square on the stage, repeating over and over again his protestations of friendship. That his friend now has Portia's mouth to kiss and money to burn in country-house gentility makes those protestations sound, at least to a modern audience, beside the point. Yet Antonio is, to borrow a lovely phrase of Montesquieu, *amoureux d'amitié*. He stands for that intense, disinterested friendship between men, a mental attitude that is inimical both to venal marriage and to the shallow and equitable relations absolved by payments of money. He is as much a relic of the *ancien régime* as Shylock, his heroic counterpart; as much even as Don Quixote himself.

Sir Walter Raleigh, writing a little later, specifically warns his son against standing surety for a friend, however dear, because of certain consequences, not of violence but of money: 'for thereby millions of men have beene beggered and destroyed, . . . therefore from suretiship, as from a manslayer, or enchanter, bless thyself.'[46] In the next two centuries, as Benjamin Nelson pointed out,[47] La Rochefoucauld, Mandeville, Montesquieu and Smith 'unmask' friendship as merely self-interest. Portia's charity suffers a similar fate at money's hands, disintegrating into Charity, defined by Bishop William Paley in the eighteenth century as 'promoting the happiness of our inferiors' through the good treatment of domestic servants, public service and 'pecuniary bounty.'[48] Hume simply abolished charity as he had abolished the gods. 'There is no such passion in human minds,' he wrote, with that love of assertion that is such a feature of his era, 'as the love of mankind, merely as such.'[49] And Adam Smith erected in its place the banausic self-interest of the small retailer: 'It is not from the benevolence of the butcher, the brewer or the baker, that we expect our dinner.'[50] Amid such profundities, is it a wonder that we still read and listen to Shakespeare?

Shakespeare had yet more to say on the subject of money and love, and we should now address, not without some reluctance, the play known as *Timon of Athens*. *Timon*, which was first printed in 1623, after Shakespeare's death, is an unco-operative piece of English: it is riddled with dramatic inconsistencies, patches of verse that aren't verse and lines so difficult or corrupt that they yield no sense without aggressive emendation. The scholars have surmised it might be the work of more than one hand or was started by Shakespeare but never completed. I will make two defensible assumptions: that it was composed by the person who wrote *The Merchant of Venice* and some years after that play.

Timon is Greek philosophy gone mad. In his leering, barking figure, Socratic irony and Diogenic cynicism collapse into misanthropy:

> Here lie I, Timon; who, alive, all living men did hate:
> Pass by, and curse thy fill; but pass and stay not here thy gait . . .[51]

It seems Shakespeare knew of the Timon story from Plutarch's *Lives*, or rather the translations from the Greek made by Sir Thomas North and printed in 1579 and 1595. In Plutarch, Timon was an Athenian of the fifth century B.C., a contemporary of Socrates and Alcibiades, who was so demoralised by the ingratitude of men he thought his friends that he could not tolerate any human society. Shakespeare may also have known, in some version or other, a dialogue by Lucian, *Timon the Misanthrope*, in which money now plays a dominant role. In the dialogue, as in Shakespeare's play, Timon is a generous man who releases one friend from debt and provides another with a marriage portion; loses his fortune and his friends; retreats to the country, where one day he digs up some gold; is inundated once again by flatterers and parasites; but this time drives them away with blows of his spade and clods of earth.

The first three acts of Shakespeare's play make excellent drama. Timon simply cannot see what the spectators can see: that all his friends are on the take and that his debts have run out of control. When his true condition finally breaks in, Timon falls to pieces. Act IV opens with Timon in the country, which is not the country of Portia, but a place of squalor, violence and an animal subsistence. Digging for roots, Timon finds some gold. In his address to the gold, which Karl Marx read with his future father-in-law and thereby, so to speak, embarked on his great intellectual quest, gold in its character as money is a sort of Satanic philosopher's stone. Instead of merely transmuting the basest metals into the noblest, as the vulgar alchemists contended, this diabolical stone turns everything into its opposite:

> Thus much of this will make black white, foul fair,
> Wrong right, base noble, old young, coward valiant.
> Ha! you gods, why this? What this, you gods? Why, this
> Will lug your priests and servants from your sides,
> Pluck stout men's pillows from below their head:
> This yellow slave
> Will knit and break religions; bless th'accurs'd;
> Make the hoar leprosy ador'd; place thieves,
> And give them title, knee, and approbation
> With senators on the bench; this is it
> That makes the wappen'd widow wed again;
> She, whom the spital-house and ulcerous sores
> Would cast the gorge at, this embalms and spices
> To th'April day again. Come, damned earth,
> Thou common whore of mankind, that puts odds
> Among the rout of nations, I will make thee
> Do they right nature.[52]

I cannot exaggerate the importance of those lines, for Timon and for Shakespeare, and for Marx and Walter Benjamin and countless others. For as money enters the system of values, and then displaces all other values like a cuckoo the eggs in a nest, reality as the world of things perceived and wanted and believed must be completely revised; and the shock to the sensitive personality is indescribable. Don Quixote simply refuses to recognise the alteration. Timon disbelieves everything.

For the relics of the Age of Faith, accustomed to reconcile all that was strange and opposed in the world by means of the godhead, the power of money to turn the universe upside down is literally divine and there can, of course, be only one God. Shakespeare has Timon recognise that in lines of blasphemous precision:

> thou visible god,
> That sold'rest close impossibilities
> And makst them kiss![53]

In such an epiphany, the old ideals of love and friendship in *The Merchant of Venice* are blasted out of existence. Antonio is and only ever was a thief and Portia a stinking, poxy whore. The wonder is not that Shakespeare could not finish *Timon*, but that he wrote so much of it! As we have said, there can be no tragedy in the age of money. *Timon of Athens* is the ruin of a great tragedy.

But human beings are resilient animals and the shock will soon dissipate. The English poet George Herbert, who died in 1633, can already make some music out of it. In his poem 'Avarice,' he addresses not gold but a silver coin:

> Nay, thou hast got the face of man; for we
> Have with our stamp and seal transferred our right;
> Thou art the man, and man but dross to thee.
>
> Man calleth thee his wealth, who made thee rich;
> And while he digs out thee, falls in the ditch.

Eventually, the enslavement of humanity by its creation will form the basis of Marx's philosophy of alienation. But meanwhile, in England and on the continent of Europe, the personality is slowly being rebuilt on new foundations of money; and that is the theme of our next chapter.

5

The Floating World

Là sotto i giorni nubilosi e brevi
Nemica naturalmente di pace,
Nasce una gente a cui il morir non dole.
                                   Petrarch[1]

There, under brief and cloudy skies, there lives a people, instinc-
tively inimical to peace, for whom death is no inconvenience.

In 1672, the French invaded the Dutch Republic. The French King,
Louis XIV, camped with his army at Utrecht, and there was panic
in Amsterdam. Johan de Witt, the chief magistrate or Grand
Pensionary of the Republic, and his brother were torn to pieces in
the Gevangenpoort prison. There was a run on the Wisselbank, the
deposit and exchange bank set up by the city of Amsterdam in 1609
and used by the Dutch merchants to settle accounts with one
another.

But let us have Voltaire take up the story. Writing from his house
near Geneva some eighty years later, he is still astonished by the
course of events:

In the midst of these disturbances and calamities the magistrates
showed evidence of virtues rarely seen save in republics. Citizens
who possessed banknotes rushed in a crowd to the Bank of
Amsterdam: they feared that their capital had been drawn upon.
Everyone was eager to be paid from the little money which was
thought to remain. The magistrates opened the vaults where the
treasure was kept, and it was found there intact as it had been
deposited over the previous sixty years: the very silver was still
blackened from the fire which had burnt down the Town Hall a

few years previously. Banknotes had thus been honoured up to that moment and the public's money had not been touched.

Having quelled the public's money anxieties, the city fathers ordered the dykes, which held back the sea from the low fields of Holland and Zeeland, to be broken. Leyden and Delft were flooded. Livestock drowned in the fields. Voltaire continues:

> Amsterdam stood like a vast fortress in the midst of the waters, surrounded by ships of war who could sail close up to the city. . . . It is a thing worthy of note that while Holland was thus vanquished on land, no longer existing as a state, she yet remained formidable at sea: it was her natural element.

On June 7, Admiral de Ruyter had engaged the French and their English allies at sea, scattered them, secured the coast of Holland and escorted the Dutch East India fleet, returning in convoy from the Moluccas, safe into the Texel, 'thus defending and enriching his country on the one side, while it perished on the other. One day, when a French consul was telling the King of Persia that Louis XIV had conquered nearly the whole of Holland, that monarch replied, "How can that be, since there are always twenty Dutch ships to one French in the port of Ormuz." '[2] The provinces conquered by the French were evacuated the next year.

Like many men of his time, Voltaire lived with one foot in antiquity; and the beautiful piece of history writing I've quoted has an antique model: it is as if Hegel were right and events really must occur twice before the spirit of world history can get through our numb skulls.[3]

In 483 B.C. silver was discovered at Laurion, about fifteen miles outside Athens. The silver mined was minted into the famous drachma coins known as Athena's Owls, after the familiar of the goddess that was punched into the reverse. Some men urged that they be distributed to the voting population at ten drachmas per family, but on the pressing insistence of Themistocles, son of Neocles, the money was used to pay the wrights to build two hundred warships. Three years later, when the Persians overran Attica, the population had been evacuated. The city was burned but Themistocles' triremes destroyed the Persian fleet for ever at the famous battle of Salamis in 480 B.C.

It was the achievement of Themistocles, as also eight years later of the poet Aeschylus in his great drama on the subject, *The Persians*, to recognise that the strength of a people need not reside in territory, provided it has men and money.[4] Surveying the flooded United Provinces of his imagination, Voltaire could also see that power had nothing to do with territory and that his amphibious republic floated on seas of money. What Voltaire did not know – though this had been suspected not only by the Dutch public but also by the most acute English and Scots commentators – was that world history had moved on a bit and the treasure of the Bank of Amsterdam on which the whole enterprise rested was not metal but faith. That faith is what we call credit: the belief, not that a person or persons have money, but that they can get it. Dutch credit, Sir Edward Forde wrote in his *Experimented Proposals how the King may have Money* in London in 1666, had raised 'their little Country (not so big, nor fruitful, as one English county) from Poor Distressed States to be Hogans Mogans, all by a real cheat, for no considerate man can believe that they have so much Money in their Banks as they give out bills for.'[5] Hogans Mogans is *hooge en mogende*, high and mighty, which was the infuriating phrase the Dutch used to address their States-General or parliament. In 1795, when the French armies – this time of the revolution, not the monarchy – overran Amsterdam and at last opened the Wisselbank's magic vaults, they found them all but empty: the merchants' deposits had long ago been lent, in the fashion of a modern bank which keeps only a fraction of its liabilities – what it owes – at home, to the city authorities and the Dutch East India Company.[6] I suspect the burned coin of 1672 was a sham, and wish I could commemorate its author.

Our age is not accustomed to distinguish between money and credit: a bank creates money at the moment it makes a loan and that's that. The abstraction of credit has long ago dissolved for us the substance of money. We are apt to forget that such an attitude is not timeless; and that even the seventeenth century resisted it. The age opens, let us say, in 1594 with the Dutch States' emissaries all but laughed out of the Scots court at Stirling for their gift to the infant Prince Henry of a life-annuity of 5,000 guilders: the Dutch envoy had to shout over the dim-witted hubbub, *Non est puf; sed est purum aurum!* You're crazy, guys, it's 24-carat gold![7] It ends in 1695 with

John Locke's antiquarian fantasies of money as precise weights of precious metal and the foundation of the gold standard.

Yet even Locke was obliged to admit that there was nothing natural about the use of metal money: rather mankind had 'consented to put an imaginary value on gold and silver, by reason of their durableness, scarcity, and not being very liable to be counterfeited.'[8] The more probable reason for the esteem of gold and silver – that they had been used in money since antiquity – escaped him as much as the evidence before his eyes: that English shillings, though battered, worn, forged or clipped at the edges, passed for full weight in transactions and that coins of different countries but of equivalent weight and fineness differed in price on the foreign exchanges. Whatever money was, it clearly wasn't exact weights of silver.

Others of his countrymen were of more empirical cast of mind. In the course of the century, first gradually, and then with mounting impatience, men begin to question money not just in its substance and appearance, but in all its political, moral and commercial entanglements. From the 1620s, tracts on money pour off the presses in London and Edinburgh, sometimes crowding out those on religious and political topics: they are all fruits of the century's wholesale inquiry into inherited notions of authority and human purposes. In these books, money emerges from out of the precious metals, from the hoarding of the bullionists, the restrictions of the usury doctrine and the agonies and nostalgia of Shakespeare, and begins to reveal an uncommon power: not just to make possible a far-flung trade in luxuries and equip armies and fleets but to conquer tyranny, chance, shipwreck, fire, even death itself, and to reveal, to its adepts, the secret mechanisms of society. The medieval dream of a fixed world of stable commercial and moral values, of good money and just prices, earthly duty and heavenly reward, gives way to a floating world, in which land and people and things are tossed this way and that on billowing tides of money. New monetary types – the banker, tradesman, projector, gamester, beau, economist, whore – take shape and precipitate into journalism, drama, novels and verse. In Defoe's unforgettable phrase, 'the gay humour' comes on.[9]

Of course, the seventeenth century's trouble with money was more practical than philosophical. It was the usual headache of getting enough of the stuff: not just as currency to settle the daily

scores among men and women without their coming to blows, but
as what we now call working capital: that is, the to-hand liquid
resources that permit an enterprise or nation to pay its employees
and suppliers and engage in commerce or warfare. In Holland, those
problems were cracked with the founding of the Wisselbank at the
beginning of the century and the creation of 'bank money,' a
compulsory system of book entries for settling accounts. England
suffered chronic shortages of money, only partly made up by traders'
tokens and forgeries, until the 1690s, when the Bank of England was
floated in a welter of inflationary banknotes.

Scotland followed with its own bank in 1695 and several other
note-issuing banks in the eighteenth century; but France, stunned
by the failure of John Law's Banque Royale in 1720, sat out the
revolution in credit with consequences disastrous to its self-esteem;
while the North American and West Indian colonies, obliged to
ship out their silver coin to pay for goods from the Old World, had
to treat as money whatever lay to hand: cotton wool, tobacco,
Muscovado sugar, wampum, lead bullets, dried cod, beaver skins,
indigo, unchipped logwood, unconvertible paper money and the
Mexican and Peruvian pieces of eight (that is, eight-real or 'eight-
bit' dollars) that were so clipped or light that nobody else wanted
them. When Anne Bradstreet sang in Massachusetts to her husband:

> I prize thy love more than whole Mines of gold
> Or all the riches that the East doth hold

the hyperbole gains an additional tenderness from the deplorable
monetary conditions in the New England of the mid-seventeenth
century.[10]

The English and Scots writers on money, whose pamphlets are
scattered in their hundreds through the iron stacks of the British
Library, were no Montaignes, staring out over an indifferent
landscape, disillusioned and wise. Their thoughts on money arise in
the graft of loading in the Bristol docks, weaving in the Home
Counties, promoting lotteries in Covent Garden and projects in
'Change Alley, tabulating receipts in Westminster and Dublin, or
raising armies and fleets for war; and hovering grossly before them,
or maddeningly just out of view, are those infernal Dutch. The
United Provinces fascinated and repelled the English of the seven-

teenth century as later Germany their successors of the 1890s and Japan of the 1970s: for the Dutch Republic challenged all inherited ideas. Obviously, it was a thoroughly bad place, a flat plain of mud, whores, tobacco, republicanism, drink and avarice; and yet . . . and yet . . . How was it that a people, whose very territory had been reclaimed from the sea, who made nothing but cheese and pickled herring, could nevertheless engross – monopolise – all the trade of the world, send the Spaniards packing, shrug off discriminatory Navigation Acts and resist the most bare-faced English aggression?

In the midst of the second of the three Anglo-Dutch commercial wars of the century, in November of the plague year 1665, Pepys went down to Erith on the Thames to inspect two captured Dutch East Indiamen, *Phoenix* and *Slothany*, and recorded in his diary a sort of terror at the sheer opulence of the adversary. The ships had already been plundered:

> Lord Bruncker . . . and Sir Edmd Pooly carried me down into the Hold of the India Shipp, and there did show me the greatest wealth lie in confusion that a man can see in the world – pepper scatter through every chink, you trod upon it; and in cloves and nutmegs, I walked above the knees – whole rooms full – and silk in bales and boxes of Copperplate, one of whom I saw opened. Having seen this, which was as noble as ever I saw in my life, I away on board the other ship in despair . . .[11]

In the course of the century, British inquiry began to collect round the Dutch relationship with money, which seemed to mark the most progressive aspect of Dutch society, at least against the backwardness of Spain and England. The United Provinces appeared to break every law in the bullionist book: there were no mines in that sodden land, no laws against the export of bullion, and rates of interest were the lowest in the world, and yet . . . and yet, coin and credit were abundant and wages, prices and rents high. To what was later to be called by Swift the 'money'd interest,' the Dutch appeared to have uncovered some magic of credit; while to the landed men, who were to become the Tories of the English countryside, the whole world seemed to be sliding unstoppably into the clutches of the Bank of Amsterdam.

The *puf* is frozen on the courtier's face. After 1672, the English know they can't beat the Dutch and might as well join them. Writing that year in Ireland, where he is engaged in mapping that country, Sir William Petty identifies three elements in Dutch society as urgently desirable: liberty of conscience, secure rights of property and a bank 'to encrease Money.'[12]

The problem was the political regime in which such a bank would act. Even Pepys had recognised by the 1660s[13] that a bank of the nature of the Wisselbank could not exist in an absolute monarchy such as the Stuarts were trying to preserve. His merchant friends needed no reminding. In July 1640, hard-pressed by his Scottish wars, Charles I had requisitioned £130,000 in Spanish bullion deposited at the mint in the Tower of London for coining: from that time on, people preferred to make deposits with goldsmiths, who gradually transformed themselves into private bankers. In the ledgers of Child's Bank, the receipts issued to depositors are worded like a modern banknote: *I promise to pay unto ye Rigt Honble ye Ld North & Grey or bearer Ninety pounds at demand.* One of Sir Francis Child's experimental designs, dated March 25, 1685, has the curli-cued *I* and *P* of *I Promise* that survived on the Bank of England notes of my childhood.[14]

In 1688, England and Scotland imported William of Orange from Holland to be their king. The City's opportunity came in 1694, when, despite a successful lottery loan of £1 million, William still needed money to prosecute war with the French. In return for a further £1.2 million, which was subscribed in just ten days of glorious sunshine at the end of June, the investors in the bank received an exclusive banking concession and the right to issue bills (that is, banknotes) for the same amount. In other words, the English crown gave up to the City its hard-won monopoly of making money, and its exclusive royalty. The articles of the Bank of England are a bourgeois *magna carta*: what the barons had started at Run-nymede was completed at Mercers' Hall in Cheapside.

The new banknotes were attended by an inflation, which the age misunderstood: it was thought to arise in the debased silver coinage. In the great debate of the next two years over the rate at which the battered shillings would be recoined, Locke's arguments won the day not for their good sense – they were refuted without effort by Hodges, Barbon, North and Temple – but at least in part for their republicanism: for if money drew its only value from its weight of fine silver or gold, then the prince's stamp added nothing and the British monarch was a stuffed shirt, as he or she has been ever since. The International Gold Standard even in its heyday was not obviously a submission to British authority: the empire of British commerce, financed by a common world currency and the universal 'bill on London', became entangled in notions of mission and dominion only in its twilight.

The Bank was not the grandest consequence of a mere need for cash. For in their impatient search for money for trade and war, and to locate themselves and their friends in a society set at its ears, the pamphleteers were forced to look into the very marrow of money: to ask what it is and how it's made and what it's for. If the tracts have anything in common beyond their slapdash printing and disintegrating bindings, it is their claim to distinguish appearance and reality: not just in the forms and purposes of money but in teasing out from the 'what should be' of Christian teaching and divine-right political theory the 'what is' of civilian self-interest. One hears, first faint, and then shrill, the modern notion that money and its pursuit are the predictable and scientific processes in society; for conscience, religion or honour – the Shakespearean bag – almost certainly mask 'hypocrisie,' as John Briscoe wrote in 1696, 'but in Interest we know there is none.'[15]

There is something Promethean in the writers, as if they had stolen money down from heaven, and would now deploy it to emancipate their suffering fellows from the tyranny of dilapidated gods. John Asgill, who promoted a bank based on land security, also wrote a pamphlet denying the obligation of death (which was burned for blasphemy by the hangman in Dublin). Sir William Petty, when challenged to a duel in Ireland by Sir Aleyn Brodrick, readily accepted, though he was so short-sighted as to be purblind. He merely asked for choice of weapons and selected, according to Evelyn and Aubrey, 'an hatchet or Axe in a darke cellar.' Sir William went to sea at fifteen, became a doctor of medicine at Oxford, made an epoch-making survey of Ireland, and was very rich, with an income from estates in Ireland and England of £11,300 in 1685 alone; but Evelyn's wonderful character of him, perhaps the finest written of anybody, vibrates with the beauty of his personality:

> When I have been in his splendid Palace, who knew him in
> meaner Circumstances, he would be in admiration himselfe how
> he ariv'd to it; . . . Lord, would he say, what a deale of do is here,
> I can lie in straw with as much satisfaction.[16]

He is forever teetering on the brink of some stupendous theory of
everything before his sparrow mind darts off somewhere else. At
one pregnant moment, he employs the mathematics used to value
land – twenty times its annual income or 'twenty years' purchase' –
to calculate that an English person is worth £86/13/4 'from whence
we may learn to compute the loss we have sustained by the Plague,
by the Slaughter of Men in War, and by the sending them abroad
into the Service of Foreign Princes.'[17]

Out of this speculative ferment, there grew the powerful monetary utopias of John Law, which is the subject of our next chapter;
and of Adam Smith, who scrubbed and organised his predecessors'
ideas without giving them credit, to the confusion of modern
economists who, too busy or diffident to read the pamphleteers, are
under the delusion that Smith inaugurated economics instead of, as
we shall see, singing its swan song.

Evidently, for money to be studied, it should obey some underlying law as objects submit to gravity. Evidently, its value was not
just its silver, for the clipped shillings passed for full value in
transaction and some coins were at a premium on the foreign
exchanges. Nor were gold and silver necessarily wealth in the world,
as the example of Spain seemed to show. Some writers thought of
money as a merchandise, like a consignment of silk or pepper,
which responded in value to the pressure of human wishes; others as
a mere instrument of commercial profit; others as congealed labour
or even 'coin'd dirt,' depending on their social allegiance. In the
pamphlet war over the recoinage in 1695–6, which distilled the
monetary insights of over seventy years, Locke's opponents
produced definitions of great sophistication. Hodges located money
squarely in the imagination, for the 'whole Value that is put upon
Money by Mankind, speaking generally, is extrinsick to the Money,
and hath its real seat in those good things, through the Estimation
providentially put upon it, which it is capable to purchase.'[18]
Nicholas Barbon is briefer: '*For Things have no Value in themselves;*

it is opinion and fashion brings them into use and gives them a value.'[19] Locke triumphed with his notion of a special and timeless value to silver, not just because men were alarmed by Barbon's subjectivity; but because the revolution was over: the merchants could afford to embrace the ideas of their betters; and anyway they wanted their rents paid and loans extinguished at 5s an ounce of silver, not 6/3d.

Deflected from money itself, the merchant writers sought their law in human attitudes to money. John Briscoe, in his *A Discourse of Money* of 1696, saw money as collecting and resolving all human wishes; and that the passions, however discordant and jarring, 'combine and unite in the Service of this one Idol Money, whose *Mysteries* in such a *Babel* of worship, we are not to wonder should be so hard to unfold.'[20] Sir William Petty not so much simplified human nature as abolished it, or rather converted it into the abstraction known as labour. His scheme, which was taken over by Smith in his lectures at Glasgow and in *The Wealth of Nations*, is breathtaking in its ambition. Political arithmetick, as he called his new science, will reduce the world to a set of numbers. It will seek, as he sets out with admirable clarity in *The Political Anatomy of Ireland*,

> to make a *Par* and *Equation* between Lands and Labour so as to express the Value of any thing by either alone.

Having achieved that 'most important Consideration in Political Oeconomies,' it would unlock the secrets of society. Money (or some other algebra) would price not just the tangible products of land and labour, but Art, Opinion, Favour, Acquaintance, Interest, Friends, Eloquence, Reputation, Power, Authority.[21]

Towards his arithmetical end, Sir William Petty uses Ireland, a place evidently of living and breathing human beings, with the cold violence he had once used on corpses:

> Furthermore, as Students in Medicine, practice their inquiries upon cheap and common *Animals*, and such whose actions they are best acquainted with, and where there is the least confusion and perplexure of Part; I have chosen *Ireland* as such a *Political Animal* . . .[22]

That his patient might suddenly wake up under the knife did not occur to him: though once at his anatomy lesson at Oxford, a young woman hanged for felony did just that (and he let blood and with spirits and other means recovered her to life, and the young scholars joined to make her a little portion, and she married and had several children and lived fifteen years more).[23] In political arithmetick, there is no place for the individual, for Sir William intends

> to express my self in Terms of *number, weight,* or *measure*: to use only arguments of Sense, and to consider only such Causes as have visible Foundations in Nature; leaving those that depend upon the mutable Mind, Opinions, Appetites, and Passions of particular Men, to the consideration of others.[24]

Human beings are thus interchangeable. The passions of Shakespeare, with their sudden beginnings and immense consequences, are replaced by the mechanical or banausic pursuit of gain, of which money is an infallible measure. From here it is but a step to the board-school anthropology of Adam Smith, in which an entire system of thought is erected on a supposed instinct in human beings 'to truck, barter, and exchange one thing for another.'[25]

Meanwhile, the individual pursuit of gain, far from being destructive of the welfare of the commonwealth, guarantees it. Such arguments had been deployed by landlords in their movement to enclose common lands for their exclusive benefit. Joseph Lee, an enclosing minister at Catthorpe in Leicestershire, disposes of scripture – 'Did not *Moses*, in all his afflictions with the children of God, aime at his own advantage?' – before prefiguring Adam Smith.

> The advancement of private persons will be the advantage of the publick.[26]

The metaphors come from physics and medicine. Newton's laws are riveted onto society, with the role of gravity taken by self-interest. Money circulates in society, vivifying each social organ and limb, even the poor, as Harvey's blood circulates in the body. Human beings, all subject to desire and need conveyed by money, and each restrained by all the other users of money, are capable of good order and need no kings or priests.

This system of belief, combining as it did City self-interest and garbled fashionable science, had its ludicrous side. Its apotheosis of luxury, of male avarice and female vanity, was lampooned by Pope and Swift, by Addison in *The Spectator*, and turned on its head in Gay's wonderful *Beggar's Opera*. But those writers could not deter Adam Smith from his *robinsonades* or prevent his thoughts gaining a wide currency. The reason is too obvious to name. People want money – even Pope speculated in South Sea stock in 1720 – not merely because they live in cities and must have it to feed but to make actual or imaginary their wishes, which, because they are also gratified by money, take on the character and urgency of need; and they will subscribe to a system of belief that promises to moralise and justify such satisfactions. The economic ideology was impregnable fifty years before *The Wealth of Nations*. It saw off the country critics just as it was later to repel the Romantic assault launched by Sir Walter Scott and reinforced by Marx, Carlyle and Proudhon and their successors.

★

If the Dutch of the seventeenth century had mastered money, they were also subject to its mastery. I have in mind the speculation in the bulbs of variegated and plain tulips that reached its peak in Haarlem and the other Dutch cities at the beginning of 1637. That chain of events has fascinated the English-speaking world ever since Charles MacKay devoted a chapter to it in his *Extraordinary Popular Delusions and the Madness of Crowds* in 1841. With its warning of the unreasonable conduct of people in mass, the book tends to be reissued in the United States at the peak of bull markets or just after they have broken. Indeed, the lecture has become so wearisome that the economists now claim that the tulip trade of the 1630s, but for its final phase, was eminently calm and sensible: naturally, if you believe the market is all-wise, then, well, so is any particular market.[27]

Financial booms and crashes are exemplary forms of history, for they appear to present that fata Morgana, an empirical or measurable psychology. You need merely record the money price of the security, or of an index, at the height of the boom and the depths of the crash to have what seems to be a quantity of human joy and misery; rather as the experience of battle is measured in the number of dead men and captured guns.

There were wild speculations before the Dutch *tulpenhandel*, for example in the stock of the Dutch East India in the first quarter of the century; and there have been countless since, from the railway shares in the 1840s to Florida real estate in the 1920s and Internet stocks in the 1990s. Trade in futures existed before 1636: farmers had anticipated their harvests and fishermen their catches since the dawn of money. The interest of the tulips lies in this: that in a society that is only just learning to think in stock-market categories – Keyser's new Bourse was completed only in 1611, and for a couple of years the Dutch East India still paid its dividends in pepper, nutmeg or mace – the records are likely to be more symptomatic and the narrative more revealing.

Financial markets are quite indifferent to the objects and activities represented by their stock symbols: the famous Main Street question, What does XYZ Corp do?, is answered on Wall Street, It goes to 100 and splits, and goes to 100 and splits. Bourses reduce all reality to a money symbol. It is merely that in selecting for their speculative fancy natural things of such ravishing, almost otherworldly beauty – flowers that had delighted the East for centuries and bloomed in Kashmiri gardens and Hafez's lyrics and the plates and tiles of Iznik – the Dutch revealed the perverse idealism of the stock-market investor. Money, as we have seen, is congealed desire: the speculators preferred, over the sensuous beauty of actual flowers, the imaginary potential of money (which might include flowers). In the process, they exemplified that destruction of quality as a mental category for organising the world that we noted as a characteristic of the age of money since Friar Pacioli. The modern Polish poet Zbigniew Herbert described the process better than I can:

> The order of the stock market was introduced into the order of nature. The tulip began to lose the properties and charms of a flower: it grew pale, lost its colours and shapes, became an abstraction, a name, a symbol interchangeable with a certain amount of money.[28]

However, that attenuation cannot be completed but can be reversed. At some point, the abstraction shudders back into form. Men saw that tulips are flowers and not money. They woke from their dream. Crash. There is an anecdote that attempts to reproduce the epiphany: it's the one about the sailor who, coming on a bulb of Semper Augustus, worth as much as an Amsterdam town house and garden, thought it was an onion and ate it with bread. As always with such stories, it matters less whether the event occurred as told than that a story was told and remembered.

We are fortunate to possess a set of three contemporary satires on the speculation, the first published in the eye of the storm at Haarlem in 1637, and called the *Samenspraeck tusschen Waermondt ende Gaergoedt nopende de opkomst ende ondergang van Flora*, or The Dialogues between True-Mouth and Greedy-Guts on the Rise and Fall of Flora. They are censorious, but they are contemporary; and I have preferred them to the later reconstructions of MacKay or the economists.

Because the dialogues are cast in dramatic form, one can draw some conclusions about the social class that provided the speculators and what they thought they were up to. Gaergoedt is a weaver, and it is clear that, in its peak phase, the boom is driven by non-professionals of small means but some ability to borrow: like the speculators in houses in London and southern England in the 1980s. The trade takes place not on the Bourse, but in what are colleges – clubs, really – with elaborate rituals in public houses. The trade is in futures, and not merely for their speculative leverage, but for a reason of horticulture. The bulbs are not like gold or pictures or the other exotic luxuries of Dutch commerce, Chinese porcelain and Islamic carpets, for they are yielding assets: and the yield, which the speculators attempt to turn into money, are the buds or offsets that form on the bulb and, properly cultivated, produce another bulb. Tulips are also subject to attack by a virus whose chief effect, apart from making the bulb sickly, is to produce streaks and patterns on the flower. It was these broken flowers that had caught the European imagination and were eagerly sought.

Tulips flower in April and May for about ten days, die back and may be taken out of the ground in June, but must be returned to it by the autumn. Originally, according to the dialogues, bulbs were bought and sold by growers by the piece or, occasionally, by the bed and only for immediate delivery in June. But from the summer of 1634, excited by the fashion for broken flowers in Holland and France, non-professionals entered the trade; growers were able to sell bulbs in the ground for delivery next season; and a market grew up in the offsets of rare bulbs that could only be separated once they had reached a certain size. Since the heavier the bulb, the more offsets and thus more future bulbs, they came to be sold by weight: by the *aas* (plural: *azen*), which was about one-twentieth of a gram, or by the thousand *azen* or even by the pound.

Just evident in the dialogues is the makings of an investment theory: that these curious and novel flowers, first mentioned in Eastern Europe only in 1554 and passing by way of Vienna, the Fuggers' garden in Augsburg, Brussels and Paris to Holland only in the first quarter of the new century, hitherto the fancy of princes, noblemen and *grands bourgeois*, must soon colonise the gardens of all the little or middling people and bring spectacular capital gains to the owners of the root-stocks:

> *Gaergoedt:* You can barely earn ten per cent on the money that is in your business and even then only by giving security, but with Flora you can double your money. Yes, even ten for one, a hundred for one, and sometimes a thousand.
>
> *Waermondt:* I've wasted my life in hard work, and so did many parents with their toil and starvation.[29]

There is always something visionary in great speculations: else they would not be speculations. The tulips *have* colonised the world. The annual trade of Holland alone in tulips is worth almost five hundred million guilders; and new varieties, even in the age of genetic intervention, are valuable. Did Gaergoedt see in a vision the endless tulip beds outside modern Haarlem and Leiden and the nurseries laid out in South Africa and Zimbabwe? Not clearly, any more than the speculators in John Law's Mississippi Company in Paris in 1720 could foresee the petrochemical industries of Baton Rouge. The delusion lies in the conception of time. The great stock-market bull seeks to condense the future into a few days, to discount the long march of history, and capture the present value of all future riches. It is his strident demand for everything right now –

to own the future in money right now – that cannot tolerate even the notion of futurity – that dissolves the speculator into the psychopath.

Prices rose steeply throughout the 1635–36 season. By the next season, the trade had lost all relation with any physical object. The trade was, in the phrase the Dutch had taken over from the Italians, *in blanco*: 'in the white' or 'in the space' or what we would now call short-selling. The seller sold *azen* of bulbs he did not possess against a value, usually but not always money, which the buyer did not possess, round and round. Neither party intended to deliver anything. They were simply betting on the future price of bulbs: and on settlement day the loser paid the difference between the price of the contract in the college and the current price in the market. By then, even plain tulips, those unaffected by the virus that caused the streaking, were traded:

> *Gaergoedt:* Single Coleuren were . . . auctioned by the thousand *azen*. Everything was worth money and so current that one could get in exchange almost anything one desired. And all this with promises and vouchers, while the bulbs were in the earth. If this had gone on, all payments would have taken place in flowers, as they say in some places of East India with conches, and many payments had already done so.[30]

Jan van Goyen, the famous painter of landscapes, paid in canvases and bankrupted himself.

The pearl of the tulips was a variety called Semper Augustus. It has, alas, like all the speculative varieties but for Zomerschoon, vanished from the earth, prey to the actual or speculative virus:

> *Gaergoedt:* That is a beautiful flower. One can see it at the houses of only two people, one in Amsterdam, from which it comes, and also here at the home of one who will not sell for any money; so they are in close hands.
> *Waermondt:* How much is such a flower worth?
> *Gaergoedt:* Who knows? But I will tell you what I have heard about it. About three years ago, [a bulb] was sold for 2,000 guilders, transferred at once at the Bank [of Amsterdam], with the restriction that the buyer could not sell or alienate it without the consent of him from whom he bought it.[31]

And what was 2,000 guilders? Reckoned in the guilder's gold equivalent at the gold price of 1997, it would be about $20,000 today; reckoned against the 1,600 guilders paid to Rembrandt to paint *The Night Watch* at the summit of his fame, it would be tens of millions of dollars. Money prices belong in their times and cannot be compared across the centuries: comparisons are, in Zbigniew Herbert's beautiful phrase, taken from the air and evaporate back into the air. For what it's worth, we are told that in the mid-seventeenth century in Holland, the weekly wages of a mason or other skilled workman were generally less than three guilders. Another bulb, of the variety Vice-Roy, was sold not for money but for two cars of wheat, four carts of rye, four fat oxen, eight fat pigs, twelve fat sheep, two barrels of wine, four barrels of best beer and one thousand pounds of cheese, not counting some household goods.

By the winter of 1636–37, the growers at Haarlem were becoming anxious that they would soon be left with beds of worthless stock. According to the *Samenspraeck*, confidence cracked on February 3. By the next day, markets in Haarlem were in full retreat. A meeting was held in Utrecht on the 7th, which prepared the way for a full conference of growers at Amsterdam on the 24th. The conference attempted to enforce all new-season contracts at 10 per cent of the price agreed, but in the devastated market, even 10 per cent would not hold. In Haarlem, the reckless buyers were instructed by the Mayor and Governors to put up 3½ per cent, but most, it seems, paid nothing at all. Cultivation of tulips shrunk back to the environs of Haarlem and Leiden; and though the Dutch were to fall prey to speculations in hyacinths in the 1730s and gladioli in 1912, it was never with such abandon.

The tulip mania was but one, overhasty instance of the Dutch discovery of a monetary reality behind appearances. In the course of the century, the discovery was to lead to new ways of confronting the uncertainties of existence: fire, accident, even death itself. The primitive lotteries, risk pools and tontines of Italy are, during the century in Holland and England, refined into modern insurances. The revenues of the state, a perennial headache since antiquity, assume their modern form. In the public administration, financial corruption makes a counter-weight to nepotism. These prodigies of finance were wrenched by the economists out of the realm of philosophy and we must now restore them.

In the Middle Ages in Europe, human beings confronted uncertainty with faith in God and a supposedly static picture of society and the cosmos. Such mental attitudes were, as we have seen, undermined by money, and by the discoveries of the book-keepers, Columbus and the astronomers. Men sought to reconstruct the old certainties on the foundation of money.

In the new world, first, there is no such thing as providence, merely probability, which can be studied at the gaming table. Second, there is such a thing as usury: whatever Aristotle and the Gospels say, money *is* productive of more money, it *does* breed, and on Sunday, too. Calvin had told a questioner in 1545, 'If we wholly condemn usury, we impose tighter fetters on the conscience than God himself,' and that would never do.[32] Once that is believed – and already by 1612, with Bacon's great essay *On Usury*, the problem is of high interest not usury, of expediency not sin – all manner of avenues open to the ingenuity. Third, the church is quite wrong and human beings are all more or less alike. Reality is thus reconfigured on the basis not of an immortal soul and a benign providence, but of probability and compound interest, which become, essentially, the theology of modernity.

Property/casualty insurance is the lottery in a mirror. Both imagine a cataclysm, of vanishingly small probability, value it in money and distribute it around a population so as to mitigate its force: in one the event is good, a prize of cash or an annuity or, as in many of the Dutch municipal lotteries, furniture or silver or a carpet; in the other, it is that fire will break out in a baker's shop and burn your house to the ground, or a storm run your ships aground. The law establishing the London Chamber of Assurance in 1601 describes, in undisguised delight, how a mere 'consideracon of Mony to other persons' ensures that 'upon the losse or perishinge of any Shippe there followethe not the undoinge of any Man, but the losse lighethe rather easilie upon many, than heavily upon fewe, and rather upon them that adventure not than those that doe adventure.'[33]

Faith in God is displaced by faith in credit: faith that the lottery promoter or insurance corporation will not abscond with your ticket or premium and beyond that in the ability of the community to enforce public and private debts. The mental shift is evident in England in a single generation. Nicholas Barbon, whose father, Praise-God Barebones, MP, had preached hell-fire in Fleet Street in the 1630s, lucidly contrasts the advantages of mutual and share-holder-owned fire insurance in his *Letter to a Gentleman* of January 26, 1684.

Life insurance takes the mental procedure one step further. It was Johan De Witt, among others, who showed that the chances of death, if they could somehow be tabulated, could be combined with an allowance for compound interest to give the present value of a life annuity; and those could be sold either by private promoters or to finance the state. In other words, money could not defeat death, as Witt's murder showed in peculiarly ghastly fashion in 1672, but it could dull its effect on a man's survivors and posterity. O Death, where is they sting? A burgher's wife could be as richly left as Portia with all the acres of Belmont. What a property of money: that it could take a man's affection for his wife, freeze it, and then, after his death, thaw it out to succour the grieving widow!

The mathematical work was done by Edmund Halley, the great astronomer and discoverer of a famous comet, working from the bills of mortality of the city of Breslau in Silesia for the years 1687 to 1691; and the whole process clothed, in the unctuous language of a company promoter of 1712, in terms of common sense. The man who did not provide for his posterity

> ought to forfeit the Name of a Rational Creature, and be no more ranked among Men; for who is there . . . who can think of leaving a near Friend, a dutiful child, or a tender Wife unprovided for, without the utmost Grief that Human Nature can suffer.[34]

In fact, that particular project, like so many insurance schemes, was not taken up. The charm of insurance and lotteries is that you collect your premiums and sell your tickets before you have to pay out on a claim or prize, so you can start up without money, and disappear without trace. The first permanent life office had to wait till 1762, with the foundation of the Equitable Life Assurance Society and the invention, in its deed of settlement, of that strange and barbaric individual (usually Scots): the actuary.

For the English country gentlemen, obliged to watch these spectacular projects raining money on the City, it was all intensely frustrating. There they were, on their thrones and acres, with not two guineas to rub togther! The City, which could capitalise the nebulous future income of the wildest money scheme – lottery tickets, excise revenues, orphans' income, even, in a famous scheme of 1720, a secret plan of which nobody was to know – had little interest in the future rents of land. The Bank of England was the last straw: 'The Current of Money,' John Briscoe wrote in 1695, 'being so greatly turned into the Bank, has made it Difficult to Supply real Securities with Money.'[35] Having learned from their excursions into 'Change Alley to look beyond appearances, the landed men now revived the old landed ideology – the gardens of Belmont, as it were – in the new language: it was land, not money, that was the core reality, for it was 'the *primum mobile* of all things,'[36] and without it nothing can be made that is made: Asgill went so far as to say that commodities were merely '*land severed* from the *soil*' and 'man deals in nothing but earth.'[37] There arose a host of schemes for land banks – by Briscoe, Chamberlen and Law in Scotland and England, Franklin in Pennsylvania – which argued that loans raised against land would be so secure they could be used as currency. In other words, the bank would issue notes secured not on deposits of coin (as at the Wisselbank) or a government debt (as at the Bank of England) but of 'England itself,' source of all monetary as well as patriotic value: truly, a precious stone set in a silver sea.

Eventually, the antagonisms of country and town are resolved by rising land values and by finance: by the Royal Bank of Scotland's pioneering invention of the overdraft and by the contract at Lloyd's. The first, known as cash-credit and introduced in 1728, converts the personality, as expressed in its possessions, into money: so that a man, as Hume put it in high enthusiasm, 'may find surety nearly to the amount of his substance . . . and does hereby in a manner coin his houses, his household furniture, the goods in his warehouse . . . and employ them in all payments, as if they were the current money of the country.'[38] Under the second, the gentlemen and ladies retain the use of their lands and moveable property at home, but must be prepared without warning to sell them to pay claims from a distant shipwreck, fire or storm. By 1776, Adam Smith was to detect no tension between London and the provinces; and, in truth, in our times, London has simply colonised the country. Just as the Marquis of Sligo in Ireland, during the famine years of the 1840s when he drew no rents, survived on the proceeds of letting out his box at Covent Garden; so the modern manor and country house derives its income not from farms and fields and woods, which yield nostalgia and expense, but from stock-market dividends. That gives to English country life, even at its most Arcadian, a decidedly metropolitan air.

In London itself, let us quickly sketch in some other monetary personalities: bearing in mind that insight from *The Spectator* of June 12, 1712 (No. 403), where Addison sees the capital as a sort of oriental city, 'as an Aggregate of various Nations distinguished from each other by their respective Customs, manners and Interests.'

Most gorgeous of these figures is the beau, who will eventually transform into the dandy. Clad in the finest French or India stuffs, he is a permanent affront to the warmongers and the bullionists: for the Hindoos will not wear English woollen and the East India trade is a drain of precious silver. He is the masculine or hermaphroditic equivalent of those women who flout in their costume a deteriorating balance of payments: the Marquise de Nesle, say, who appeared in the Tuileries gardens on July 17, 1715, in a dress embroidered 'in the Indian manner on linen of that country' and was reported to the Minister of Police,[39] or those women who embraced Dior's New Look in London in February 1947.

Whereas the lord inherits distinction, and the merchant buys it, the beau borrows it without any intention to repay. He lives off retail credit, or rather effrontery, and that is his challenge to the pompous mercantile credit of the City, the aristocratic honour of the shires and the virtue of ladies. He obliges the tradesmen to carry an immense capital. Ten thousand pounds, enough to build a country house, was barely capital enough for a lace-man in London in 1747, according to one of the many commercial manuals of the time; and even then the fellow 'must have confidence to refuse his Goods in a handsome Manner to the extravagant Beau who never pays'; as for tailors, 'they make a handsome penny, and would raise Estates soon, were it not for the Delays in Payment among the Quality.'[40]

The dandy is the beau taken beyond all economical sense. The name dandy was imported from India, or Scotland, in the seventeenth century, according to the dictionaries; but in truth the dandy is a man without attributes: he has no father, mother, coat of arms, friends, wife or child, or any property, for his clothes, carriage and plate are not paid for. Within the dandy's world there are postures that do not concern us – homosexual or transvestite pose, nostalgia for Eton and that facetious confusion of the artifical and natural that we admire in the conversation of Wilde – for these have been studied *ad nauseam*, notably in France. Our concern is with his monetary doctrine. The French theorists of dandyism in the 1840s, including Barbey d'Aurevilly and Baudelaire, were able to locate the dandies' origins in time (heirs to the beaux of the Restoration) and place (Covent Garden, that is, equidistant between the City and the West End) but were unable, being French, even to begin to understand their economics.

The dandy as financier is active only on the right or liability side of the balance-sheet. That is his spiritual *point d'honneur*, and cannot be renounced, as was shown in the passion and death of the greatest of dandies, Brummell. The reader will forgive me if I discuss his career out of sequence, for it is the perfection of a seventeenth-century psychology.

George Bryan Brummell, the leader of male society under the British Regency of the early nineteenth century, ran out of money and credit – to the dandy, they are indistinguishable – on the evening of May 16, 1816. He drank a bottle of claret – *Système physiologique anglais*, Barbey notes ethnographically[41] – and wrote to Scrope Davies:

> My dear Scrope, send me two hundred pounds. The banks are shut and all my money is in the three per cents. It shall be paid to-morrow morning.—Yours, George Brummell

Davies' reply came back with the messenger:

> My dear George, 'tis very unfortunate, but all my money is in the three per cents.—Yours, S. Davies[42]

Let us peel back the layers of heroism and affectation to reveal the meaning of that celebrated exchange. The 3 per cents are the British government bonds, paying an interest of 3 per cent, known since the financial reforms of the 1750s as Consols or Consolidated Annuities: a perpetual issue is still outstanding and quoted at a heavy discount in the *Financial Times*. They are loans, arising on the left-hand side of the balance-sheet, and to the State of all things; and since they carry the faith and credit of the United Kingdom are almost without risk of default or non-payment. In other words, they are the absolute reverse of dandyism. Brummell's claim that he has money in the Funds, that he is some suburban *rentier*, is a fabulous piece of invention that Scrope's answer matches and respects, though with that habitual rudeness the dandies use in their internal communications. Scrope's seems to me a thoroughly dandy-like reply, and I'm sure Brummell thought the same: he went out to the opera. Next morning, he set off for Dover, overnighted there, and arrived in Calais, refuge of British debtors, on May 18. His property was auctioned, and men paid high prices in money for souvenirs, notably his snuff-boxes: presumably, everything else was repossessed by the tradesmen.

Brummell died in the poor-house of Bon Sauveur at Caen in Normandy in 1840. In his beautiful encomium of the Englishman, which was published in 1845, Barbey deplores his choice of ending:

> *Quand on meurt de faim, on sort des affectations d'une société quelconque, on rentre dans la vie humaine: on cesse d'être Dandy.*[43]

> [To starve to death is to abandon the affectations of a particular circle and return to humanity: one ceases to be a dandy.]

It is hard to imagine an analysis more thoroughly mistaken. To save his life, Brummell might have worked for money or put something aside; but such existences required that he embrace the division of labour and submit to money's dominion. To choose the starving fraction of humanity, to pass among the raving destitutes in ruins of cambric and silk, is the triumph of the dandy's perversity, his self-immolation. The best commentary on Brummell is not Barbey's essay, but the life of Baudelaire, which I shall address in Chapter 8: Proust says somewhere that Baudelaire's sympathy for the poor arose from *anticipation*.

What the beaux had grasped long before Brummell is that once money becomes the chief form of wealth, or rather when all wealth is available in the form of money, it can be borrowed or stolen. The tragedy of the Jews of medieval Europe, murdered and mulcted of their wealth because it is in money, becomes the comedy of the Restoration. The identification of the beau and the gambler is not accidental: nor is their common passion for venal duelling, what we would now call armed robbery. The great confrontation between Law and Wilson in Bloomsbury Square on the evening of April 9, 1694 – an event as important to our history as the founding of the Bank of England that summer, as we shall see – is summed up by Evelyn in two words: that Law killed the boy 'not fairly.' As for cards and dice, to which Law brought a mind of extraordinary analytical power, we need merely consult the manuals of the century – Charles Cotton, say, or Theophilus Lucas' *Lives of the Gamesters* – for their mixture of the new mathematics, theft and murder. We come on rich young men who are *bubbleable* and can be *taken* or *rooked*, with dice *loaded* or *swept*; and if probability or cheating fail there is always cold steel.

The gambler has not even the beau's insolence. Money is his whole personality: money that is drained of all mortal wishes and exists solely for the game. Lucas saw into his nature with great acuity:

> There appears to be no middle condition; the triumph of a Prince, or the misery of a beggar, are his alternate states. He that is worth 4 or 5000 pounds at noon, shall not be worth a farthing by night; and what can be a greater scandal for noblemen than to play with fellows who have no other visible livelihood than that of shaking the elbow? who are so very poor, that if ill luck strips 'em of all their money, they must borrow half a crown of the maid that cleans their shoes, with which gaming in Lincolns-Inn-Fields, among the boys for farthings and oranges, till they have made up three pieces, then they return to the Rose-Coffeehouse, or some other place for raffling with hopes of retrieving their late losses.[44]

Cotton had this to say about the dice game known as Hazard or Hazzard:

> Certainly Hazzard is the most bewitching game that is plaid on the dice; for when a man begins to play he knows not when to

leave off; and having once accustom'd himself to play at Hazzard he hardly ever after minds [considers] anything else.[45]

On the distaff side, we must celebrate not only the great lady gamblers of the Restored Stuarts – the Duchess of Cleveland lost £8,000 in a single sitting – but also its whores: over the court of Charles II presides that 'Imbezling C—t' which draws, in the words of one poet, all the money of the kingdom into its maw.[46] In such a perilous world, prudent families with a dynastic cast of mind naturally attempt both to inhibit the mobilisation of property into money and to imprison money into things. For Defoe, the tradesman becomes a gentleman only at the instant he sells up and 'has converted his money into solid rents. He has, then, laid down the *Tradesman* intirely, and commenc'd *Gentleman*.'[47] The seventeenth century also saw the spread of the 'strict settlement,' or estate in entail, which sought to make an estate insoluble to a profligate heir. To Dr Johnson, who liked the idea of subordinating an individual to his family history, entails in moderation were a useful curb to the mobilisations of money.[48] Marx, in contrast, whose fondness for feudal pageantry was inflamed by his wife's grand Scots ancestry, marvelled that in Britain men did not inherit land but vice versa.[49] Less sentimental than either, Jane Austen will eventually show us that the English passion for real property is mostly sham: her characters can recite the capitalised money income of a Mansfield Park or Pemberley down to the last red guinea. She never forgets that these places, for all their comfort, amenity, rank and display, are money. But then she and her sister lived on £20 a year.

But let us leave England and touch briefly at another society transformed by money and gaiety in the seventeenth century: I mean Japan.

★

You should save money. It will be another parent in your life to add to your father and mother.

Saikaku[50]

At the turn of the seventeenth century, Japan gained a stable central government (known as the Toshugawa Shogunate), a trusted currency based on a hierarchy of gold, silver and copper coins and some minor exposure to Dutch ideas, through the Holland traders permitted to do business at Nagasaki. Those brought to birth, in a society vastly different from that of England and Scotland, a new way of regarding the world that still evokes nostalgia in modern Japan.

The picture of the world, which does not long disguise its monetary foundation, is known by the Japanese term transliterated as *ukiyo*. That word was originally written with the characters that mean 'sad world' and expressed a feeling for the evanescence of phenomenal reality – appearances – in Buddhist doctrine. In the course of the early seventeenth century, the word was refigured with the characters that mean 'floating world' and is defined early for our purposes in a passage of the samurai writer Asai Ryōi in 1661:

> Living only for the moment, gazing at the moon, the snow, the cherry blossoms and the maple leaves; singing songs, drinking wine, diverting ourselves in just floating, floating; caring not a fig for the penury staring us in the face, refusing to be disheartened, and floating like a gourd in the river current: that is what we call the *floating world*.[51]

It is irresponsible pleasure, the money to buy that pleasure, and the essential instability of both. In the passage, there is a melancholy, a slight pressure on the spirit: over the Floating World hover the ghosts of penury, which frustrates desire, and mortality that extinguishes it.

The Floating World is peopled not by samurai, the warriors of feudal Japanese society, nor by peasants or artisans but by the lowest and richest estate, the townspeople or *chonin*, merchants who are beginning to make large fortunes from the expansion of trade and population. They are excluded from the world of feudal power, and must find some other outlet for the wishes embodied in their silver. The markets of their desires are certain walled commercial entertainment compounds erected on the outskirts of the big cities in the course of the century: Yoshiwara at Edo (Tokyo) in 1617, Shinmachi is Osaka in 1620, Shimabara in Kyoto in 1641. To describe these districts as brothel or red–light quarters would be quite correct –

Yoshiwara, rebuilt out in the rice fields after the fire of 1657, soon comprised 150 houses with some 3,000 indentured women – and yet would give a wholly wrong impression. They are privileged spaces where the feudal rigidities of social position and sexual relation dissolve in the sea of money; or rather, since the *chonin*'s world is quite as rigid as its feudal counterpart, are reconfigured in the language of money. In these 'cities without night,' in the 'world of flower and willow,' in the Kabuki theatre and the *tayū*'s gorgeous sash and robe embroidered with plovers, the *chonin* escapes the gloom of Buddhist piety, the rigid official confucianism, the draconian laws on sexual morality and the bullying of the samurai. For here, money rules, and the samurai will not impress the girls with his stipend of rice:

> In the Yoshiwara
> The way of the warrior
> Cannot conquer.[52]

In this highly circumscribed space, the *chonin* may also take his consolation for his utter political impotence: for the gay quarters (as they were known to an earlier generation of writers) exist to preserve the feudal system and to prevent the merchants converting their money, as in England, into power in the state. In fact, Japanese feudalism will survive, cut off from the world, until the arrival of Commodore Perry and his flotilla in 1853.

The novelist of this world of money and pleasure is Ihara Saikaku, who is not much read in the English-speaking countries. Born, probably in Osaka, in 1642, he was well known as a poet, though a certain quality in his *haikai*, either formal innovation or outlandish imagery, caused him to be dubbed 'Dutch Saikaku' (*oranda saikaku*). In the course of the 1680s and early 1690s, he wrote a series of stories that are a reworking in the language of money of the great novels of the feudal epoch, such as *The Tale of Genji*. A predecessor of Defoe in England, he has been compared to the Englishman: and indeed, one finds in Saikaku that admiration for the townsman, for his resilience and common sense, that is such a feature of *The Complete English Tradesman*; also the meticulous price lists of *Moll Flanders*. Yet is it hard to imagine Defoe ever giving his Moll the terrifying vision of the Amorous Woman: her ninety-five abortions wearing their placentas like lotus-leaves on their heads, dripping with blood from the waist down and shrieking. 'Carry me on your back! Oh, carry me!'[53]

Saikaku is more fascinated by money even than Defoe: there is more coined money in his stories than in any others, unless it be *Manon Lescaut* (the novel of the Law epoch in France) and Balzac's *Comédie Humaine*. We learn down to the last copper *mon* how much it costs a girl to rent her working costume for the night; how much, in the rigid monetary stratification of the licensed quarters, it costs a man to visit the highest rank of girl in Kyoto (five hundred and fifty-one *momme* of silver with tips); even, at one point, the *capital* cost of loving such a woman (five hundred *kamme* of silver).

In these novels, money is the complete personality. Just as the women of the licensed quarters are defined by their tabulated fees, so is the man by his capital or 'storehouse' (a solid locked building by his house where he keeps his rice and money).

> Money is the townsman's only pedigree. A man may be descended from the noblest of the Fujiwara, but if he dwells among shopkeepers and lives in poverty, he is lower than a monkey-showman.[54]

In Saikaku's Floating World tales (known as *ukiyo-zōshi*), one senses for the first time the deranged reality of the modern city; and that is no accident, because I suspect Edo, Osaka and Kyoto were already as densely populated as London and Amsterdam. In the city, all actions are transactions: everything costs money. The reality of country and season, where desire is conveyed directly rather than through an intermediary and must often wait on nature for its satisfaction, disintegrates, and Saikaku records that disintegration with great care. This is how the second story of *The Japanese Family Storehouse* (1688) opens:

> The plum, the cherry, the pine and the maple – these are what people like having in their houses. But more than those, in truth, they want gold, silver, rice, and coppers. [The rice here is not food but money, and coexisted with coins in some districts.][55]

The introduction of money has also demolished the ethical basis of society. The famous Chinese *Twenty-four Examples of Filial Conduct* is rewritten by Saikaku as *Twenty Examples of Unfilial Conduct in Japan* (1686). Wang Hsiang, who had melted river ice by lying naked on it to bring his stepmother carp out of season, or Meng Tsung, who had searched in the snow for early bamboo-shoots, are compared, wittily, with their money counterparts:

> Bamboo-shoots in snow may be had at the greengrocer's; and there are always live carp in the fishmongers' tanks.[56]

The first story in the collection establishes money as the paramount connection between men and both material and spiritual worlds:

> Many are the ways of making a living. . . . Some spend the whole year painting banners of Benkei on the Gojo Bridge. . . . You can rent what you need for a Buddhist service – sacrificial food, flower-vase, candlestick, censer and a gong as well – all for twelve *mon* a night. A lying-in-room couch, including the large pillow, will cost you seven *fun* [a weight of silver coins] a week. At the season of making rice cakes they rent steamers for three *fun* a day and two a night.

(There follows an account of a Kyoto money-lender who makes secret loans against future inheritances at usurious rates.) By the time Saikaku came to write 'Reckonings That Carry Men Through the World' in 1692, money has fully displaced the natural calendar: it is only by paying his debts on New Year's Eve that a man can pass into the new year. One poor tradesman dreams that night so vividly of money that he is transubstantiated: his wife wakes up beside a heap of gold *koban*.

In these cities of desire and temporary satisfaction, sexual love has a paramount authority; for where men have no beliefs or traditions or curiosity or power, money and pleasure alone seem real and come together in their most overpowering form in the body of a girl. That is the meaning of the admirable second story of *The Japanese Family Storehouse*, called 'The Wind That Destroyed the Fan-maker's Shop in the Second Generation.' The wind is, of course, love, which demolishes a fortune built up in two generations of business. Going to the Shimabara to deliver a letter and a coin he had found dropped accidentally in the street, the younger fan-maker is overwhelmed, squanders 150 hundredweight of silver coins in four or five years and becomes destitute.

That theology of money and love will become the theme of a great series of paintings by the artist Utamaro at the end of the eighteenth century. In his Floating World pictures (*ukiyo-e*), say *Ten Types in the Physiognomic Study of Women* (1792–93) or *Array of Supreme Beauties of the Present Day* (1794), Utamaro is seeking to penetrate into the very nature of happiness. His gorgeously dressed figures, half- or three-quarter length against mica or yellow backgrounds, are not portraits of actual women who might have names. They are incarnations of sexual gratification in the clothing of Yoshiwara, which is money. The summer clothes, which locate the girl precisely on the scale of fees, are disordered by a step, and there's a flash of sexual allure. In *Five Shades of Ink in the Northern Quarter* (c. 1794–95), Utamaro even gives faces and gestures to the lowest category, the one-and-a-half *momme* street girl. His appetite for femininity is insatiable: in inscriptions to the series *New Patterns of Brocade Woven in Utamaro Style* (c. 1796), he describes his artistic mission in metaphors of the female body.

And yet there is a monotony in these pictures: not because Utamaro can't draw (he can), but because his project is utterly hopeless and is doomed to repeat itself. Utamaro is attempting with his brush to uncover the secret of happiness, to find a permanent satisfaction, to extinguish desire; but desire is not extinguished by a brush-stroke, any more than it is extinguished by the payment of one and a half *momme* of silver. It is extinguished by sickness and death. One comes away from these great masterpieces bored, to death.[57]

Long before Utamaro, Saikaku had reached the same conclusion. From the beginning he saw that money, while opening up a world of pleasure and love to its possessors, delivers to countless miseries those that do not have it, men and women. By the end of his life, and no doubt because of a slowing of the business expansion, his Floating World is ceasing to float. Money breeds as women breed, and makes money. Those who have it soon have more:

> Now it is only silver than can produce more silver. In these times it is not so much intelligence and ready wit that bring a man profit, but simply the fact of already possessing capital.[58]

The gay humour had passed.

Saikaku was now fifty-two, by the Japanese reckoning, and thus had outlived the traditional Japanese life span of two-score years and ten. He had tried, as hard as anybody, to find the reality behind appearances: as hard even as the T'ang poet Li Po, who 'died drunk / He tried to embrace a moon / in the Yellow River.'[59] He had thought that reality was money, as millions have done since, but understood it isn't, and he too was weary of monetary appearances, to death. His death poem is this:

> I have gazed at it now
> For two years too long –
> The moon of the Floating World.[60]

6

Mississippi Dreaming:
On the Fame of John Law

1

Un jour, au milieu de cette cour de France, autrefois si militaire, un jeune Ecossais parut, qui venait vanter à des fils de preux ruinés les prodiges de la banque.

Louis Blanc[1]

In that court of France, once so martial, one day a young Scotsman appeared, come to unveil before those bankrupt lordlings the stupendous possibilities of banking.

Man's great inventions are, as we have seen, words and money, and words about money are therefore of double interest to us. The word I have in mind is the word 'millionaire,' a word of some importance in the history of money. Its coinage can be dated and placed quite precisely, and with much less labour than generations of American philologists have devoted to the useful abbreviation O.K.

The word 'millionaire,' which is French and means *celui qui possède un million d'argent*, was invented in the open air in a little street near what's now the Centre Beaubourg in Paris known as the Rue Quincampoix or Quincenpoix in the autumn of 1719. (That it was not admitted by the Académie Française till 1762 merely shows the caution of that body.)[2] It is the legacy to the languages of the world of a moment when the world turned and of the master and instigator of that manoeuvre, M. Quincampoix himself, the Scotsman John Law of Lauriston.

The man known as Law, Lawe and Laws in English, Lauw in
Dutch and Las, Lass and Laze in French is one of those human
beings in whose biography history itself changes direction. In the
all-encompassing financial system, known now as the Mississippi
Scheme, that Law established for a few months in Regency France,
he was looking back to an age when both prosperity and salvation
were domiciled in the Indies: back through the mercantilist companies of the seventeenth century, English state piracy and Columbus' great letter from Jamaica to the geographical and metaphysical
fantasies of the Middle Ages. In his notion of money as pure
function, he looks forward to our own era: to the final collapse of a
metallic standard in 1971 and the virtual moneys of electronics.

At the summit of his power, a period lasting somewhat longer
than five hundred days, Law ruled France more completely than its
absolute monarchs. He controlled its foreign trade, mints, revenues
and national debt, as well as half of what is now the United States
(excluding Alaska). Though he cared, as Montesquieu noted sourly,
less for his riches than for his ideas, and died without a sou, he was
for a few months rich as nobody before or, once an adjustment has
been made for the greater liquidity of modern societies – they use
more money – since.[3] Law owned one-third of the Place Vendôme
in Paris, most of the undeveloped land in the Faubourg St-Honoré,
the Hôtel Nevers (now the Bibliothèque Nationale) and the Mazarin
Palace, the block of streets at the site of today's Bourse, fifteen
country estates in France, much of what is now the U.S. state of
Arkansas, a library of 50,000 books and 150 million livres tournois
(£5–£10 million in the sterling of the time) in securities.[4] In a
single bear operation against the English East India Company in
1719–20, Law lost at least £370,000: more than anybody had made
in the City of London in a lifetime.[5]

We do not need to believe, with the Duc de Richelieu, that he
had an affair with the Regent's mother, for pornographic fantasies of
royalty are not the exclusive property of modern England: we simply
note the anxiety of the age that Law, a foreigner and a Protestant, a
gambler, adulterer, convicted murderer, slaver, and coward (also the
handsomest man in Europe and possessed, as even his enemies
conceded, of peculiarly beautiful manners), had cuckolded a throne.
It may also not be true that the Papal Nuncio kissed Law's little

daughter at her birthday party: all we need record is the age's recognition that that act of condescension by the representative of the representative of Our Saviour confirmed the true location of spiritual authority, a hundred years before Heine's famous ejaculation that money is the religion of modernity. The great ecclesiastical disputes that had so tormented seventeenth-century France were settled, as Voltaire noted, in 1719: the French were too interested in money to bother about Jansenism; and 'pleasure succeeded where *Louis XIV* had failed.'[6]

Into the ruin of French absolutism, the gambler insinuates himself and shakes it till it totters. In the solvent of Law's money, power and duty are disarranged for ever; relations between the sexes disintegrate; the estates promiscuously mingle and the duchess, raising her glasses from the river of diamonds on a neighbour's chest to the face above, recognises her cook. The great revolution is present in embryo: in the furious debates on money in the National Assembly in September 1790, Law is a phantom auditor, leaning against the Tribune.

The System, as Law called his invention, may be tackled at different levels of difficulty, like a video game. At its most elementary, it was a breathtaking device to convert the debts of France's bloody and capricious past into charges on a brilliant future, secured on the simplest fiscal regime ever devised and the potential of what is now the United States. At a somewhat more demanding level, it sought to create the most powerful nation on earth – Scotland, England, Savoy, France, Denmark, Russia, depending on the client – without strain and above all without violence. (That Law later took to violence to maintain his scheme in France is an element that we will introduce at the dramatic moment.) At a level more ambitious still, it sought, through the institution of a great commercial trust in which every citizen would risk his savings and enjoy his reward under a disciplined monarchy, to enfranchise society. And yet further, between the lines of Law's writings in English and French, for all their lucidity, one senses something else, wide and slow and undammable as the Mississippi itself: a river not so much of money as of happiness, of which we saw but the springs in Saikaku and Defoe. The activities and artefacts of the Regency are drenched in happiness: Manon and Des Grieux are reunited on the

Mississippi, Watteau's lovers are preserved for ever embarking for their inflationary Cythera, the Italian Comedy returns from its twenty-year exile, *galants défunts* smile in secret recollection from Rosalba Carriera's pastels. The moment passes, the river flows on, past the graves of martyred Jesuits and *sauvages nobles* thigh-deep in the wild rice, the gaunt financial ruins of Turgot and Necker, and the corpses of kings and revolutionaries and prostitutes, till it issues at last at the famous city that Law helped found and that still carries his air of risk and magic and incorrigible delight, the city of New Orleans.

In the autumn of 1719, the Venetian painter G. A. Pellegrini, having lost the competition for the cupola of St Paul's in London, accepted a commission to paint the vault of the Salle de Mississippi at Law's bank. The ceiling was 130 feet long, 27 feet wide and 4 feet from cornice to apex: Pellegrini worked on it for eighty days, painting more than one hundred figures, while the bank collapsed around him.[7] The ceiling was destroyed when the Hôtel Nevers was converted to house the royal library in 1724, but I have reconstructed it from the catalogue of an exhibition of Pellegrini's drawings at Venice in 1959[8]; from an iconographic *esquisse* or programme, almost certainly composed by Law, that is preserved in an eighteenth-century life of the French royal painters;[9] and from a brilliant article by Claire Garas in the *Bulletin* of the Musée hongrois des Beaux-Arts in Budapest in 1962.[10]

The ceiling is the great lost work of modernity, for it was the first and only attempt ever to portray money as grace: to glorify a financial enterprise in the pictorial language of absolutism. At its centre, the infant Louis XV, supported by Religion and the Hero (a portrait of the Regent, the Duc d'Orléans), is engulfed in a swirl not only of the usual allegorical virtues, sciences and vices but by the Genius of Commerce, Riches, Credit, Security, Invention, Arithmetic, Book-keeping, Industry, Navigation, the Seine and the Mississippi, Vessels Laden with Louisiana Produce, and Princes of the Indies. Glimmering above the entrance door, idyllic and serene, 'the STOCK EXCHANGE is represented by a portico around which merchants in their different national dress conduct their business.'

2

A grand imagination found in this flight of commerce something to captivate. It was wherewithal to dazzle the eye of an eagle.

Burke[11]

How is it that Law, that gorgeous sinner, that paragon of masculinity and finance, has so fallen into obscurity, his works unread, his tombstone in Venice effaced by the sandals of tourists unaware that they travel by a system of credit that owes much to John Law? Partly, I suspect, it is because the very modernity of the System, which makes it reasonably clear to our age, perplexed two and a half centuries: in the writings of his time, one keeps coming on explanations and motives that have more to do with magic, alchemy and court rivalries than business. In the *Mémoires* of the Duc de Saint-Simon, we can see Law flattering the vain old thing much more clearly than Saint-Simon himself. Law finally captures the duke by financing the purchase for the French regalia of an Indian diamond 'the size of a greengage,' then being hawked round Europe at a price of two million livres.[12] (It is now in the Louvre.) With the collapse of the System in May 1720, and the death of the Regent three years later, the *rentiers* that Law despised were restored, French finance fell into the hands of his business rivals and his reputation into those of Montesquieu and Voltaire, who disapproved of him. Law's ideas languished until they were revived in the *assignats* and *mandats* of the National Assembly: the enthusiasm of 1790 produced an excellent edition of Law's writings, edited by General Senovert with an introduction that breathes the pure spirit of that year. But the hyperinflation of the *assignats* had its reaction in Bonaparte, whose mind was closed to credit and, with his sanguinary conquests and picturesque titles, was everything that Law was not: he sold Louisiana to the Americans for four cents an acre, an oceanic discount to the future earnings of the Mississippi basin. And even in my childhood, the French from De Gaulle downward had a secret horror of fiat money and a deep attachment to the precious metals.

In England, the System was confounded with its City imitation, the South Sea Scheme of 1720, which was, as Adam Smith correctly noted, 'a meer fraud':[13] though it is worth noting that Walpole, who knew a thing or two about both power and speculation, had a regard for Law and was ready to employ him. In Holland and Scotland, one would expect better things; but the Dutch were burned in the collapse, and their best commentary is the collection of obscene and satirical prints of 1720, modelled on the tulip prints of the 1630s and called *Het groote Tafereel der Dwaashied* (*The Great Mirror of Folly*). In Law's homeland, Smith, with that peculiar ruthlessness of the eighteenth-century Scotsman on the make, speaks dismissively of Law in *The Wealth of Nations* (though, on the evidence of the *Lectures on Jurisprudence*, he was a little more conscientious in lecture). The Jacobite economist Sir James Steuart really did understand the System, for he had a strong intelligence and the lonely diligence of the exile, but he, too, is overshadowed by Smith. None the less, a deaf-mute Edinburgh antiquary called John Philip Wood (whom Walter Scott loved and described as a man 'of very powerful [memory] and much curious information') collected all the material he could find on Law, and his *Life*, published in 1824, is still by far the best printed source for Law's biography.[14]

By the middle of the nineteenth century, Law's reputation was a battleground between the *rentiers*, who blamed him for debauching French money and morals, and the romantic socialists who chose to forget Law's general villainy in his modernity: the great chapter in Louis Blanc's 1847 history of the Revolution refashions Law as a man of the people. Fortunately, Marx was at hand to resolve the non-existent contradiction in a single sentence in the third volume of *Capital*, which ascribes to Law the psychological ambiguity of all great financiers: 'the pleasant character mixture of swindler and prophet.'[15]

In the era of the gold standard, Law was considered, if at all, to be a dangerous ignoramus: one comes on smug little comments which make curious reading after a decade in which the value of gold has more than halved in terms of paper currencies. As late as the 1930s,

Charles Rist was calling Law a crank and jeering at him for not knowing the difference between money and credit. In reality, that was no monetary howler but policy: in a paper-money economy, as we have seen, the distinction can barely be detected.[16] In the United States, with its tradition of popular agitation against gold, there are good nineteenth-century studies of both Law and the *assignats*: Davis' *An Historical Study of Law's System* (1887) is the first systematic treatment of the scheme in English since Steuart. In our century, Keynes does not appear to have heard of Law; but the break with gold in 1914, the bull market of the 1920s and the Depression communicated a new interest in the father of paper inflation, with some diligent work by Dutch and Italian scholars in the archives of Amsterdam and Turin and Paul Harsin's great *Oeuvres Complètes* of 1934. Post-war references to Law for a while came labelled with apprehensive obeisance to 'Earl J. Hamilton's forthcoming study' or 'Prof. Hamilton's *magnum opus* on Law': as if, with the author of *American Treasure and the Price Revolution in Spain* already in the field, lesser knights should keep well clear. I don't know what happened to that work, but a fragment, delivered in an address to the annual meeting of the American Economic Association in San Francisco in December 1966, was distinctly unenthusiastic: Hamilton clearly disliked Law's gaming, household arrangements, and un-American despotism.[17] Vilar found contradictions in Law's economic thought, but seemed to forget that Law was a prime minister of France trying to establish a revolutionary economy over the hostility of much of the court, the *parlements* (appellate courts) and the *rentiers*, and the intense competition of the City of London.[18] Vilar's plea that we not ascribe too great a genius to Law was amply granted in the most recent French biography, Edgar Faure's *La Banqueroute de Law*.[19]

There is, no doubt, still evidence to be turned up in the French national archives, the accounts of the Bank of Amsterdam, the letter-books of the London bankers and the police reports of Paris, Genoa, Turin and Venice. In this chapter, I'd like to try, however clumsily, to bring Law out from the shadow of the economists and reveal him not as the greatest financier of history – a shabby enough laurel – but as the greatest of all Scots.

If there is a moment that I'd choose to embody Law it is that moment in the fall of 1719 when the stocks have gone through

10,000, and the Earl of Islay calls on his countryman. In the deafening hubbub of the Palais Mazarin, Islay, to his great surprise, is shown straight in to Law's office, where he finds him all alone, writing to his gardener at Lauriston. They play at piquet for half an hour.[20] It is this moment, in the still eye of a storm of history and money, in the tumult beyond the double doors – the princes of the blood slapped by the Swiss valets for pushing, the duchesses confounded by their clothes – that is for me the essence of Scotland: not, I mean, the Scotland of leaky castles, fulminating ministers, kail-yards, clipped coin, rig-and-furrow agriculture and Edinburgh slops, but of two men a long way from home, and alone in the world, but for their intelligence, their faces and their impregnable effrontery.

3

Belzebub, gewan Law,
Law, gewan de Bank,
De Bank, gewan Missisippi,
Missisippi, gewan SISTEMA . . .
        Het groote Tafereel, 1720

The Devil begat Law, and so forth.

In No. CXLII of Montesquieu's *Persian Letters*, there is a facetious mythology that begins: 'In the far Orkneys, there was born a boy, the son of Aeolus and a Caledonian nymph . . .' The reference to Aeolus, the god of the winds in Homer and an important figure in early financial iconology – the god of *trading in the wind, puffs, bubbles* and *inflation* – makes clear about whom we're talking. In fact, Law was born in Edinburgh, the son not of a god but of a successful goldsmith-banker who had bought the estate of Lauriston at Cramond on the Firth of Forth and one Jean Campbell, by all accounts a pretty formidable sort of nymph. The baptismal record is dated April 21, 1671. According to Wood, who had access to sources of information now lost, the young Law really did shine in algebra in school; another Scots antiquary mentions a skill at tennis.

Law's early biography is encrusted in mythical dissipation. He bursts into documentary history in the *London Gazette* of January 3–7, 1695. This, the first mention of Law for the purpose of publicity, is worth giving in full:

> Captain John Lawe, a Scotchman, lately a Prisoner in the Kings-Bench for Murther, aged 26, a very tall black lean Man, well shaped, above Six foot high, large Pockholes in his Face, big high Nosed, speaks broad and loud, made his escape from the said Prison. Whoever secures him, so as he may be delivered at the said Prison, shall have 50 l. paid immediately by the Marshal of the Kings-Bench.

Sir William Petty valued a person at twenty years' purchase of his or her earnings:[21] at that prospective multiple, nobody was going to sell Jessamy John Law for fifty quid.

Law killed a man named Edward 'Beau' Wilson in the evening of April 9, 1694, running him through the stomach fifty yards from where I am writing this, in Bloomsbury Square. He was found guilty at the Old Bailey of murder and received a sentence of death which was commuted by the King, who took a fairly light view of duels. Not so Wilson's family, which appealed; Law was remanded in the King's Bench prison; and escaped.

It is impossible to be sure of the cause of the quarrel. The jury was told that Wilson had insulted a lady at Law's lodgings; but that did not satisfy fashionable London. Wilson had no obvious source of income but lived in very high style, and even sophisticated people racked their brains to understand how. Evelyn's sentence is important: 'It did not appear he either was kept by Women or Play, or Coyning, Padding; or that he had any dealing in Chymistry.'[22] But those professions – coyning is counterfeiting coins, padding is highway robbery, chymistry is what we call alchemy – were being joined, as we have seen, by new ways of making money. After all, 1694 was the year of the founding of the Bank of England, the first great credit inflation and the Million Lottery.

Money floated in the hot London air as never before. It seems at least possible that behind the honour of the lady – a Mrs Lawrence, according to the trial report – there glittered something yet brighter, which is the subject of our history: Wilson's family, at least, thought so.

Affair of honour or armed robbery gone hopelessly awry, the duel, like so much in Law's biography, remains shrouded: even the Wanted notice, sandwiched between advertisements for a Collection of New Ayres for Two Flutes and Lost or Mislaid: Two Goldsmith's Notes, is inaccurate in important particulars. I suspect it was inserted by Law's allies to help him slip out of town.

If the causes of the duel are obscure, its effects are not. The duel is of capital importance in the story of money, not as anecdote, but because of its effect on Law: it drove him to Scotland and the Continent, out of respectable finance and bullionist theory, into scientific gaming, lottery promotion, stock-jobbing and paper. Law flickers in and out of continental police reports. We know he witnessed the near-failure of the Bank of Scotland in 1695, gambled in Italy, possibly spent time in Holland studying the Bank of Amsterdam, was definitely expelled from Paris in 1701.

Law opposed the union of the English and Scots parliaments, not out of some precocious nationalism, but to save his life: for with union would come the warrant. It is self-preservation that is the motive behind his first indubitably authentic piece of writing, a little book in the British Library in bad condition called *Money and Trade Considered, with a Proposal for Supplying the Nation with Money*, and dated 1705 at Edinburgh.

The book contains the germ not only of the banking schemes Law presented ten years later to princes in France and Italy but of the System itself. At its heart is a notion of money as something without substance: if it must represent some anterior value, that need not be some scarce and unwieldy metal, however much it charmed men such as Locke, or indeed anything more concrete than the productive power of a nation. In other words, Law presented precisely the theory underlying the modern banknote, which is a claim not on the gold in the Bank of England or Fort Knox but on the wealth of the nation embodied in the central bank.[23] Law goes further. Money is pure function:

Money is not the value *for* which Goods are exchanged, but the Value *by* which they are exchanged: the use of Money is to buy Goods, and Silver while Money is of no other use.[24]

This sentence is the spring of Law's beliefs and of his activity. For Law, the chief purpose of money is to mobilise the energies of people and the riches of the natural world. After all, a gambler does not hoard money, but stakes it again and again. In attacking the bullionists and Locke, Law shows he is aware of money in its other aspect: that it is the object of desire in itself and comes robed in all sorts of imaginative fantasies. He later exploited that complex of emotions in the Quincampoix but, as it were, against his better judgement: and it destroyed him, as we shall see.

Law then moves on to the condition of his homeland, which really was in a desperate situation. A series of bad harvests, a crisis in fishing and the failure of a colonial scheme at Darien on the American isthmus had driven the country to despair. Gaping deficits in trade with both England and Holland meant that coin just flew away: the Scots money at this period was a mish-mash of copper, old English coins, some going back to Elizabeth, Northern European eccentrics, cheese, oats, beasts, chickens and so on. Rates of interest were half as high again as at London. Law believed that in Scotland there were what the economists term idle factors of production – Law uses the old-fashioned economic expressions 'men,' 'arts-men' and 'lands' – that only a shortage of money kept out of employment, and he now proposed to remedy that shortage.

How was this to be done? He rejects the old remedies of exchange control, coining plate, 'raising the Money' (that is, devaluation) and even credit through the mediation of banks such as the new Bank of Scotland: it was just too slow, 'sound credit' at least, for a man on the lam. Instead, and since money is a matter of pure function, Law proposes a paper issue secured not on deposits of coin (as at the Amsterdam Wisselbank) or a sovereign loan (as at the Bank of England) but on the only category of commercial value in Scotland besides its people: land. There is little argument but that is as ingenious as ever: since land, Law says, is the ultimate source of goods and services, paper mortgages issued against productive land and circulating as currency would match demand with output. But

Law's scheme was, as we've seen, just one of many land-bank notions floating round England and Scotland in the war atmosphere and, if it was ever presented to the Parliament in Edinburgh, it was rejected: Scotland went meekly into union in 1707 and Law into exile. What is important is that one element of the System – a stimulatory paper currency – was already in place.

Once more, Law passes out of respectable view. At some point, he gains a partner, a certain Lady Catherine Knollys, who left her husband for him. Of her surviving portraits, that in *Het groote Tafereel* shows a very handsome woman in a tricorn hat captioned with the coarse riddle that had been invented for Louis XIV's mistress, Mme de Maintenon: *Je suis ni épouse, ni veuve.* (I'm not a wife and not a widow.) The others, in a set of Dutch playing cards in the British Library, are pornographic caricature.[25] Saint-Simon says she had a birth-mark on one cheek but was otherwise 'well-made, tall, haughty, saucy in her speech and manners, receiving compliments, making few or none, going out rarely and only to select addresses, and fully in charge of her household': he was greatly impressed by Law's consideration to her.[26] Prévost simply called her 'a lively lady' (*enjouée*).[27] She bore Law two children, but they never married, even after her husband died: when the scandal became public at the fall of the System, the Regent cancelled the annuities Law had bought for her and the children and left her destitute.

Law is definitely in Paris in 1707, and is expelled once again: not for running a high game, he claims, but for promoting a bank of issue. Thanks to the work of Prato in the Turin archives, we know he was at the same business with the hard-pressed Vittorio Amedeo II of Savoy in 1711 and 1712. Later in 1712, the British ambassador reports him at Paris. On July 21, he opens an account for £100,000 at the Bank of Amsterdam. He is by now dealing actively in British securities through the banker George Middleton in London and laying side-bets on the Dutch lotteries. He buys a house in The Hague and from there commutes to Paris. He has amassed, by his own account, a fortune of 1.6 million livres tournois (at 28*l* to the mark of silver) in French money and securities.[28] The story is that Louis XIV, when presented with a Law scheme, asked if he was a Roman Catholic: when the answer was negative, the King changed the subject. If not true, it is highly in character and expresses a historical reality: paper money was felt at the time to be a mischief of the Protestant powers – the Netherlands and England, Sweden, Scotland and New England – while the Catholic countries clung to the righteous certainties of gold and silver. But even great kings must die, leaving utterly ruined kingdoms to their infant great-grandsons, and on September 1, 1715, Law had his opportunity.

4

Today, a duchess kissed M. Law's hands. Who knows what other parts of him the other ladies might salute!
                                    Madame, October 6, 1719[29]

France in 1715 was not Scotland in 1705, but she was bankrupt in all but name. The long wars of Louis XIV's reign, the expenses of his court and a chaotic system of revenue collection had left the Duc d'Orléans, who had been appointed Regent for the duration of Louis XV's minority, with an intolerable burden of debts: the authorities mention totals of between two and three billion livres tournois. A portion of the debt was secured on branches of the revenue, under the old practice of the French monarchy of capital-ising and selling off as annuities – *rentes* – any source of income as it arose; but, according to Law, some 90 million livres tournois in annual payments were now four years in arrears. In addition there were some 600 million livres tournois in miscellaneous army and navy scrip and household bills; pensions and sinecures had gone unpaid; and revenues had been anticipated as far forward as fiscal 1718. The French monarchy had lost all its credit, while a pig-headed monetary deflation at the close of the great king's reign had caused a depression in trade and reduced (as Law wrote later) 'an infinite number of families to beggary.'[30] Above all, as the Regent's mother, a German princess usually known by her title of Madame, reported the troops had not been paid; and there was danger that the King of Spain might contest the succession of the infant king. Something had to be done and quickly.[31]

The Regent considered and rejected bankruptcy, in favour of a partial repudiation of debts, a spanking devaluation and a retrospective profits tax on the only deep pockets in the kingdom, the merchants who farmed the tobacco, salt and other duties for the crown. The funded debt was reduced arbitrarily to 1,750 million tournois at a rate of 4 per cent, and the floating debt to 250 million tournois, also at 4 per cent, for which so-called *billets d'état* were issued. As these instantly sank to a discount of up to 75 per cent (that is, to a quarter of their value) in the Quincampoix, the public had little confidence of receiving either interest or principal. I suspect only one man was buying those busted obligations, and that was Law. At the same time, the most powerful figures in French finance were mulcted: Antoine Crozat, the proprietor of Louisiana, was assessed at 6.6 million tournois, the great Samuel Bernard voluntarily disgorged 6 million.

From his assembly of Law's scattered papers, Harsin came to the conclusion that all the main elements of the System were in mental place by the end of 1715. One document, a memorial dated October 4, entitled *Restablissement de Commerce*, describes a vast commercial trust that would eventually engross all the trade and revenue of France, and a national bank which through an elegant scheme, set out in a lucid flow-of-funds statement, would amortise the debts of the crown over twenty-five years. Carrying Law's signature, and a note to say it was given by him to Montesquieu at their meeting in Venice of August 29, 1728 – *Donation par M. Law. Montesquieu* – it looked far too good to be true, and Harsin, in deep sorrow, later rejected it. In contrast, a letter to the Regent of December 1715 has never been challenged and is worth quoting for Law's astonishing self-assurance:

> Your Royal Highness will remember one day at Marly . . . I had the honour of saying to him that the bank proposal was by no means my most considerable and that I had another by which I would furnish 500 millions without cost to the people. [Actually it was 1,600 millions, for reasons I shall explain.] . . . The bank is

not the only or the grandest of my ideas. I will devise a scheme that will astonish Europe by the alterations it will make in France's favour, alterations more radical than those procured by the discovery of the Indies or the introduction of credit . . . that will establish order in the public finances, revive agriculture, manufactures and commerce, increase population, lift useless and onerous taxes, increase the King's revenue while simultaneously relieving the people, and reduce the national debt without injuring creditors.

This great Kingdom, well governed, will be the arbiter of Europe without recourse to violence. . . . Your Royal Highness's regency, well employed, will suffice to increase the population to 30 millions, national product to 3,000 millions and the King's revenues to 300 millions. . . . By my efforts, I will make the Indies redundant [*je rendrai les Indes inutiles*].

And how would all these circles be squared? By lowering the rate of interest by increasing the supply of money (*non pas par des Lois, mais par une abondance des espèces*). And what did Law need for that great enterprise? Not money, the King's confidence or staff: just protection (*je ne demande qu'à travailler et à estre protégé*).[32] I confess that I cannot read this letter without the deepest pleasure; but recognise that others might find it unsettling.

The Regent, a man of wide horizons, a certain indecision and a weakness for the bottle, was evidently ravished; but the council called to consider Law's bank proposal, which included expert testimony from Bernard and other financiers of the old guard, rejected it at a session on October 24, 1715. Law was permitted, however, to open a private bank with 6 million tournois in equity capital, Law & Cie, which was licensed by edict of council the following May. The French would be introduced to banking, as it were, gradually. The Banque Générale, as it was known, was a clearing bank and its notes were not legal tender. Modelled partly on the Bank of Amsterdam, it served the same function in providing a means of settling merchants' accounts without resort to coin, which was liable to the arbitrary changes in metallic content to which the French monarchy was addicted. Inevitably, its notes are now rare and valuable, but they turn up among the dealers round the Bourse in Paris and it is clear that they are simply receipts for deposited coin: they are convertible into coin 'at the weight and fineness of this day,' which is written in.

The bank was an immediate success, and the notes went to a premium – the famous agio of the Wisselbank – over coin and on the foreign exchanges. Law was also aggressively discounting commercial bills and the injection of credit soon had its effect in quickening trade. The bank's other important feature was that it was capitalised only as to one-quarter in money and three-quarters in *billets d'état*: since, as I have said, those were at a discount of 70–75 per cent, Law and his friends needed to subscribe only about 1.3 million tournois of those instruments (that is, 30 per cent of 4.5 million). In fact, Law or a collaborator later said that no more than a sixteenth of the bank's equity capital was subscribed in cash, or just 375,000 tournois (less than £20,000 in the sterling of the time): never was supreme power sold so cheap.[33]

By early 1717, the banknotes had become legal tender for the payment of taxes. In August that year, Crozat the Rich's concession in Louisiana was annulled and passed to a new Compagnie d'Occident, capitalised in *billets* at a nominal 100 million tournois, with Law as director-general. The next year the bank was nationalised: its notes were marked not in coin but in livres tournois (and are as common as dirt in the modern collectors' market). In the course of 1719, in a deluge of partly paid stock and banknotes, the company took over the moribund trading companies of Colbert's era, the East India and China companies and the slaving companies of West Africa, the mints, the lucrative General Farms of the taxes, the tobacco monopoly and all the debts of the crown; and began the construction of 24 ocean-going vessels of 500 tons each. In 1720, bank and company, now named the Compagnie des Indes, were amalgamated.

This astonishing scheme was not simply plucked out of the air. The principle, as Jacob Price rightly states in his very learned study of the tobacco monopoly, *France and the Chesapeake* (1973), was the principle of the English South Sea company of 1711–12: capital is subscribed in government obligations, the interest on which provides the working capital for the company's operations. Law went a stage further. In refunding the debts of the state, he clearly intended to make good the public creditors not from arbitrary and unpopular taxes but from commercial profits. That was bold in the extreme: for in converting the *rentes* and *billets* into shares in a national commercial venture (with a dividend he guaranteed, but still risky withal) he challenged attitudes embedded in the French nature. In his great letters to the Paris Parlement and the *rentiers*, published in the *Mercure de France* as the system was disintegrating about him in early 1720, alternately lucid and deranged, he speaks of a future in which 'the whole Nation becomes a body of traders.'[34] What Law did not recognise, because the nineteenth century was still, as it were, to come, is this: that between the *rentier*, living on money whose source he cannot even imagine – indeed, he cannot see the world through the veil of his little annuity, *Neuf, dix pour cent; & après moi le déluge!*[35] – and the worker and the trader confronting reality in all its obduracy, there is an unbridgeable gulf. So the System crashed.

It crashed because of its astonishing acceleration. In the speed of Law's promotion and the blizzard of edicts from the Regency council, one senses an abnormally quick mind that cannot tolerate the pettifogging slowness of things. There were also good political reasons for extreme despatch. Law had enemies at court, among the old-line financiers and new men such as the Pâris brothers, the powerful *intendants* in the provinces and the *rentiers* championed by the Parlement. Stair, the British ambassador, was sending poisonous despatches back to London. Competing schemes, the so-called *Anti-Système* of the Pâris brothers, the re-organised South Sea Company and other bubble ventures in England and Holland, were drawing liquidity out of Paris as soon as Law created it. To amortise the debts of the crown, he had to move quickly: he couldn't afford the twenty-five years of the *Restablissement*. In August 1719, Law offered to lend the crown 1.2 billion tournois at 3 per cent, which he then raised to 1.6 billion. He would become the crown's sole creditor and the sole public debtor. But to finance the loan, he had to draw the nation's entire liquid capital into the company, and for that he needed a bull market in its stock. For the only time in history, a great speculation arose in the calculated will of a single man.

To drive up the shares, Law employed tricks that, though incomprehensible to his age, are commonplaces of today: margin loans, partly paid shares, call options. To win the *rentiers*, he promised a secure 4 per cent dividend. Above all, he issued banknotes, backed by nothing more substantial than his own brilliance, which, coursing round the Parisian economy and finding little to buy, were converted into shares in the Quincampoix. According to the person known as Dutot, who is very precise and may have been Law's cashier, the bank issued 2.7 billion tournois in banknotes that in effect doubled the money supply in less than a year: nowadays, the German Bundesbank becomes alarmed if the annual increase is more than 6 per cent. Interest fell to 2 per cent or less. The counterpart of cheap money is expensive property. Dutot says that land, usually priced at 20–25 years' purchase of its income, was now being sold at 80 years' purchase: in modern language, it went from a 4–5 per cent yield to one of 1.2 per cent.[36] The company's stock, which carried a dividend of 200 tournois, was priced at its peak at the turn of 1720 at 50 years' purchase.

I do not think Law's System was a fantasy or fraud. Dutot, Steuart and Smith in lecture all say that the scheme was, to use a term from modern Wall Street, doable. Dutot's profit-and-loss for the company of early 1720 shows an income of 80 million tournois, enough to cover the promised dividend, which in turn supported the shares in the hands of the public; Law himself gave a figure of 91 million.[37]

Those profits arose chiefly from the interest on the royal loan and the tax farms and had nothing to do with Louisiana, which was still a howling commercial waste. There were fewer than four hundred colonists scrabbling a miserable existence: felons, vagrants and whores were being pressed and shipped there in the worst conditions, as we know from *Manon Lescaut* and the operas made from it. (Law himself preferred to keep French labourers at home and send German volunteers at his own expense.) Law's promise to supply tobacco exclusively from Louisiana by 1721 (rather than buying it in the English market) clearly could not be honoured: even in 1763, the Mississippi crop could fill only one ship a year.[38]

Yet tobacco, as Warren Buffett reminded the world, is a good business: 'make it for a penny, sell it for a dollar and it's addictive.'[39] With the fashion for snuff, consumption of tobacco rose steeply in the course of Louis XV's reign: Voltaire complained in 1768 of the millions of livres that left the country each year 'for stuffing up our nose a stinking powder from America.'[40] And the shares even at

10,000, more faithfully reflected the potential of the Mississippi basin and the risks in unlocking it than Bonaparte's four cents an acre. Who knows what might have been done with the colonial economy had Law survived?

Speculators poured into Paris in their tens of thousands from all over Europe. The memoirs and popular songs of the time recount extraordinary scenes in the Quincampoix and later in stockbrokers' emcampments in the Place Louis-le-Grand (Vendôme) and the garden of the Hôtel de Soissons. These anecdotes fall into four groups as they describe the avarice of the nobility and princes, the extreme immodesty of ladies, the powerful sexual aura that surrounded Law himself and the promiscuous mingling of social class. In her letter to her sister of November 23, Madame outdoes even herself in coarseness. Law had been accosted in his garden by a group of women demanding the right to buy company shares: '"A thousand pardons, ladies, but I need to piss so badly, if you don't let me go, I'll burst." The ladies answered, "Piss away, sir, just so long as you hear us out." So he did and they just stood there.'[41]

What struck the age as ominous was a murder that occurred in the Quincampoix the following March, or rather the murderer's fate. A young nobleman, the Comte d'Hoorn, stabbed a broker for his *portefeuille* of banknotes on March 22 and, against the appeals of his royal relations, was broken on the wheel four days later. The greatest privilege of the nobility, an unspectacular end, had dissolved in the ocean of money: the Terror takes form and begins its progress into history.

The System was still incomplete. We know Law had in mind a fiscal reform, which would replace all direct and indirect taxes by a single property rate or real estate tax of up to 1 per cent. This *denier royal* had been first mooted as a tax by Vauban in the previous generation; in Law's visionary and humane proposal, it would fall on everybody in the kingdom, including the nobility – of which he was a member several times over by virtue of his estates – and the clergy, and excluding the poor and nascent industry.[42] But by the spring of 1720, Law was, in Senovert's wonderful phrase, 'no longer master of the movements of his machine.'[43]

Inflation had to spread out from the Quincampoix like a town fire. According to Hamilton, who studied the account books of various charitable foundations in Paris, wholesale prices had first responded sluggishly to the flood of money: France really must have been desperately underemployed at Law's arrival.[44] But by December 21, Madame, a careful housekeeper, was complaining that food and other household prices had risen three-fold;[45] Hamilton's basket of goods had risen over 70 per cent in price by the new year. Confidence in Law's money was ebbing.

He was also having difficulty maintaining the shares. Capital was flowing out to competing ventures in London and Amsterdam, and Law's attempts to break the bull market in London were going drastically awry. I do not believe with Hamilton that he was 'maddened by jealousy.' To establish his India Company, he had to capture capital from the older Dutch and English versions: he was attempting to discharge through money commercial rivalries that would take a hundred years to resolve in blood.

On September 19, 1719, Law had very publicly offered to sell Thomas Pitt, Earl of Londonderry, £100,000 nominal of English East India short for £180,000, for delivery the next August 25. English East India was then trading in the market at about 200 per cent of par, that is for £200,000, and Law was therefore showing the market that he thought it would fall at least 10 per cent. By May of the new year, in the midst of the speculation known as the South Sea Bubble, East India was at 300 per cent of par and Middleton was scrambling to buy stock at ever higher prices as the delivery date loomed. In the end, Middleton was to spend £372,000 in fulfilling the bargain and, when Law's property was confiscated, was forced to declare bankruptcy.[46]

Law also had a crisis at home.[47] As a condition for his appointment as Controller-General of Finances in January 1720, Law had converted to the Catholic faith; and a good Catholic would naturally have repudiated Catherine. Law's confessor, the Abbé Tencin, somehow skirted or ignored this irregularity, but Catherine did not follow her husband into the church and one senses in Law a growing isolation. By March, Stair was sending putrid gossip about his eccentricities back to London. Saint-Simon said he had become hard, bad-tempered and often rude in argument.[48] Cantillon, who was shorting Law's shares, thought it prudent to leave Paris.

Desperate to maintain the credit of the banknotes and the shares,

Law tampered with the coin and issued a string of despotic edicts, culminating in that of February 27 banning possession of coin to a value over 500 livres. The public was rattled. Merchants and speculators were selling notes for any kind of hard asset that might hold its value in the inflation: Boule, the famous cabinet-maker, had an order-book worth 80,000 tournois at his workshops in the Louvre that spring. Finally, on May 21 came the fatal edict, reducing in stages the face value of the notes by half and the shares from 9,000 tournois to 5,000.

This edict has perplexed all students of the Regency: nobody can understand why Law pricked his own bubble. In his own account,[49] Law impatiently explains the difference between real and nominal values. I suspect Law had simply lost touch with the world of people and things, and thought that a gradual deflation, which favoured the shares over the banknotes and thus would cause people to sell notes for shares, was no great thing. He was quite wrong. Value was revealed for what it is, mere will; and the revelation shattered confidence in him, his shares and his money. On May 22, Steuart wrote, 'A man might have starved with a hundred millions of paper in his pocket.'[50]

That is exaggeration. According to Hamilton's researches, prices continued to rise until September: that would not have happened if the banknotes had become valueless. An important witness is Pellegrini's sister-in-law, Rosalba Carriera. As the first woman to support a family by painting portraits, she was naturally very interested in money: her diary/account-book, written in villainous Venetian dialect, records payments in coin from that October. The Coutts & Co records for September, studied by Price, show a plummeting rate of exchange in London and then 'no exchange.'

The edict of May 21 was revoked, but that merely compounded the public's insecurity. There were runs on the bank/company. On July 17, according to Saint-Simon, ten or twelve people were crushed to death at the entrance to the Palais Mazarin. Law's coach and house were attacked. It is said St Bartholomew was invoked: that was code for a massacre of Protestants. The Parlement was reported to be planning to capture, try and execute Law, all in a day. He took refuge in the Palais Royal, where Madame records, in a mixture of great tenderness and even greater exasperation, his terror for his life. The Parlement was rusticated, and then recalled in December. Law asked the Regent's permission to retire to his estate at Guermande outside Paris. He received passports to leave France, arriving in Brussels on the 22nd. All his property in France was confiscated and Catherine was forbidden to leave. When Rosalba Carriera called at the bank on the 21st, she peeped into the Salle de Mississippi and saw it covered from top to bottom with books of useless banknotes.[51]

And so ended, in Voltaire's words, 'that stupendous game of chance, played by an unknown man, and a foreigner at that, against a whole nation.[52]

5

> If at times he [Law] used specious arguments when he considered them a necessary road to the truth, it was with so fine an art that one found oneself brought suddenly into brilliant light without noticing that one had passed through darkness to get there.
>
> John Law[53]

On October 25, 1721, there was a performance of *The Alchemist* at the Drury Lane Theatre in London. In the silence that followed the collapse of the System and, in short order, the London and Amsterdam bubbles, one recognises that compound of shame and euphoric recollection that is the residue of great financial speculations. To Jonson's drama of greed and folly, the company had appended a dreary epilogue:

> Well! since we've learn'd experience at our cost
> Let us preserve the remnant not yet lost,
> By sober arts aspire to guiltless Fame . . .

But that night, the actor-manager broke open the last heroic couplet, with the hopeful, recidivist verse:

Though L-w from France has landed on the coast!

and bowed at a tall man in the boxes. The *Whitehall Evening Post* reported the next day: 'Last night, their Royal Highnesses the Prince and Princess of Wales were at the Theatre in Drury Lane and saw the *Alchymist*. There was a splendid appearance of the Nobility and Gentry: the famous *Mr Law* and his son were *there also.*' All that was left of Law, apart perhaps from the royal pardon for murder he'd picked up that afternoon, was his fame.[54]

The end of the story is suitably brief. Law hung round London, dealing in this and that, and lobbying Walpole, till his novelty had more than worn off. At the Regent's death, he gave up hope of restoration in Paris. Instead, he returned to Venice and his old occupation of gambling, devoting his mornings to *mémoires justicatifs*, trying to recover the million and a half livres tournois he'd taken into France in 1714, affairs of gallantry and the emissaries of bankrupt powers. Montesquieu, as blind to Law's ability as to the beauty of Venice, still found in him a certain pathos: 'He was still the same man, with small means but playing high and bold, his mind occupied with projects, his head filled with calculations.'[55] To the senator Contarini, Law said, 'I have spoiled my life. It is here I should have stayed and developed my talents, dreaming of little pleasures and little scandals . . . and so heedlessly coming to die as one suddenly comes up against the night on the threshold of a doorway.'[56] That is how I like to remember him: seated at his place in the Ridotto, unmasked, beside him 1,000 pistoles in gold, but piling up the little wagers of the tourists who will go back home and say, I played at Hazzard with the famous Mr Law, two pistoles to a thousand pistoles of gold, and the odds, of six sixes in one throw, confound the odds![57] He gets up; pockets his billets-doux; and, striding to the door, sees he has killed the day, and night come down on the Calle Valaresso.

Law believed money was a distillation of human relations and might be turned to purpose – more easily than the antique machines of politics and custom – to create a prosperous and just society. That wasn't a mere rococo utopia, because he damn near pulled it off. His fault, if he had one, was the fault of Pellegrini's ceiling: money and absolutism cannot happily cohabit. Law thought he could somehow smuggle money and its liberties up a back stairway in the

Palais Royal. He remembered too late that the public banks of the Netherlands and England had been erected on the ruins of absolute monarchies.

In the last week of Carnival in 1729, he caught pneumonia, collapsing in a gondola after dining with the English resident. He lay dying, far from his lady and children, hag-ridden by Jesuits and French spies. They forced him to make a will though he pleaded he had no assets but his playing money. It is said the fate of Pellegrini's ceiling haunted him like an omen. At his death on March 21, the French ambassador impounded all his papers and then, unforgivably and but for one box, lost them.

Of his family, Lady Catherine lived in respectable poverty until 1747. Their son fled his father's creditors to Maastricht, where he died of smallpox, their daughter was immortalised in Rosalba's *La Jeune Fille au Singe* in the Louvre. One great-nephew became a marshal of France under Louis XVIII, another perished in the Pacific with La Pérouse. The marshal's grandson showered his fortune on a girl in the Rue St-Georges, gaily enlisted in the ranks in Algeria, returned as the third Napoleon's chief of ordnance.[58] Lauriston was ruined by lawsuits: the judge and memoirist Lord Cockburn remembered from his childhood 'a bare solitary keep, fenced from the farmer's cattle by a crumbling Galloway dyke, with scarcely a comrade tree, and staring on the Firth as if it had been looking out for the reappearance of the South Sea schemer that was once its master.'[59]

In France, the word 'bank' was not employed for the rest of the century: the French went back, in Steuart's phrase, to 'coming at money at the best way they could.'[60] But Law's inflation had one important effect: it permitted not just the monarchy but also farmers and working people to pay off their debts in a depreciated currency; and France was able at last to enter the eighteenth century. The revolutionaries of 1790 thought that Law's only error was to serve an arbitrary master, not recognising that tyranny can wear a Phrygian hat. Eighteen-fifteen ushered in the ninety-nine-year summer of the *rentier*, preserved for us in the obsessions of Balzac.

But the System had, in Voltaire's grudging compliment, 'illuminated the spirit, as civil wars hone the courage.'[61] For though Law disappears from economics, he still flickers through imaginative literature as once in the reports of police agents and diplomatic spies: in *Manon Lescaut,* where he is reborn as Des Grieux, a man determined to be ruined by love;[62] *Faust,* where Mephisto takes on his character and gives a paper currency to the world; in Thackeray's *Barry Lyndon*; perhaps in the Guermantes of Proust; and in a little book by Dostoyevsky (that same Dostoyevsky who saw that, in the prisons we make of our societies, money is our coined liberty). That book, called *The Gambler,* written in six weeks for money and still the best commentary ever on its psychology, ends like this:

> And there really is something special in the feeling when, alone, in a strange country, far away from home and friends and not knowing what you will eat that day, you stake your last gulden, your very, very last!
> Tomorrow, tomorrow it will all come to an end!

7

Coined Liberty: His and Hers

> Money is coined liberty, and so it is ten times dearer to the
> man who is deprived of freedom. If money is jingling in his
> pocket, he is half consoled, even though he cannot spend it.
>
> Dostoyevsky[1]

Money, we have seen, had come in the course of time in Europe,
Japan and the Americas to be identified with freedom: freedom
from want and from a fixed pattern of society. Money, which
delivered the serf not into idleness or happiness, but to a market of
indifferent wishes, also clipped the wings of princes, forced them to
devolve their power to parliaments and public creditors and set in
train civilian settlements that culminated in the foundation of the
Bank of England in 1694.

This freedom did not offer equality. Money, as we have seen and
as Saikaku complained at the end of his life, entrenches social
inequality: its possessor can, without any sacrifice, accumulate more
money through interest or speculation in the public funds or through
rent and profit. The career of John Law showed us just how much
money a man could amass, and how rapidly, in the age of credit.
Yet money's neutrality, its indifference to the character and station
of its temporary possessor, and the ease with which it is administered,
present the possibility of freedom to the imagination even of the
destitute. Naturally, for those wishes to have any conviction,
somebody must be seen to be gratifying them; and societies tolerated
or even worshipped the new rich in their exemplary function. The
rich are loved for making actual the wishes of everybody; while the
poor, conversely, are despised as lackeys of unattainable desire.

Adam Smith did not like this worship of the rich, but he saw it was indispensable to his utopia. Admiration of the rich and contempt for the poor were morally idiotic, 'the great and most universal cause of the corruption of our moral sentiments,' but they were, alas, necessary to 'maintain the distinction of ranks and the order of society.'² In the course of the seventeenth and eighteenth centuries, freedom thus was defined as money: an imaginary equality of opportunity and an actual inequality. Eventually, that double aspect of money was enshrined in the U.S. Constitution: as Madison wrote in 1787, the first object or prime purpose of government is to protect 'the different and unequal faculties of acquiring property.'³

In *The Complete English Tradesman*, Defoe had seen his merchant-turned-gentleman as invulnerable. 'Nothing,' he wrote, 'can break in upon the security of this man's affairs, but some public calamity, such a war as should expose us to publick invasions . . .; and even in such a case they should not carry away the land; the fee-simple [freehold], with after-years of peace, would restore all again.' If there was a danger, it came only from the imbecile vanity of the gentlemen class: 'from the *kitchen* and the *stable*.'⁴ Social climbers always seek to kick the ladder from beneath them: Defoe ought to have seen his petrified society would be an offence to the next generation of tradesmen. Law's days in Paris showed to clearer heads the revolutionary potential of an inflation: that paper money could 'dissolve' not just a monarchy⁵ but the past itself as it is embodied in the innumerable money claims of the creditor class on the present and future. The collapse of the System had restored the monarchy, the creditors and the *soi-disant* precious metals, but they had lost their invincible aura.

Not surprisingly, Law found his first disciples in North America. Constrained in their trade by the mother country, forced to buy most manufactures from England and to remit taxes thither, the British colonies could never hold on to metal money: even in the seventeenth century, the Bay Colony, as Massachusetts was known, issued paper bills to finance an invasion of Canada. To pay for the revolt against Britain eighty-five years later, the American revolutionaries pioneered a patriotic taxation which has ever since been popular in wartime: the issue of an unbacked paper money which then inflates away, leaving everybody – soldier and civilian, debtor and creditor – bailing the same boat of equal and patriotic poverty.

Benjamin Franklin, writing from Paris on April 22, 1779, was scathing about the monetary slowness of the Europeans:

> This Effect of Paper Currency is not understood on this Side the Water. And indeed the whole is a Mystery even to the Politicians, how we have been able to continue a War four years without Money, and how we could pay with Paper that had no previously fix'd Fund appropriated specifically to redeem it. This Currency, as we manage it, is a wonderful Machine. It performs its Office when we issue it; it pays and clothes Troops, and provides Victuals and Ammunition; and when we are obliged to issue a Quantity excessive, it pays itself off by Depreciation.[6]

As a printer, Franklin had an affinity to paper money, and had done very nicely from a contract for the Pennsylvania currency in the 1730s.

In 1786, seven of the states had paper currencies outstanding for the discharge of public and private debts. The great constitutional debate of that year and the next, which attempted to crystallise the relative powers of the centre and the states left floating at the Articles of Confederation of 1776, also sought to answer the question of what the American money should be: debtor confetti, such as the farmers wanted and had won the war, or a hard, centralised money that would guarantee private property and public creditors against the populist impulses in state legislatures? In other words, was the revolution to proceed through the door of liberty to equality.

Among the aristocratic party in the United States, later termed Federalist, there was particular concern at the various state debt-forgiveness measures such as tender acts, which made payment in kind legal for debt discharge, or so-called stay laws, which postponed collection. At the front of everybody's mind were the disturbances in western Massachusetts in the fall and winter of 1786, in which hard-pressed farmers under the leadership of a former army captain, Daniel Shays, tried to prevent the county courts from sitting. Shays' Rebellion was put down by a militia raised by the merchants of Boston and manned by college boys, but not before it had injected a sense of urgency, even panic, into the preparations for the Constitutional Convention, called for Philadelphia for the following May. Madison wrote to his father on November 1 that among

Shays' farmers 'an abolition of debts, public and private, and a new division of property are strongly suggested to be in contemplation.'[7] Washington wrote to the younger Madison from Mount Vernon four days later that General Knox, just back from Massachusetts, had informed him that for many people in the state 'there creed is, that the property of the United States has been protected from confiscation of Britain, by the joint exertion of *all*, and therefore ought to be the *common property* of all.'[8]

The Constitutional Convention was about a great deal more than paper money: though Americans will recall that Article I of their great constitution, emitted on September 17, 1787, bans the use of anything but gold and silver coin as legal tender for the payment of debts.[9] The convention established a strong executive and President, whose despotic power is hampered by bewilderingly frequent elections, a federal capital, a standing army and 'checks and balances' as curbs on executive power, rather than a supreme legislature. But to a British student of these years, the U.S. Constitution looks suspiciously like a Restoration that extinguished the spirit of '76; or, in the language of the time, the triumph of creditor over debtor, money over virtue and religion, commerce over liberty. No doubt fortunately for their successors, the framers resolved not to be free but rich, not good but rich, not equal but rich.

The series of articles known as *The Federalist Papers*, composed by Hamilton, Madison and John Jay from October 27, 1787 to August 15, 1788, were designed to persuade the state of New York to ratify the Philadelphia constitution. Signed simply 'Publius,' a pseudonym evoking the worthy who had established the Roman republic after the expulsion of the Tarquinian kings, the articles are littered with references to paper money, which is merely a synonym for injustice or, as Madison put it, 'any improper or wicked project.'[10] According to the modern editor of the *Papers*, Captain Shays is mentioned six times.[11] In the contributions of Hamilton and Madison, one senses a role for money, hard money, at the very core of the new state: not just in making possible a powerful, well-armed commonwealth on the English model but in occupying the energies of fallen men and dissipating their natural aptness to faction.

Hamilton was just thirty when he conceived the project, and wrote the lion's share of the essays (fifty-one out of eighty-five),

producing them at a rate sometimes of one every three days. Born
on Nevis in the British West Indies in 1757, 'the bastard brat of a
Scotch peddler,' as John Adams called him, he came to New York
at the age of sixteen, studied at Columbia, and rose in the war to
become Washington's aide-de-camp, responsible for organising and
financing the revolutionary armies. With the help of his wife's
fortune, he entered the Continental Congress in 1782, and formed
an unlikely alliance with Madison in pressing for the convention.
Madison, in contrast, was born in 1751 to a long-established family
in Virginia, and supplied in precision and industry what he lacked of
Hamilton's dash.

For Hamilton, money is not only the lifeblood of a modern state:

> Money is, with propriety, considered as the vital principle of the
> body politic; as that which sustains its life and motion and enables
> it to perform its most essential functions.[12]

It is also the occupation of the citizenry:

> The prosperity of commerce is now perceived and acknowledged
> by all enlightened statesmen to be the most useful as well as the
> productive source of national wealth, and has accordingly become
> a primary object of their political cares. By multiplying the means
> of gratification, by promoting the introduction and circulation of
> the precious metals, those darling objects of human avarice and
> enterprise, it serves to vivify and invigorate all the channels of
> industry and to make them flow with greater activity and
> copiousness.[13]

Dr Johnson had memorably stated in London in 1775 that there are
few ways in which a man 'can be more innocently employed than
in getting money.'[14] Madison, in his famous No. X, saw the pursuit
of money as not merely innocuous. The clash of commercial interests
it fomented and the unequal distribution of property it made possible
were guarantors of the new state: the old *divide et impera* of tyranny
in its republican clothes.

> Those who hold and those who are without property have ever
> formed distinct interests in society. Those who are creditors, and
> those who are debtors, fall under a like discrimination. A landed
> interest, a manufacturing interest, a mercantile interest, a moneyed

interest, with many lesser interests, grow up of necessity in civilised nations, and divide them into different classes, actuated by different sentiments and views. The regulation of these various and interfering interests . . . involves the spirit of party and faction in the necessary and ordinary operations of government.[15]

For these men, as earlier for Locke in England, Montesquieu in France and Hume and Smith in Scotland, liberty is pre-eminently the unequal right to property, commerce a substitute for morality and money for religion. Against such splendid arguments, the Anti-Federalists, older men who dreamed of small, innocent, virtuous, parsimonious and democratic republics on Spartan or early Roman models had no chance. In capitulating to the Federalists' coup d'état, Patrick Henry told the delegates at the Virginia ratifying convention:

When the American spirit was in its youth, the language of America was different: liberty, Sir, was then the primary object.

But, he added,

I will be a peaceable citizen . . . I wish not to go to violence, but will wait with hopes that the spirit which predominated in the revolution, is not yet gone, nor the cause of those who are attached to the revolution yet lost.[16]

They were fobbed off with a Bill of Rights.

So important is the Federalist conception of money, not just for the United States but for those parts of the world that admire the United States, I shall devote a separate chapter to its later history, Chapter 10. Let me just say here that the matter was far from settled in 1787, and Hamilton and Madison soon fell out. Madison went on to be the fourth President of the United States. Hamilton never saw old age. As dark and handsome and brilliant as Law, like his great countryman he was a duellist: on July 11, 1804, he took a ball in his guts from Burr under the sunlit cliffs of Weehawken in the most thrilling tableau of the United States in its heroic era. He was carried to Greenwich Village, and for years, each morning as I set off for work uptown, I passed the street where he had bled to death.

The ideological dispute suppressed at the ratification conventions erupted again in 1860. The Confederacy of southern states fought not merely for state power against the centre but for a radically different notion of society which, because it authorised slavery, diminished money: its monuments are the busted bonds that can be bought for nothing in American and English junk shops. Except for a seventy-year period in this century, the United States itself has always been an international debtor: it simply doesn't have the savings for its ambitions, and like all ambitious spendthrifts, it has a tendency to creeping default. Meanwhile, the virtuous or Spartan disdain of money surfaced in the Utopian communities of nine-teenth-century New England, in the hippie settlements of 1960s New York and California and in those backwoods paradises that erupt into our consciousness only at the moment they disintegrate in spectacular gun battles with federal agents.

But let us return to France, where the view of society embodied in money followed a different course. France eventually woke to Franklin's lecture. The issues of paper money by the French revolutionaries are not, as I was taught as a child, simply a by-way of the Great Revolution, of interest only to financiers, but the revolution itself. I mean not merely that one sees reflected, in the rates of exchange of the *assignats* and *mandats* into coin, the triumphs and abominations of the years 1790 to 1797 in France: during the September massacres, for example, one of the most ghastly episodes in the annals of inhumanity, the discount on the *assignat* actually narrowed. I mean that the revolutionary paper moneys seem to drive the revolution on. In the career of these pieces of paper, one sees condensed the idealism of 1790, the chaos of war and invasion, the massacres at the Salpêtrière and the triumph at Valmy, the guillotine in the Place de la Révolution, the quaint New Age months and years and weights and measures and festivals of the Supreme Being, Saint Just's pastoral fantasies on the eve of *thermidor*, the despotism of Bonaparte and the communism of Babeuf and finally Balzac's profiteering nouveaux riches. Edmund Burke, who was terrified and fascinated by the events in Paris in equal measure, saw the first issue of *assignats* by the revolutionaries as 'a centre from which afterwards all their measures radiate.'[17]

The word *assignat* had been used, ominously enough, in Russia, to describe obligations of the state issued by Catherine II in 1768. After the fall of the Bastille, the young National Assembly attempted to come to grips with the desperate state of the nation's finances. It was Talleyrand, a bishop, who suggested confiscation of the lands of the church, which were duly placed 'at the disposal of the nation' in the decree of November 2, 1789. The *assignats*, as first conceived in the decrees of December 19 and 21, 1789, were originally designed as a measure to anticipate the proceeds from the sale of the church and crown lands: 400 million livres in *assignats* were to be issued to the state's creditors against the future sale of those lands and benefices, were a fraction of their realisable value, carried a high denomination of 1,000 livres (face value), paid interest, and were supposed to be extinguished with the sales. But in the course of 1790, the *assignats* were made legal tender in the public administration and a further issue of 800 million livres was authorised, this time paying no interest. In other words, the *assignat* became just a means of funding the expenses of a revolutionary state unable to levy taxes. By the end of 1791, the issues already exceeded the theoretical real security, and throughout 1792 hundreds and then thousands of millions were printed at denominations as low as a few livres to feed and pay fourteen armies to defend France from counter-revolutionary invasion. The next year, Cambon, the financial expert in the Convention, adopted a series of measures that partly restored the value of the *assignat*: those measures included the consolidation of all state debt into obligations of the revolution. But the issues continued unabated. By the time the *assignats* were demonetised on the 30 *pluviôse An IV* (February 19, 1796) some 45,581,411,618 livres had been printed, excluding counterfeits, in denominations as low as half a sou. Unlike Law's banknotes, the *assignats* had always been at a discount to metal money, but they were now worth less than 5 per cent of what they had been. The Directory experimented with another paper money, the *mandat territorial*, exchangeable for the *assignat* at one for thirty, but that too inflated to almost nothing and was finally demonetised on the 16 *pluviôse An V* (February 4, 1797), and was exchanged for what became known as the Germinal franc, the money of nineteenth- and twentieth-century France, at a rate of 1:100. Therefore, a revolutionary patriot who received 3,000 livres in *assignats* in January 1791, could hand them to the government's contractor on February 4, 1797, and receive, in exchange, a single franc coin.

The economists, inasmuch as they are aware of those extraordinary events, see in them only a confirmation of their quantity theories of money; while the moralists, notably in the post-bellum United States, draw lessons of the perils of a paper currency unbacked by metal. I think their interest lies deeper. Just before the plates and other equipment associated with the *assignats* were burned or smashed in the Place Vendôme on February 19, 1796, Dominique Ramel de Nogaret, the minister of finance, delivered an oration that may be paraphrased thus: You made us what we are, and we do not yet understand what we owe you, but you are killing us.[18]

The *assignats* began life purely as an emergency means of maintaining the credit of the revolution, at the disposal of the assembly rather than the executive embodied by Necker and the Caisse d'Escompte (a sort of primitive central bank). Already, there is a decisive break with the Federalist model. By the time of the great debates of August and September 1790 over a second issue to increase the circulation to 1,200 million livres (face value), the *assignats* have become a touchstone of revolutionary zeal. In his speech on September 27, 1790, Mirabeau presented the new issue as the liquidation of the *ancien régime*. France, he said, was burdened by history in the form 'of a debt the centuries of despotism and civil disorder have piled on our heads.'[19] The creditor class will now be obliged to support the revolution! *Oser être grand!* (Dare to be great!)

As for the use of *assignats* as money, Mirabeau (and his collaborator/speech writer, the Genevan Solomon Reybaz) resurrected all the arguments of the land-bank theoreticians of a hundred years before: 'I ask all the philosophers and all the economists of every land on earth whether there is not more reality, more veritable wealth, in that entity of which our *assignats* are the symbol, than in that thing adopted under the name of currency?'[20] On the benches of the Right, the Abbé Maury waved a sheaf of Law's worthless Banque Royale notes, which he compared, in the metaphorical language much favoured in those days, to buoys placed over shoals 'to commemorate for ever a tremendous shipwreck.'[21] On September 29, the issue was approved by 508 votes to 423.

Necker had already resigned and, from exile, he told the French precisely what would happen. Because the *assignats* could finance the revolution without taxes or economies, they allowed the revolutionaries to dream. They enfranchised the assembly 'from the domineering yoke of reality, and allowed the law-makers to deliver themselves up more trustingly to their own abstractions.'[22] Burke, in his *Reflections on the Revolution* of 1790, called the *assignats* 'the finance of philosophy'.[23]

As the *assignats* poured off the presses in the next three years, they became part of the apparatus of the Terror: the counterpart of the scaffold in the Place de la Révolution and then its substitute. The confiscated property of nobles, émigrés, enemies of the revolution and then mere suspects were added to the notional fund that backed the *assignats*: in the tumult of blood and money, men could no longer distinguish purposes: *on battit monnaie au place de la Révolution.* In the last weeks of the Terror, to refuse an *assignat* or even to inquire about a discount on it became punishable by the guillotine. Thus an instrument invented to mobilise the property of the privileged classes and put it at the disposal of the revolution's creditors became an instrument of destroying them both. It converted the past into paper money precisely because paper money can easily be destroyed. As the revolution progressed and envenomed, the *assignats* turned into a mass liquidation. Liquidate the clergy! Liquidate the monarchy, the estates, all property, chivalry and religion and inequality and liberty! Liquidate, in the horrible paroxysms on the eve of Robespierre's fall, the revolution! Liquidate, in Edmond Dubois de Crancé's astonishing outburst in 1796, money itself:

> *Tuez ensuite l'argent: oui, tuez l'argent . . . que l'assignat soit la seule monnaie républicaine.*[24]
>
> [Go on, kill money. Yes, kill the damn thing . . . so that the *assignat* may be the sole republican currency.]

In Burke's great philippic, it is hard to see what appals him more, the mistreatment of Marie Antoinette or the contempt for metal money. To Burke, gold and silver were 'the two great recognised species that represent the lasting conventional credit of mankind, which disappeared and hid themselves in the earth from whence they came, when the principle of property, whose creatures and representatives they are, was systematically subverted.'[25] All in all, the glory of Europe was extinguished for ever.[26]

The events of 9 *thermidor*, when Robespierre, Saint-Just and Couthon were dragged out of the Committee of Public Safety and guillotined, ended one form of the Terror and left the revolution with only the other, the *assignat*. A popular song recorded, with exquisite irony, a certain regret for the source of revenue in the middle of the Place de la Révolution and its operator, Charles Henri Sanson:

> *O Guillotine aimable*
> *Nous chantons tes exploits!*
> *Grand Trésorier de France*
>   *O sublime Sanson!*
> *Combien dans la finance*
> *Tu surpasses Cambon!*
> *De notre République*
> *Tu grossis le Trésor.*
> *Les Mines de Mexique*
> *Ont produit bien moins d'or.*[27]

[Sweet guillotine, let us hymn your achievements. Grand Treasurer of France, great Sanson! In matters of finance, you far outshine Cambon! You enlarge the treasure of our Republic: the mines of Mexico were much less productive.]

The years III and IV procured an inflation such as the world had never seen. Yet men stared into the abyss of negation and, as in the United States earlier and the Soviet Union, the Third Reich and Cambodia later, stepped back in horror. Bonaparte, if we are to believe the financier Ouvrard, didn't really believe in money, but did believe in violence: *Avec cinq cent mille hommes, on fait ce qu'on veut.*[28] With five hundred thousand men, one does as one pleases. The *assignat* had made possible the revolution, but also diverted it. It did not end inequality, it promoted it. As Burke had prophesied with great foresight in late 1790, the *assignats* ensured the creation of a bourgeois oligarchy. The confiscated lands were bought up by notaries, attorneys, merchants and rich peasants, who paid in a rapidly depreciating paper currency, and the country passed from the hands of crown, church and nobility to the Grandets of Balzac.

Whatever Mirabeau had in mind in the late summer of 1790, I'm sure it wasn't that. This shipwreck of 'equality and the rights of man'[29] was to haunt Europe for two centuries.

England, which fought both the revolution and Bonaparte to defeat, financed its side of the war with unfunded paper and went through its own restoration after Waterloo. The Gold Standard, which was a global currency backed not just by metal but by the credit of the City and the power of the English fleet, was also a guarantee against the horrors of years III and IV. It had existed, de facto, since Brazilian gold, coined into guineas, had displaced Potosí silver, coined into dollars, in the eighteenth century. With the defeat of Bonaparte at Waterloo, the gold standard became a legal concept. In a period that lasted from the aftermath of Waterloo to the preparations for Mons – that is, from 1821 to 1914 – the English authorised an autonomous control for the impulses conveyed by money, what Freud might have called a monetary Super-Ego. For that long period in the British Empire, and from the 1870s also in France, Germany and the United States, and their dependencies, the International Gold Standard served the interests of certain classes of society so obediently that those classes came to regard it as natural, perfect and timeless and, in James Grant's excellent phrase, 'the rule of law applied to money.'[30]

This is how it worked. The civilised world had a single money – gold – of which the paper moneys of individual states represented fixed and timeless sums. For example, the United States dollar, except during the greenback period of the Civil War and its aftermath, when value was said to have been conferred by Act of Congress, was always and only 25.8 grains of gold, nine-tenths fine. The U.S. and British treasuries were bound by that definition of money: they could not create money out of air any more than a commercial bank could or a private citizen. For gold was still exceedingly scarce: five thousand years of mining and dredging had brought to the surface of the earth, by the turn of the nineteenth century, only about five thousand tonnes of the metal; and even after the discoveries in California and Australia in the middle years of the century, all the world's gold could have been comfortably shipped in a single ocean liner.[31]

If a country bought more goods from abroad than it sold – that is,

gave its impulses free rein – it was obliged to ship gold abroad to
extinguish the debt that had arisen. Its money would contract with
its gold, bringing about a depression in trade, causing imports to fall
and consumption to be deferred or stifled. As that happened, it
shipped less gold abroad. That process of decay and rejuvenation,
well studied by Hume among others in the eighteenth century,
seemed to have its counterpart in Darwinian nature. Its chief effect
was a slight but continuous depression in the price of goods in
money, thus accelerating the use of technique in manufacturing,
ruining farmers and other debtors and entrenching the lending class,
the *rentiers*. Gold became, in Keynes' phrase, 'part of the apparatus
of conservatism.'[32] The English and French literature of the nineteenth century gives an impression of stability, even smugness, in
the social order. In 1888, Kipling wrote in 'The Education of Otis
Yeere':

> All good people know that a woman is the only infallible thing in
> this world, except Government Paper of the '79 issue, bearing
> interest at four and a half per cent.[33]

When an idea is so self-evident that it can be read in cheap
paperbacks on colonial railways, you can be sure it has not much
longer to run; and confidence in money, as embodied in the price
of British Consols, reached its peak in 1896. Two years later, the
West Shore Railroad in Chicago issued 4 per cent bonds maturing
in A.D. 2361: in other words, the bond buyers assumed money had
been made eternal. At which point, it fell to bits.

All the chief belligerents in the Great War detached their moneys
from gold and printed paper to pay for troops and munitions.
Attempts were made to restore the gold standard in a watered-down
version at a conference at Genoa in 1922. England returned sterling
to gold in 1925, but the drastic fall in prices and wages that ensued
provoked a general strike and gold was abandoned, not without
some relief, in 1931. Inflation became a household tool of peacetime government. The *rentiers* were mulcted: in 1958, the financial
markets recognised that lending money was inherently more risky
than owning things, when the yield on equity securities fell below
that on government bonds. In England and Scotland, the gentry
sought a *rentier* existence at Lloyd's of London, a market for re-

insurance that was, in reality, only for the most red-toothed entrepreneur. Many were ruined at the end of the 1980s.

The United States lasted longest, but, needing to finance a war in Southeast Asia, left gold in 1971. Money is still trammelled. The ambitions of politicians, the actions of speculators in markets for money and debt securities and the financial manipulations of central banks all affect the exchange-rate of a nation's money and its rate of interest; but because these are collections of men and women, they lack the abstract, alien authority of our golden Super-Ego.

These grand dramas, for all their interest, are excessively masculine in casting and we should delay no longer in examining what women felt about money in this period. For women then had a strong consciousness of themselves as women, as well as individuals and human beings, and that consciousness is still with us today. Women, if I have read and heard them right, see history as the story of the emancipation of their sex: a process that has a beginning and a middle but not, as far as anybody can descry it, an end. The emancipation is from the tyranny and caprice not just of kings and priests but of all men, and in that immemorial struggle, money has seemed to many women to be their chief or even only ally.

Money comes to a woman by three main channels, all of great interest to our story. The first is inheritance. The second is her labour, where her medieval serfdom, the toiling up of stairs with water and coal, the whole existence summed up under the motto 'a woman's work is never done,' is taken outdoors, measured, limited and rewarded by money, which then becomes hers to spend: even, if she wishes, on other women as domestic servants. The third may merely be a form of labour, though it has generally been considered a rather special form: it is her sex, which she can convert into money as a male labourer does his strength, so as to convey desires quite other than those she whispers to her entranced lover; and which may even be detached from her body and sold, like an animal's pelt. In these processes, a woman's wishes lose their specific femininity, for money is as indifferent to sex as to race or personality.

★   ★   ★

Caroline: I think I understand the difference between fixed
and circulating capital perfectly.

                                        Mrs Marcet[34]

We use the term 'bride-wealth' – the old term bride-price has
been retired – to describe the payment still made in much of the
world by a groom or his family to his wife's kin. It is intended either
as a pledge that the woman will not be ill-treated or as a compensation to her family for her loss. The payment can be in goods or, as
in the story of Jacob in Genesis, who worked seven years for Leah
and seven for Rachel, in services; in cases of gin, as in Nigeria of the
1920s; or in money; or in a combination. When I lived in the Arab
world, the limitless greed of fathers was the chief or only subject of
conversation among some young men. Thus women have been
implicated in money from the beginning.

In Islam, a wife retains her property on marriage, even if her
husband administers it, and may ask for it back whenever she pleases.
That most epoch-making of the Prophet's social reforms gave
women a measure of protection in a society that still does not like
to comment on, let alone legislate for, the inner household. And
even that modest independence was too much for some men: Sanai,
the medieval Persian lyric poet, advised men to keep slave girls; for
'At least you know when you rise in the morning / You'll see the
face of your own property not that of your creditor.'[35] In Christendom, women had greater access to the company of males but had to
wait for that elementary right of property: in Britain indeed, wives
without marriage settlements could not acquire, hold or dispose of
property without the intervention of a trustee until the Married
Women's Property Act of 1882. Women therefore played a smaller
role in the great expansion in the operations of money than their
numbers warranted: after all, as Virginia Woolf said of her mother's
generation, why make a killing on the stock exchange if you must
meekly hand the capital gain to Him?

In the course of the Middle Ages in Europe, the protection
afforded women – which authorised, like the feudal ties, all manner
of exclusions and mistreatment – was gradually subverted by the
culture of sexual love. 'What is sweeter and more delightful and
more loveable than a beautiful face? The gates of heaven can surely

not be more pleasing to the sight,' wrote Lorenzo Valla in the fourteenth century as if he'd discovered the thing.[36] Bourgeois society in Europe and the Americas became mysteriously feminine in its ornament, if less so in its structure. Social life was disarmed, domesticated, refined, even in Russia. Surveying a ballroom in early nineteenth-century Petersburg, Onegin saw that the ranks of men

> all sombre, all the same,
> Set off the ladies, like a frame.[37]

In the novels of Jane Austen, composed a few years earlier, there is a moment when her heroine wields an absolute power: the power to subject a man body and soul to her will. That dominion is so complete that it actually transcends the relations of money so carefully set out, in the manner of those manuals of political economy for girls fashionable at the time, in the first pages. Jane Austen's novels open in an English drizzle of guineas and annuities; but, as so often in England, the shower passes. In a celebrated scene in *Pride and Prejudice*, Darcy, who is rich and grand, is so demoralised by his enslavement to Elizabeth Bennet, who is lowly and poor, that he insults her. Pemberley, with all its rank and amenity and above all its capitalised income, is thrown at Elizabeth's angry head as if it were a China vase: it misses and, to the secret delight of many readers, does not break. It is at such moments that Jane Austen rises above her pseudo-cynicism, leaves the lady economists – Mrs Marcet, Mrs Martineau – hopelessly earthbound and unfurls her flattering message to her readers: that for a moment, and if she is smart and lucky, a woman has it in her power to shatter the monetary foundation of society. And all with the most perfect propriety.

That power of Elizabeth's is called her beauty. A woman's beauty conveys to the man's imagination the promise of sexual happiness; and yet that happiness, even in the imagination, has an end in that repose that Baudelaire described so beautifully in his Icarus poem:

> *Les amants des prostituées*
> *Sont heureux, dispos, et repus.*[38]

[The clients of prostitutes are happy, glutted and well.]

Money, however, sets no limit to the imagination and grants no repose; and some women (and a few men) will always prefer to the limited satisfactions of love the unlimited promise of money. After all, labourers of both sexes prefer money wages to vouchers at the company store. Prostitution would therefore seem to be the exemplary form of sexual love in the age of money, as Villon, Rochester and Baudelaire have been at pains to inform us.

In a marriage or other family relation of sexual love, there is a pattern of rights and obligations between the parties, which may be declared before witnesses or merely spoken to the bedroom walls. In its ideal form in Christian doctrine and much Western literature since the Middle Ages, the relation is one of barter: love exchanges for love, which does not submit to measure, except occasionally in the conceits of verse. Such unremunerated love is still considered the prize and consolation of human existence: a glimpse, however fleeting, of a divine bliss. Just to have experienced such a sensation is to pardon the world. Where money enters the relation, and it almost always does so, it is still felt to be an intrusion; and while it conveys desire, it is profoundly disruptive of desire. In his farewell letter to Marie Duplessis, the famous *Dame aux Camélias*, Dumas *fils* made the point with great dignity and affection: 'I am neither rich enough to love you as I'd like, nor poor enough to be loved as you'd like.'

Such attitudes survive in the West with undiminished conviction. Even now, it is still not proper for lovers to give each other presents that can be converted into money: hence we have florists and confectioners and purveyors of silk scarves, knick-knacks and elaborate underwear, which though not as perishable as sweets or flowers, yet cannot easily be sold; and, coming from the other direction, mechanical ornaments for office desks. Mercier, in his *Tableau de Paris* of 1783,[39] describes a shop near the Pont Neuf called the Petit Dunkerque, where a man might find *bijoux frivoles* 'that one gives to honest women who wouldn't for a moment accept money but will accept little golden trinkets because they have an air of respectability.' The air of respectability can be quite thin: Balzac, who liked to make his point with a mallet, has the Duc d'Hérouville in *Cousine Bette* give Josépha a cornet of sugared almonds that conceals thirty thousand francs a year in *rentes*. In all large cities, even in the times of Mercier and Balzac, there will be shops that will take a lover's or a husband's present of a jacket or a dress (and, no doubt, all sorts of women's gifts) and convert them back into money, though at only a fraction of the giver's outlay. 'A lot of Arab ladies,' such a shopkeeper in London told the reporter of *Independent* magazine, 'use clothes as currency . . . because while their husbands will buy them anything they want – maybe, three Hermès handbags at £6,000 each . . . – they won't give them *cash*.'[40]

The reticence of romantic love is three-fold. Money conveys desire: it cares not at all where that desire finds satisfaction. To give money to a woman – and here I must speak as a man – is to deny her special quality, her *irreplaceability*, and reduce her unique amiability to a commodity. Money takes away her name, while transforming her lover into a nameless customer of a market of appetites. No person likes to be thought interchangeable in love. Finally, a gift of money allows the beloved to deploy wishes in every direction, whereas her lover wants to concentrate them on himself. The English satirists of female vanity of the early eighteenth century cannot conceal a certain trepidation at the new opportunities money offered women: Addison, in *The Spectator* of February 7, 1712, and only half in joke, warned husbands against pin-money – a wife's allowance of money – 'as furnishing her with Arms against himself, and in a Manner becoming accessory to his own Dishonour.'[41] Money therefore meets a triple resistance. (The same arguments apply to women's gifts of money to men and, *mutatis mutandis*, to presents of money to children at Christmas and on their birthdays.)

At some point, as she progresses along the axes of money and sex, a woman is termed a prostitute. The word is not easy to pin down. In the famous *Histoire de la Prostitution* of Dufour, published in eight volumes in 1861, prostitution is any form of officially irregular or unwed love:[42] if we adopted such a definition, we would never pass beyond generalities or would end up writing nonsense, like Proudhon, who saw all activity by women in the money arena as prostitution and the women themselves – even George Sand – as constituting a *pornocratie* or rule of whores. The old notion that prostitution was a perversion of the natural purpose of sexual love, in that it substituted egoistic gain for the gain of the species, is hardly persuasive in an age of contraception. Any useful definition must

include some combination of the words 'sex' and 'money', though
we must remember that in modern times, and especially since the
invention of the daguerreotype process in 1839, a woman has been
able to earn money from her attributes of sex without even touching
a man or exposing herself to anything more disreputable than a still
or video camera or a telephone. If such women are prostitutes, they
are virtual prostitutes. The key lies in that passage from Herodotus I
quoted in Chapter 1. In the earliest discussion of money, there is
also a mention of prostitution. Prostitution is therefore, truly, an old
profession, if not the oldest: not because it is as old as Eve, but
because it is as old as money.

In taking payment for sex, women free themselves from the
authority of home and husband and gain the imaginative liberty of
money. But just as many men, in consenting to measure their
personalities in money, feel they have suffered a loss of manliness; so
women, in taking to a life of prostitution, are felt to suffer a penalty,
whose vagueness and severity do not long conceal an Oedipal
location: the child doesn't wish his mother to leave the house, let
alone screw around, for he will thus lose her attention. In the
sixteenth century that penalty was hell-fire, and even as late as *Crime
and Punishment*, Dostoyevsky sees a correspondence in the moral
conditions of Raskolnikov, murderer, and Sonya, whore, that seems
to us merely social, not ethical, and greatly weakens that fine novel.
The *grandes horizontales* of the nineteenth century in Europe are
afflicted by a mysterious mortality. Here is Marie Duplessis again at
the ceremony to open that Rothschildian extravaganza, the Gare du
Nord. Jules Janin was there and captured that epoch in women's
emancipation (and, while we're about it, the fame of Belgium):

> In that station, immense gathering-place of all the railroads of the
> North, Belgium had collected all her glories: the shrubs of her
> hothouses, the flowers of her parks, the diamonds of her tiaras. An
> unbelievable mob of uniforms, decorations, brilliants, gauze
> dresses cluttered the scene of the party. The French backwoods
> and the German nobility, Spanish Belgium, Flanders and Holland,
> all dripping in diamonds old-fashioned at the time of Louis XIV,
> the massy and oppressive manufacturing fortunes and one or two
> Parisian ladies, looking like butterflies in a swarm of bees, had

rushed to this celebration of industry and restlessness, of tempered steel and obedient fire and conquered time. A bizarre confusion, in which all the energies and graces of creation were represented, oak and flower, pit-coal and amethyst. In the midst of that parade of peoples, kings, princes, artists, black-smiths and professional flirts, I saw – perhaps only I saw – the entry of that lovely person, paler and whiter than usual, already stricken with that invisible ailment which would drag her to the grave.

She had come to the ball, despite her name, and by favour of her dazzling beauty! . . . An appreciative murmur marked her passage, and those who knew her bowed at the waist; but she, calm as she always was and isolated in her habitual disdain, received the compliments as if they had been due.[43]

That is all clear enough. Marie Duplessis' beauty suspends not only the traditional criteria of rank and women's virtue, but also the newer touchstone of money: she disdains even the massy industrial fortunes heaved at her feet. Imprisoned in her perfection, ill to death, she knows only boredom: Janin follows her to Spa and watches her at the gaming-table, 'appendix to her profession,' where she wastes the hours and money that men had wasted on her. At her death, in a house opposite the Madeleine, her patron saint, her effects were auctioned. Women paid fortunes for items of her intimate toilette, as if to capture the residue of her independence, that vanishing essence of money and allure.

> *Son peigne fut poussé à un prix fou; sa brosse pour les cheveux s'est payé au poids d'or . . . On a vendu des bottines qu'elle avait portées, et les honnêtes femmes ont lutté entre elles à qui mettrait ces souliers de Cendrillon.*[44]

> [Her comb was bid up to the skies. Her hairbrush sold for its weight in gold. Respectable women fought with one another as to who was to wear Cinderella's slippers.]

Verdi's opera about her, *La Traviata*, which was first performed at Venice in February 1852, recasts the story as a tragedy. It is the first sung drama of bourgeois femininity: there is little action, merely sung conversation, and all that takes place between four walls in the city or the rural suburbs. Marie Duplessis' offence to the moralists, the secret provocation of her death sentence, was to demand the masculine privilege of independence and exhaust it. Violetta's is altogether more respectable: she merely gives love precedence over propriety, an old, old story. We even have, in *Di Provenz' il mar, il suo*,[45] Germont reminding his son of that old chestnut, the primacy of real property over money. Music will make delightful all sorts of nonsense; but an indifferent performance of *La Traviata* can be gruelling.

Alphonsine or Marie Plessis, a farm girl from Normandy, began at the very bottom of the whore's ladder: her consumption, which made her too sensitive for any corsage but a camellia, was no doubt as hard-earned as her little prefix of nobility. As far as I know, women can become prostitutes out of love of love, vanity, idleness and avarice; but many do not feel any sensation of choice. Many prostitutes are prostitutes out of injury and need (even if only an artificial need, such as a drug addiction). Many women sell their sex for money because it is their only entrée to the world of actual and potential choice embodied in money, rather as a friendless immigrant will sell bags of smack in the ghetto. In a world of parity between the sexes on the field of money – which is, of course, quite blind to gender – either prostitution will evaporate or all relations between the sexes will come down onto a monetary footing.

In antiquity, among the courtesans of the Renaissance, and with increasing confidence in the eighteenth century, one hears women pleading for some other gateway to the world of money than that of their sex. For Virginia Woolf, in the essay called *A Room of One's Own* she published in 1928, money is privacy: 'A woman must have money and a room of her own if she is to write fiction.'[46] The source of the money is important. It must be an inheritance or £500 a year in gilt-edged interest, which will provide a woman with both independence and privacy without exposing her to the indignity of witnessed labour; and will, in an extremely optimistic formulation, give a woman 'the greatest release of all . . . which is the freedom to think of things in themselves. . . . Indeed, my aunt's legacy unveiled the sky to me, and substituted for the large and imposing figure of a gentleman, which Milton recommended for my perpetual adoration, a view of the open sky.'[47]

The notion that a *rentière* has some special insight into the world seems peculiarly absurd: for a writer to abandon her consciousness of class and sex to queue at the Bank of England on Dividend Day would be asking for trouble. Yet that criticism is ungallant. Existing on the margin of a society in which money is the chief reward, confined to a feminine world that is thought frivolous precisely because it is unremunerated – for 'money dignifies what is frivolous if unpaid for'[48] – even bourgeois women are desperate to enter the arena of money. In 1906, my grandfather, though still a young man, gave his sister Anna an allowance of £100 a year. It had an effect he hadn't foreseen. The next year, Anna went to India, wrote a novel and supported herself and several other people from her royalties for the rest of her life; and yet, as she wrote in her memoir, *Unforgettable, Unforgotten,*[49] 'even when I no longer needed [the annuity] he could hardly be persuaded to give it up.'

In antiquity and the Middle Ages, labour itself seemed to be dignified: what has happened is that men and women, unless they be Marxians, have transferred to money the old sensation of the dignity of labour. Housework, which seems to men such a valuable and dignified activity, has been brought into the world of money: at first, by way of a market for domestic servants and then by appliances and microwaveable recipe dishes, whose manufacture has given a great impetus to the monetary measures of national economy. By abandoning the house to the money economy, and going to work outdoors for pay, the housewife gains a double reward: she is freed of a limitless task – for there is always another pot to wash or shirt to stitch – and gains, in place of a single gruelling house, the imaginary and spotless mansions of money. She is incorporated into the mainstream of human desire, a process described to her husband by Jenny Marx with her usual dusky precision.

> In Germany, a child is still a very great honour, the cooking pot and needle still bring respect and moreover one still has the satisfaction of a duty fulfilled in return for all the washed-out, sewn-up, child-minded days. But when those old things no longer count as duties and honours and so on, when people progress so far that they consider even such old expressions to be obsolete, from then on one feels no more impulse to the small duties of life. One wants to enjoy, become active and experience in oneself the happiness of mankind.[50]

All that is painful for men to observe: so painful, indeed, that it can provoke a violent reaction, as in Iran in 1978. The pain arises not merely in the Oedipal conflict I mentioned, but also in a certain shame: no man of pride is content that money – or possessions bought with money, such as automobiles – is the foundation of his self-worth. He would be tempted to say: 'I never much cared for being chairman of Microsoft/ working down the pit/ bleeding to death on the battlefield, but you might, my love, you might.' Of course, such sentiments are intolerably provoking to women. Relations between the sexes in the Anglo-Saxon countries are so bad in this year 1997 not because women are taking men's wages – as if money or labour or desire were fixed quantities! – but because women suspect men have devalued those wages; and that women are doomed to perpetual frustration in their endeavours, are thrown back again and again on their historical condition and are for ever condemned, like an Arab wife behind the curtain of the guest-room, doomed always to eat from dishes that men have picked at and let go cold; while they themselves have lost all pride in the achievements of a feminine culture. All over the world, women confront a nightmare: that they must labour at home, as they have always done, and also in the world for money.

Yet I imagine that the equalisations of money, its impatience with both chivalry and discourtesy, will eventually dissolve the distinctions of sex. Jenny Marx's melancholy world of *Kirche, Küche, Kinder* has exploded; and though there will be reactions to that cataclysmic reordering of the most intimate sphere of existence, as occurred in Iran, money has a powerful inertia. The so-called feminine virtues of fidelity, chastity, piety and thrift long ago lost their femininity and are ceasing to be virtues. In the West, men and women experiment clumsily with each other's traditional roles. Homosexuality becomes legal and then customary; and will finally, no doubt, lose all conviction as a social posture. Children will be reared, as in ancient Sparta and the modern United States, by sexless corporations, which impose on their employees a celibacy as demanding as that of the Shaker settlements in old New England. Women will still think of themselves as women, but only to the extent that men now think of themselves as men: that is, only in the seasons of love and parentage. The differences between the sexes will attenuate to mere physique, and perhaps beyond even that: already, it is much harder to distinguish the sexes on Malibu Beach than on the streets of Kabul; and I imagine that amalgamation of the sexes will proceed until the reproductive imperative, the need to make men and women seem always new in each other's eyes – what we term fashion, which is powerful, perhaps more powerful than money – sends them off in different directions.

★   ★   ★

Les systèmes sont comme les rats, qui peuvent passer par vingt petits trous, et qui en trouvent enfin deux ou trois qui ne peuvent les admettre.

Voltaire

Adam Smith believed that the transmission of desire by means of money, uninhibited by any censor other than competing desire, was the goal of history: it was the 'obvious and simple system of natural liberty.'[51] The sovereign, he said, had no responsibilities other than external defence, the administration and execution of justice and certain unprofitable public works. That Smith was soon to be Commissioner of Customs at Edinburgh, employed at a salary of £600 per year to frustrate Scots' wishes for cravats, ruffles, pocket handkerchiefs, brandy and other requisites of natural liberty, did not appear to him too much of a contradiction; though he went carefully through his own household and wardrobe for smuggled articles.[52]

Such contradictions run through all Smith's thought on money, and have left a legacy of the greatest confusion. Every economic treatise since Smith's has accepted his account of the origin of money, as a spontaneous convenience in commerce that predates any public authority, and demonstrated its advantages in terms identical to his.[53] Yet his picture of money simply does not make sense. For, on the one hand, and as a stick to beat the bullionists, he treats money with the greatest disdain, as a mere 'kitchen utensil,'[54] while simultaneously elevating that pot or pan to be the embodiment of reason, civility, virtue and liberty. In truth, Smith is a prude of money: he is actually revolted by untrammelled desire, and prefers to the word 'money' a euphemism, 'the division of labour' – which

sounds sort of fair and equitable – as if they were identities. They
need not be and Smith should have known it. He was a fine scholar
of classical antiquity and could have seen that the division of labour
in antiquity, as analysed by Plato and Xenophon – they were in his
library, heaven knows[55] – was valued as a path not to quantity and
exchangeability, but to quality and beauty; not to pins and pubs but
to the object in the British Museum on which countless hands
worked and which is known as the Portland Vase. He would have
known that the division of labour in India had become rigid,
endogamous and perpetual: what we call caste.

At the heart of his thought is a deliberate misunderstanding of the
sensations embodied in money. While clearly aware that money
contains or conveys wishes, Smith asserts that it conveys thoughts:
that its pursuit, accumulation and disbursement are always rational,
and its effects benign. Of course he recognises that many wishes
conveyed by money are disreputable and have consequences that
look bad; and for money's effect to be benign, liberal and rational, it
will have to do something to those wishes on the way. He therefore
adopts, not without distaste but without acknowledgement, the City
ideology expounded with such cynical delight by Mandeville:

> The Root of Evil, Avarice,
> That damn'd ill-natur'd baleful Vice,
> Was Slave to Prodigality,
> That noble Sin; whilst Luxury
> Employed a million of the Poor
> And odious Pride a Million more.[56]

but attempts to give it a scientific foundation. For that purpose, he
makes use of a piece of metaphysics, a metaphor that belongs more
in a thriller than in a work of philosophy: the invisible hand.

The phrase has a curious history in meaning which we shall now
reconstruct. In Defoe's *Moll Flanders*, printed in 1722, it is a
euphemism for ill-luck or retribution, 'an almost invisible Hand,
that blasted all my Happiness.'[57] In Smith's first use of the phrase, in
his juvenile *History of Astronomy*, it is the supernatural agency to
which primitive peoples attribute irregular or alarming natural
phenomena.[58] By 1759, when Smith published *The Theory of Moral
Sentiments*, that malign and unpredictable force has become the good

god of the Stoics, who has arranged the universe so that all events, even the most alarming, work towards the prosperity and perfection of the whole. The invisible hand is now money, which captures selfish or silly human sentiments and channels them to every corner of society in a neutral form that anybody can use. The rich

> consume little more than the poor, and in spite of their natural selfishness and rapacity, though they mean only their own conven-iency, though the sole end which they propose for the labours of all the thousands whom they employ, be the gratification of their own vain and insatiable desires, they divide with the poor the produce of all their improvements. They are led by an invisible hand to make nearly the same distribution of the necessaries of life, which would have been made, had the earth been divided into equal portions among all its inhabitants.[59]

Fifteen years later, in *The Wealth of Nations*,[60] Smith's wonderful machine is promoting GDP. The merchant has no interest in the annual revenue of society; and although

> by directing that industry in such a manner as its produce may be of the greatest value, he intends only his own gain ... he is in this, as in many other cases, led by an invisible hand to promote an end that was no part of his intention.

Whatever you do, it will have a good effect! How soothing to ruthless minds and bad commercial consciences! When in the spring of 1787, late in life, Smith came down to London to enjoy his celebrity, he stayed at the Lord Advocate's villa in Wimbledon: and once when he came downstairs, Pitt, Dundas, Grenville and Henry Addington all stood up. 'We will stand till you are first seated,' said the gentlemen, 'for we are all your scholars.'[61] Indeed! For Smith had given those people, in Joan Robinson's admiring phrase, 'the ideology to end ideologies, for it ... abolished the moral problem. It is only necessary for each individual to act egoistically for the good of all to be attained.'[62] Smith had taken a religious metaphor and, without irony or even self-consciousness, applied it to money.[63] In so doing, Smith converted the self-serving business slogans of the seventeenth-century City into a creed.

At this stage, political economy is still just a system of belief, no more scientific than any other; but the political economists wanted a science, for they had always hankered after the prestige of Newtonian physics or Harveian physiology, in which a single natural law seemed to explain a whole class of natural phenomena. (Only for a while, of course, but everybody feels his beliefs are timeless.) Governor Pownall used just such Newtonian language in his letter to Smith of September 25, 1776: the goal was to create 'Principia to the knowledge of politick operations, as Mathematicks are to Mechanicks, Astronomy and the other Sciences.'[64]

In the two centuries after Smith, more mental effort was wasted on objectifying his system of belief than on any other in history, not excluding the immortality of the soul and the rentability of civilian nuclear power. The merchants and political arithmeticians had cleared the ground, by reducing human beings to indistinguishable quantities, bereft of every moral sensation and desire other than for money. The evident subjectivity of money's value had been ruled out, as we have seen, by Sir William Petty when he excluded from political arithmetick 'the mutable minds, opinions, appetites and passions of particular men.' The next stage was to discern in money and goods bought for money a value that was operative in all cases, like gravity in Newton's objects; which could then be applied to promulgate laws binding on the human community, including the pesky poor.

At times, Smith thought that value was labour: that is, that both money and objects bought for money were worth what they cost to mint or make. That curious notion was taken up by Ricardo and prolonged, far beyond the natural life of an idea, by Marx. There is something intensely poignant in Ricardo's struggle, in his last days, to find some invariable value that would give a retrospective meaning to his life. The metaphysical in political economy has never been more clearly exposed.

> It is a great desideratum in Polit. Econ. to have a perfect measure of absolute value in order to be able to ascertain what relation commodities bear to each other at distant periods.

He thought this thing would be like a yard or pound, constant, and, rather as the yard is long and the pound heavy, valuable in itself: he was still unwilling to recognise that the value resident in money and commodities is not an external convention but a subjective sensation: if money can measure reality, it is as a foot and thumb do, not twelve inches. Yet Ricardo's last written words are honourable and courageous: 'It is still exceedingly difficult to discover or even to imagine any commodity which shall be a perfect measure of value.'[65] Unfortunately, Marx did not see those passages. From his reading of Smith and Ricardo in Paris in the spring of 1844, Marx decided that political economy, so clearly an ideology of the bourgeois, might somehow be captured for the poor; and the instrument of that brigandage was to be the labour theory of value. If money and commodities are congealed labour, then interest and profit must somehow be stolen from the labourer, who, on entering the market to recoup his strength, gets his work back, as it were, less those deductions.

Mill and Jevons talk about a thing called value, another called utility and a third called price, but I cannot, for the life of me, tell if they are meant to be identities. What is value? What you want. What is utility? What you want. What is price? What you pay in money for the above. Marshall came at the problem from another direction: he thought that desire itself was a fixed quantity; or rather that human motives could be measured in the events they give rise to, not in the modest, poetical sense of 'see what a rent the envious Casca made,' but in a hard arithmetic of prices, wages and the rate of interest (the price of money). He opens his *Principles of Economics* with a humanity simplified out of existence:

> The steadiest motive to ordinary business work is the desire for the pay which is the material reward of work. . . . The motive is supplied by a definite amount of money; and it is this definite and exact money measurement of the steadiest motives in business life, which has enabled economics far to outrun every other branch of the study of man. Just as the chemist's fine balance has made chemistry more exact than most other physical sciences; so this economist's balance, rough and imperfect as it is, has made economics more exact than any other branch of social science.[66]

Marshall thus managed to re-introduce the mental affections into economics, but in caricature. Meanwhile, Edgeworth saw no particular obstacle to devising a Unit of Pleasure (presumably to be named the Pound Sterling).

Though the economists had manifestly failed to find their gravity, they proceeded as if they had. They became like drunkards who have lost their house keys, and search under the street-lamp, not because they dropped the keys there, but because the street-lamp casts a faint artificial light. Le Play, in his collection of annual household budgets called *Les Ouvriers européens*, sought to reduce the most abject human misery and degradation to units of money. Here is the ragpicker, dignified and commemorated for all time in Baudelaire's *chiffonnier* poems, in his last items of discretionary consumption *per annum*:

> Chewing tobacco (cigar butts picked up in the street) . . . . 34 f
> Toys and other presents for the child . . . . 1 f [67]

Yet such is the prestige of mathematics, and the charm of talk about money, that the economists have imposed their arithmetic on the world. Though in their own existences, most people recognise that money and happiness are not co-terminous; yet they will accept whatever money quantities are fashionable with the economists – national product, balance of payments, consumer price indices or whatever – as measures of national welfare; and because those sums, being sums, have a technically rational sound about them, people forget there are other goals of national, as there are of individual, aspiration. That the economists can't measure any of their quantities even to their own satisfaction, can explain neither prices nor the rate of interest and cannot even agree what money is, reminds us that we deal here with belief not science. As for myself, if my long residences on the Arabian Peninsula and in Iran taught me anything, it is that contentment and peace are only accidentally contiguous with rising GDP and large reserves of foreign exchange.

In truth, the economists were aware all along that there was something very unscientific about money. Mill wrote:

> As it is always by means of money that people provide for their different necessities, there grows up in their minds a powerful association leading them to regard money as wealth in a more peculiar sense than any other article; and even those who pass

their lives in the production of the most useful objects acquire the habit of regarding those objects as chiefly important by the capacity of being exchanged for money.

But he then reverted to pots and pans:

> There cannot, in short, be intrinsically a more insignificant thing, in the economy of society, than money; except in the character of a contrivance for sparing time and labour. It is a machine etc.[68]

Like Mill, Marshall could not entirely ignore the capital feature of money: that it is imaginary gratification of all possible wishes, eminent satisfaction. He gingerly drops his comment into a footnote, as one would dispose of a maggoty rook in a park bin:

> We do indeed hear of people who pursue money for its own sake without caring for what it will purchase, especially at the end of a long life spent in business: but in this as in other cases the habit of doing a thing is kept up after the purpose for which it was originally done has ceased to exist etc.[69]

Keynes, who was a little more worldly than his master, fished out the corpse, hosed it down and restored it to the main text, if only a piece of journalism:[70]

> The love of money as a possession − as distinguished from the love of money as a means to the enjoyments and realities of life − will be recognised for what it is, a somewhat disgusting morbidity, one of those semi-criminal, semi-pathological propensities which one hands over with a shudder to the specialists in mental disease.[71]

I hardly know which is less preferable: to ignore the avarice that is the chief feature of modern society, or to wish it away! In attempting to restore the ethical component to political economy, Keynes turns virtue on its head: his economics are a sort of Black Mass. Smith had reluctantly agreed with Mandeville and Johnson that private vices were public virtues; for Keynes, the old private virtues (prudence, thrift, kindness) are public vices. In place of Sir William Petty's no ethics, we have bad ethics, for a despot will loll on a vacated throne. Keynes may have sensed he was not getting very far, for he soon gave up with motive, though he attributes that failure of will to the public, which he and his friends had so comprehensively deluded:

the money-motive . . . apart from certain admitted abuses . . .
does its job well. In the result, the average man averts his attention
from the problem, and has no clear idea what he really thinks and
feels about the whole confounded matter.[72]

That 'well' is superfluous, because Keynes cannot conceive of a
better or worse outcome: whatever job it does, money does its job.
The world we have is not the best world or the worst: the world
we have is the world we have. Dimly aware of those tautologies,
economics since Keynes has retreated into algebra: whose singular
virtue is that it needs no counterpart in human experience, no
meaning. A profession that begins with priests, runs through crooks
and speculators, and then professors and gentlemen, ends with
hermits. Political economy is now, I suspect, in the same condition
in which Scholastic learning found itself on the eve of the Discoveries. It is about to explode.

Because economics is not a science, it cannot be proved or refuted
– for that is a definition of science – merely exposed to the
recommendations of history and experience: that is, lampooned. I
copied out the quotations above, not merely out of boisterousness
but also out of sorrow; for I have watched the most able men and
women of my generation, who might have created unexampled
monuments in moral philosophy, mathematics or engineering, waste
their lives in a prattle of non-accelerating inflation rates of unemployment or rather, since such matters cannot long occupy an
educated mind, in interminable telephone conversations with their
stockbrokers.

It is Dostoyevsky, once again, who restores reality to the economists' money; and if I have given him the last word for a second
chapter running, it is because of that ability of the Russian nineteenth
century to follow an argument to its furthest reaches of delusion and
violence. Pushkin had made fun of Smith in the first book of
Yevgeny Onyegin, and in this passage Dostoyevsky is no doubt paying
homage to his master:

> Science tells us, 'Love yourself before everyone else, for every-
> thing in the world is based on self-interest. If you love only
> yourself, you'll transact your business as it ought to be transacted
> and your coat will remain whole.' And economic truth adds that

the more successfully private business is run, and the more whole coats, as it were, there are, the more solid are the foundations of our social life and the greater is the general well-being of the people. Which means that by acquiring wealth exclusively and only for myself, I'm by that very fact acquiring it, as it were, for everybody.[73]

And while Luzhin rabbits on, in that hot, tiny, crowded room, Raskolnikov is lying on his filthy sofa under a pressure of guilt so palpably conveyed it is worse for the reader than his own worst nightmare. Raskolnikov's guilt arises not from an offence against law or custom, which the author shows us to be quite arbitrary in Tsarist Petersburg; but from pursuing the economic ideology to its conclusion. In prosecuting his economic interest in the blood and brains of an old woman money-lender, Raskolnikov has destroyed his very humanity. For that is the end of economics: the world reduced to a scorching slum, its women to whores, its men to murderers.

8

Death in Dean St.

> The future smells of Russian leather, blood, godlessness and
> many whippings. I should advise our grandchildren to be
> born with thick skins on their backs.
>
> Heine

In certain masculine novels of the turn of the nineteenth century,
an unwilling young man from a commercial family is for ever setting
out on horseback into new mental country. He may, as in the best
of those books, Goethe's *Wilhelm Meister* of 1794–6, be on assign-
ment to collect some debts of business but quite early in his journey
falls in with crags, waterfalls, travelling actors and women; or as in
Rob Roy, which Sir Walter Scott wrote in 1817, meets a Highland
freebooter and is himself mistaken for a highwayman.

Georg Lukács, who made a study of the historical novel from the
Budapest of the 1940s, thought that if *Rob Roy* were successfully to
be filmed, it must first dispense with Francis Osbaldistone and his
family counting-house, so that Rob might stand free in all his wind-
swept Scotch magnificence; and that has indeed been the case with
the most recent films with a debt to Scott's great novel. But these
films betray the author's intention, for it is precisely at that moment
when Francis falls under suspicion in Chapter 3 of *Rob Roy* that
Scott speaks directly to the reader and unveils his literary enterprise.

Here is the passage:

> A man in those days might have all the external appearance of a
> gentleman and yet turn out to be a highwayman. For the division
> of labour in every department not having then [1714] taken place
> so fully as since that period, the profession of the polite and

accomplished adventurer, who nicked you of your money at White's, or bowled you out of it at Marybone, was often united with that of the professed ruffian, who on Bagshot Heath, or Finchley Common, commanded his brother beau to stand and deliver.... A young man, therefore, in my circumstances, was not entitled to be highly indignant at the mistake which confounded him with this worshipful class of burglars.[1]

The passage intrigued me at first with its submerged echo of Law's duel in Bloomsbury Square, and with the word 'worshipful,' an honorific used then and now of the merchant livery companies in the City of London, but here transferred in the manner of Gay and even Shakespeare to their underworld shadows; but it is at the phrase 'division of labour' that Scott throws down his challenge. For the apostle of the division of labour is none other than a certain elderly Commissioner of Customs at Edinburgh whom Scott had met in his youth, Mr Adam Smith, LLD. And it is here, at the beginning of *Rob Roy*, by means of the literary artifice that he was in the process of perfecting and we now call The Historical Novel, that Scott strikes his blow at the world of money whose scripture is *The Wealth of Nations*.

The two men met at Smith's house in the Canongate, Edinburgh, some time in the 1780s and their confrontation, though its arena was a sugar bowl, is also worth recording as one of the turning-points in this history. In those days, Smith lived with his maiden cousin and housekeeper, Janet Douglas. Scott must have been in his early teens and his reminiscence is full of that facetious spite that barely conceals, in an ambitious young man, an intense frustration at the elders in the way:

We shall never forget one particular evening, when he put an elderly maiden lady, who presided at the tea-table, to sore confusion, by neglecting utterly her invitation to be seated, and walked round and round the circle, stopping ever and anon to steal a lump from the sugar basin, which the venerable spinster was at length constrained to place on her own knee, as the only method of securing it from his most uneconomical depredations. His appearance mumping the eternal sugar, was something indescribable.[2]

That is part of a long portrait of Smith, which is mere caricature: we learn nothing of the economist's great classical learning, his powerful ethical sense, his wit and his kindness. But Scott's enterprise was not just to dislodge the absent-minded old celebrities blocking the exiguous Scots sun; it was nothing less than to take the age of money – for which Smith's euphemism was the division of labour – and infuse it with all the splendid values of its predecessors; to bring back the banners, duels and princesses; and to inject into commercial credit (as embodied by the honest merchants of the novel) the wild and unpredictable aristocratic honour of Rob Roy MacGregor.[3]

This feudal pageant was primarily a literary exercise, though it was embodied in stone in the house Scott built by the Tweed at Abbotsford and in the celebrations he staged for the visit of King George IV to Edinburgh in 1822. In itself, it was Quixotic. Scott wrote for money; indeed, he was the first man in Europe, unless that was Beaumarchais in France, to make a fortune from literature. In 1809, Scott had been deeply offended by Byron's jeering at *Marmion* and his 'prostituted muse' at £1,000 a trick;[4] but when his publishers failed sixteen years later, he possessed the honour (and the credit) to shoulder their liabilities of £130,000. 'I will dig,' he wrote in his diary on the dark day of January 24, 1826, 'in the mine of my imagination to find diamonds (or what may sell for such) to make good my engagements.' On February 16, his works in progress (*Woodstock* and the *Life of Napoleon Buonaparte*) have become simply 'funds' for the debt.[5]

Mingling with influences from Germany and England – Shelley, Hölderlin, Schiller, Goethe – this neo-Quixotry spread out to colonise a century. Though reactionary, and utterly hopeless, it passed into social theory with Marx and Proudhon, banking, public administration, painting and photography, and still astonishes us every day in the architecture left from the Victorian age. For the monumental buildings of the nineteenth century, though built in and to serve the world of money, seem at first sight to be other things: a castle, a cathedral, a mosque. Only closer inspection reveals that that *thing* in Bombay is a railway station. These buildings, which in my childhood were held to be ludicrous precisely because of their fatal confusion of purpose – their helpless ignorance of what they actually were – their religiosity and indiscriminate nostalgia, now move us to tears. For who has not sat at a Victorian railway station, anxious or delayed, and felt overpowered by the yearning in the architecture? For, in reality, those buildings are acts of worship. They celebrate, in awe and fear, the God-like power of money to bring together so many distant and estranged impulses and concentrate them at a single point of space and history.

It is in the reproduction of wilderness – that is, of the world that cannot even conceive of money – that the Romantic artists feel most painfully the presence of money; and that feeling has, if anything, increased in intensity in our lifetimes. Whereas at school I was taught the feudal system of medieval Europe till it came out of my ears, as if to inculcate in me a Carlylean longing for social relations unmediated by money, my children are fed the rain forest or what still remains of it. Education, it seems, is in a condition of permanent homesickness for a vanished world.

The wilderness, as an object of Romantic contemplation and source of emotional supplies, had been invented in December 1777, when Scott was just six but Goethe was twenty-eight and residing at Weimar in Thuringia, where he was employed as a sort of economic consultant by the little local court at a salary of 1,200 talers a year. A hunt had been ordered, so as to deal with some wild boar that were annoying the villagers in the Eisenach region, and as the court train rumbles and jingles through the soft countryside, in the damp early-winter air, something extraordinary happens. It was captured by Goethe in a poem of great beauty and precision, the 'Harzreise im Winter' ('Winter Journey in the Harz Mountains'). The prince's coach, as it bounces over the turf, is suddenly transfigured into Fortune's car, which we recognise without effort from the prints of Law's scheme and the Haarlem tulips and sixteenth-century Antwerp:

> *Leicht ist's, folgen dem Wagen,*
> *Den Fortuna führt,*
> *Wie der gemächliche Tross*
> *Auf gebesserten Wegen*
> *Hinter des Fürsten Einzug.*

[It's easy enough to follow Fortune's car, like the gaggle of hunt
followers that trip down the trails blazed for the Prince's progress.]

and then, as if he cannot control himself, and yet so self-consciously
that he writes not of his feelings but of those watching him, Goethe
turns off, leaves the ride, vanishes into the thicket, falls out of the
world.

> *Hinter ihm schlagen*
> *Die Sträuche zusammen,*
> *Das Gras steht wieder auf,*
> *Die Öde verschlingt ihn.*[6]

[Behind him, the bushes whip back together. The grass stands up again.
The waste engulfs him.]

These verses, set to music later by Brahms and eventually recorded
by the doomed British contralto, Kathleen Ferrier, are the quintess-
ence of the Romantic sentiment in its heroic phase.[7]

Up to that moment, as Goethe rides off on his own and sees an
eagle soaring above a hill-top, the wilderness has been a place
waiting for exploitation. It is seen as a value, but one that is still
hidden or imprisoned until it can be released by agriculture,
grazing, metallurgy, hunting and all those economic activities that
Goethe, pre-eminently among the great Romantic artists, had
mastered and understood. In other words, it was waiting for
conversion into money. What Goethe sees in the wilderness is not
explicitly stated, except that it isn't money: a more precise definition becomes, as it were, the Romantic task or project. In the
'Harzreise' it is God's unpredictable but ever-present mercy; for
Wordsworth in the 'Ode' on immortality, it is the painful residue
of childish states of consciousness; while in the landscape paintings
of Caspar David Friedrich, it appears to be nothing less than intensity itself as a quality. These sensations arise and draw their creative
and destructive power – and I don't believe this has been said
elsewhere – from an agonising contradiction within the psychology
of money.

The distinctive aesthetic experience of nature – what we used to
call Romantic and now term environmentalist – begins at a great
remove from nature. The farmer who ploughs a stony field, or stays

up all night on Christmas Eve to keep his new-born lambs from freezing, does not generally regard nature with a contemplative eye or feel that soft sorrow, that sense of estrangement from a lost paradise that we think of as the proper Romantic or environmental response to nature. He welcomes the by-pass if it will speed his journey to or from market. He'll grow trailers in his fields as happily as soybeans. The song 'Summertime' is a celebration not of the beauty of the cotton bush but of the strength of the market for it: the living is easy *because* the price of cotton is high.

The portraiture of natural landscape, for some interior value rather than as an arena or background to human activity – a village wedding, a madonna among lilies, an English duke before a window opening on owned acres – presupposes a distance from it and a break in our ancient or ideal unity with it. It is the expression not of a rural existence but of an urban yearning; and the ghastly perversity of it all is, as Georg Simmel well noted, that *only the possession of money permits us to take flight into nature*. Simmel did not mean merely that only money allows us to pass from city to wilderness, from Oxford Street to the Himalayas: it is money that makes us need to do so! How bold we feel, setting off from Kathmandu towards the mountain. We feel that we are passing out of the world of money and can now enjoy our primordial natural inheritance, which might include 110 mph winds and an agonising, lonely death. In reality, of course – and here we must extend Simmel's argument – we drag money with us and leave it there, like the oxygen tanks and corpses that litter the second base camp on Everest.

There is nothing more heart-breaking than to return to a favourite location – say, the Vale of Kashmir, which I visited in 1978 and again in 1986 and again in 1996 – only to see the hill-sides cleared of timber, the lakes half-drained and the town overrun either by soldiers or tourists, of which we were mere harbingers. For the tourist, ever since the time of the railways and Thomas Cook in the 1840s, and possibly even earlier, has only one means of communicating with the places and people he burdens with his visit. Money is to the tourist what questions were to Herodotus, verse to Goethe and the rifle to H. M. Stanley. The tourist has not time to master the language of the country he visits, let alone its monuments of thought or architecture, but he can, with difficulty, master its money and he uses it to buy things which, consumed there or carried home, give him the impression he has experienced a foreign land; although, all the while, he secretly believes his own money at home to be privileged and natural and all others to be departures from it, as all languages from his mother tongue. Tourism, therefore, is the Romantic excursion at retail, *Harzreise macht Spass!* (It's fun to travel in the Harz!) Not surprisingly, tourism alters a landscape as comprehensively as open-cast mining.

The case is most clear in America, for we know already from Las Casas, Montaigne and Locke that the American hemisphere was a sort of Eden, to which the Europeans introduced the serpent money. The first school of Romantic landscape painting in the United States is associated with the Hudson River in New York, which seemed to the open-air painters of the 1820s and 1830s to be sufficiently like the Rhine to merit Romantic depiction. That it was very much grander and more beautiful than its counterpart in Europe was not seen as too great an impediment. In those days, Europe was the source of authentic Romantic sentiment: indeed, even now, the Hudson's banks are still littered with the *Schlösser* of forgotten millionaires, while the small town where for a while I kept a $500 Dodge Aspen, subsiding imperceptibly onto its four punctured tyres, is even named Rhinecliff.

In the most thrilling of the pictures of the Hudson River School, *Kaaterskill Falls*, painted by Thomas Cole in 1826, right in the middle of the canvas, too small to be distinguished as an individual or to display anything more than the immense size of the falls, is an American native. Thirty years later, in George Inness' *The Lackawanna Valley*, the redskin has been replaced by a railway train: one could not hope to have the serpent's introduction more literally depicted. The cut trees that litter the front of the picture, which was commissioned by the Delaware, Lackawanna and Western Railroad, convey not regret but triumph: there is not a trace of irony. Those painters who do not wish to portray money must go west, south and north: to the Rockies, Sierras and the Rio Grande, to Venezuela or Cotopaxi, or finally, as in one or two masterpieces of Frederick E. Church, to the polar regions.

What these views have in common – and have in common even

with the photographs of Ansel Adams – is a certain inaccessibility: not in the literal sense, for the artist is literally there, in his sun-hat, pocket-book bulging with dollars, as in Asher B. Durand's 1849 portrait of Cole with the poet William Cullen Bryant at the Falls, *Kindred Spirits*, in the New York Public Library; but in the sense that there is in these views something internally unattainable, which is, in the beautiful English of Simmel's translators, 'a promise that is never fully kept and an entity that responds to our most passionate devotion with a faint resistance and strangeness.'[8] For they are seen through a veil of money, which makes us desire them while simultaneously repelling us, like the chador worn by my girl students when I was a teacher in Isfahan. All attempts to pierce the veil are doomed. Press too close to nature, examine it too long, survey it, set novels in it, photograph it, and its Romantic essence evaporates like the God of the cathedral, leaving just a husk, good for nothing then but to be cast off like a worn-out shirt, thrown to the world of money for its more brutish exercises: mining, sub-divisions, tourism or even – as in the famous *Siebengebirge* on the original or European Rhine – raucous *thés-dansants* where elderly Dutch couples revolve with glacial slowness in a stupor of married affection, arthritis and drink.

In the United States, where the worship of nature coincided with the colonisation of a vast continent, whole territories were set aside for Romantic contemplation: the Grand Canyon, Yosemite, part of the Alaska North Slope. I have loved these national parks, which seem to express the magnanimity of a nation worthy of its beautiful domicile; and yet with their rangers and rustic picnic architecture and bizarre regulations, they are as artificial – shaped by money – as the Empire State Building. And all will be paved over, if not perhaps in our lifetimes. For the sensation of beauty cannot survive in the age of money: for any beauty must be exploited, reproduced a million million times by every medium open to commercial ingenuity, till one can only cover one's eyes and stop one's ears. The sole aesthetic sensation of modernity is nausea: permanent, lethal nausea.

These contradictions lie at the heart of the great sadness of our civilisation: that by using money, we convert our world into it. Humanity is, to use a word that will assume an importance in the second half of this chapter, estranged by money from its natural habitat, without any hope of appeal. We are also – and here the Romantic movement loses its self-control and, like the Don himself, becomes violent – estranged by money from one another. It is this sense of a community of people atomised by money, where all human relations are disrupted by money, that is the second great Romantic legacy to our age and we will now address it. Its roots lay in the poets – Shelley and Schiller, above all, and through them in Shakespeare and the antique writers – but were transplanted to the stony field of German philosophy. The story is embodied for us in the ghastly figures of Karl and Jenny Marx.

*

If human misery could be said to leave a deposit, if all suffering were materially commemorated, then one could not walk down Dean Street in the Soho district of London except in tears. For on the eastern side of the street, above an Italian restaurant, at No. 28, is the wretched apartment in which Karl and Jenny Marx lived and suffered. Their sorrow seems to beat in gusts in the street.

Let us select one moment, in the wet spring of 1852, which Jenny Marx remembered years later as the essence of her devastated life. It is the evening of April 14. The flat has two rooms, and costs £22 per annum. All the surviving members of the family – Karl, Jenny and their daughters, Jenny Eleanor, Jenny Caroline and Jenny Laura – are seated together in the front room; in the back room is the body of a child. In the memoir she made for her daughters in 1865, *Brief Outlines of an Adventurous Life*, Jenny Marx wrote:

> At Easter, 1852, our poor little Franziska fell ill with severe bronchitis. For three days the poor child wrestled with death. She suffered much. Her little lifeless body rested in the small back room; we wandered out into the front room, and when night fell we made our beds on the floor, and the three living children lay with us, and we wept for the little angel who lay cold and lifeless next door. The death of our beloved child took place at the time of our bitterest poverty. . . . With anguish in my heart I ran to a French *émigré* who lived near us and used to visit us. I begged him for help in our terrible need. He at once gave me £2 . . .

and with the money the small coffin was bought, and there my poor child now slumbers peacefully. She had no cradle when she came into the world, and for a long time she was refused a last resting-place.[9]

Jenny, who had been brought up in comfort in Germany, believed all her life that Jenny Franziska might have been saved with a little money for medicine or the sea-side: the little corpse in the back room embodies money more completely than anything else in this story. Marx's dead and bastard children seem to be manifestations of a desperate psychological disorder, as in a Strindberg play; and have their counterpart in a chaotic set of writings about money which tormented his adult life and which he not so much never completed as never really began. They are sketches for a great compendium or philosophy of money which, like all obsessive projects, gains with time not in wisdom but in bitterness: from the Paris manuscripts of 1844 to the London manuscript of 1857 known as the *Grundrisse*, from the anti-Semitic tract of 1843–44 called the *Judenfrage* to *Capital* itself, there is a progressive darkening of tone and distortion of emotion. It is only on the last page of the manuscript of the last volume of *Capital* that Marx attempts to explain his notion of social class: it is as if the New Testament ended with the words: Now, by God we mean . . .

These writings simply cannot be understood without a notion of the family's relations with money. As Marx himself wrote to Engels in 1859: 'I do not think anyone has ever written about money who was so lacking in it.' Marx was not simply a masculine head thinking thoughts, but a man surrounded by skimping women and generous men. We must be aware of the Argyll silver, the banknotes sent by Engels, the legacies and begging letters and imaginary stock-market coups, the beer-sprees and singing-lessons for the girls, taking as our text the complaint of his mother that Marx remembered on his birthday in 1868: 'It's a pity little Karl didn't make some capital, instead of [just writing about it].'[10] For there was no economical reason why the Marxes were so short of money. Jenny was from the comfortable small German nobility, and Karl's uncle founded the famous Dutch electric company, Philips, which still exists and prospers. Even in the worst years at Dean Street, their income was probably never less than £200 a year, or nine times their rent, a multiple most city-dwellers would envy: for comparison, a bank clerk in those days earned £75 a year and a domestic servant less than £20. They could have lived like bourgeois and often wanted to.

Karl was born in 1818 in Trier, a handsome old Roman town on the Rhine, the son of a lawyer, who was himself descended from a long line of rabbis. Father Heinrich Marx had converted to Christianity to preserve his position in the Prussian regime that took over the Rhineland after Waterloo: he was baptised the year before Karl was born. His wife, Henrietta Pressburg, was of a Dutch family and seems to have remained more Jewish in attitudes and practices; but she, too, was baptised in 1825.

Some Jewish scholars have liked to discern a residual Judaism in Karl, or at least a vestigial Jewish self-consciousness. They see him as a sort of secular rabbi, poring over old commentaries: why bother oneself with worrying about upkeep, when life is only given us to learn the Talmud? Some Christians, notably R. H. Tawney, portray him instead as the last of the medieval Schoolmen, who had somehow slept through three centuries of monetary enlightenment.[11] The poet Marcel Herwegh, with whom Marx quarrelled in his characteristic way, said Karl 'would have been the perfect incarnation of the last Scholastic. A tireless worker and great savant, he knew the world more in theory than in practice.'[12]

I believe the contradiction is the essence of Marx's biography and thoughts: else why did he marry a Christian and write the *Judenfrage*? His Jewishness is both the Alp or historical succubus that sits on the breast of the living, as in the famous opening of *The Eighteenth Brumaire of Louis Bonaparte*, and also the source of that unbearable sense of loss that was later to inhabit his concept of estrangement. In one of his very earliest writings, an essay at the Friedrich-Wilhelm Gymnasium at Trier on the subject of a passage in St John's Gospel,[13] he speaks of man 'as the unique being in nature whose purpose is not fulfilled,' for man is for ever in an agony of yearning for union with God.[14]

From his father, he learned to read Voltaire and Racine, works of the Enlightenment, but early in youth he came under the influence of a Prussian official, Ludwig von Westfalen, who read him Homer and Shakespeare, interested him in the Romantic drama, and walked with him in the woods. Ludwig's father had married a Jacobite refugee from Scotland, Jeanie Wishart, who communicated – mediated or *vermittelte* in Hegelian language – pieces of Scottish folklore: the nick-name Jeanie or Jenny, which Marx's wife and daughters all bore; a remote kinship to the Dukes of Argyll, of which Karl was inordinately proud; and a silver tea service engraved with the arms of the Campbells of Argyll, which gleams intermittently through the Marx biography, as it passes into and out of money at pawnshops in Paris, Brussels and London. Karl does not seem to have been aware that he was kin, by way of his wife and Jean Campbell, to great Law himself; and, alas, that sensational genealogical discovery of mine has never excited my Marxian acquaintances.

The Rhineland of Karl Marx's youth was backward almost beyond description. It was barely touched by manufacturing capital, and in some districts had barely shaken off serfdom. We should not imagine an England or Lowland Scotland, where monetary habits of thought are already so entrenched as to appear self-evident, or even a France, where Balzac has just discovered money and set himself up as the artistic cashier of the bourgeois monarchy. The great event or rather process in Germany for his and our purposes occurs in the territory of philosophy, where the empire of Hegel, which had been supreme throughout the German-speaking lands in the 1820s, had disintegrated on his death more comprehensively than that of Alexander the Great. Hegel's successors, known as the Young Hegelians, squabbled over the provinces of the mind as once the Diadochoi over Syria and Egypt; and it was Marx's doomed ambition to try to restore that shattered dominion.

Hegel's thought was itself an attempt to organise the space left empty by the evaporation of religious faith. At its heart is a view of history – that is, the story of human society – that is not an account of the unfurling of God's grace in the world; or even, as many people felt even then, of one damn thing after another; and certainly not the uniform repetition of events according to laws patterned on those of the physical sciences of the seventeenth century, as the economists pretended; but as a *process*, an intelligible process by which human potentiality or freedom is made progressively actual.

This potential he called spirit or *Geist*, a word that has caused many students of Hegel – and, heaven knows, they are not a numerous band – to dismiss the whole thing as a sort of mumbo-jumbo. In reality, the fault – if it has one – is the fault of much German thought, which is its excessive rationality: we are whisked from *a* to *z* by way of *m* and *p* in a high-powered logical vehicle in which both clarity and common sense must sit, terrified and enraged, in the back.

At the foundation of Hegel's view of history is Christianity, filtered through Kant and Lessing and the economic philosophers of Scotland, notably Sir James Steuart, whose fame, as we have seen, was destroyed by the anti-Jacobite prejudices of Smith and Hume. But it is in Schiller, in his prose and verse, that we must look for the depiction of that concept of alienation that so captivated the Young Hegelians, and particularly Karl Marx. In the fifth and sixth letters of Schiller's *Über die ästhätische Erziehung des Menschen (On the Aesthetic Education of Man)*, which was published in 1795, we learn that civilisation, or rather the division of labour, has destroyed the antique wholeness of man, and opened a gulf between men and nature and within human beings themselves. In this fragmentary state, 'enjoyment is divorced from labour, the means from the end, the effort from the reward.' Man is reduced to a mere off-print or 'impression of his business and his knowledge.'[15] This faint and fragmentary personality is further inhibited by moral law and religion, which men persist in regarding as external to themselves and to which they ascribe an omnipotent authority. Those notions, pondered by Hegel and his successors, Ludwig Feuerbach and Moses Hess, develop into Marx's macabre, even Promethean attacks on money and religion. They are distilled in his famous notion of money as fetish: an object, which though merely an expression of human relations in society, has gained a secret dominion over the lives of men and women.

Most young men quarrel with their parents about money, for it appears to them to promise their emancipation from their elders: that it is a sort of apartment they can inhabit alone. From Karl's letters so painstakingly and, as it were, belatedly assembled in the *Marx-Engels Gesamtausgabe*, one hears a grim rumble of resentment over money at Henrietta Marx. In 1836, Karl became engaged to

Jenny, the belle of Trier society, and passed under Caroline Westfalen's control. The young people, who seem to have been very fond of each other, married in 1842 and, after an improvident honeymoon in Switzerland, they moved to the little Rhineland spa town of Bad Kreuznach, where Karl read in the Gymnasium library and attempted to make his reckoning with Hegel, Germany and his Jewishness. He wrote two articles that appeared, after his move to Paris at the end of 1843, in a short-lived journal he co-edited called the *Deutsch-französische Jahrbücher* (*Franco-German Annual*).

The first of these, 'Contribution to the Critique of Hegel's Philosophy of Right: Introduction,' is very brilliant. It shows Marx at his most polemical and unfair: for his attack on Hegel – or critique, a word much in vogue with the Young Hegelians – distorts Hegel rather than, as Marx claimed, 'sets him on his feet again.' Hegel's fault, it seems, is to claim a universality to ideas that arise only in particular conditions and eras. Hegel starts, like Plato, from a standpoint of law and the state, whereas those seem to Marx to be merely expressions of the material conditions of life at any particular time and place. History, for Marx, is not a battleground of incarnate ideas but of warring social classes. Much more interesting for our purposes is the essay that appeared in the same and only double volume of the *Annual* in February 1844, called 'On the Jewish Question.' This text has always embarrassed the Marxians, for a question demands an answer and we have seen, most particularly in the banknotes of Theresienstadt, abominable answers. But anti-Semitism is a stage in the history of money, even among those of Jewish inheritance, and it would be foolish to avert our eyes from it out of propriety or squeamishness.

The question in question at Bad Kreuznach appeared to be a political one. Since 1816, Jews under Prussian rule had not enjoyed full civil rights and the question was whether they should be accorded them or deprived of those rights they had. In reality, it was a private philosophical quarrel with two other Young Hegelians: Bruno Bauer, whose 'Die Judenfrage' had appeared at Brunswick in 1843, and Moses Hess, who had submitted an article on the philosophy of money, 'Über das Geldwesen,' to the *Annual*, which Marx felt free to plunder. Marx invites his reader to forget the political situation in the Rhineland for the moment and instead consider what social element stood in the way of Jewish emancipation; and that element is not Judaism or Jewish manners or customs – for how could it be, one senses, when the author is baptised – but money. Already the tone is so disagreeable that one yearns for the dignity and restraint of Shylock:

> What is the profane basis of Judaism? *Practical* need, *self-interest.* What is the worldly cult of the Jew? *Huckstering.* What is his worldly God? *Money.*[16]

And what is money? It is, as religion was for Feuerbach, 'the supreme practical expression of human self-estrangement':

> Money is the jealous god of Israel, beside which no other god may exist. Money abases all the gods of mankind and changes them into commodities. Money is the universal self-sufficient value of all things. It has, therefore, deprived the whole world, both the human world and nature, of their own proper value. Money is the alienated essence of man's work and existence; this essence dominates him and he worships it.
>
> The god of the Jews has been secularised and has become the god of the world. The bill of exchange is the real god of the Jew. His god is only an illusory bill of exchange.
>
> The mode of perceiving nature, under the rule of private property and money, is a real contempt, and a practical degradation, of nature.[17]

In other words, and no doubt others are called for, money, which was invented to convey human wishes, has acquired independent status and is seen by men and women not as a conveniency to satisfy common human wants but as an objective or free-standing institution possessing eternal and impersonal authority. Or, to revert to Marx's language to make the point as clear as it will ever be to anglophone readers:

> Just as man, so long as he is engrossed in religion, can only objectify his essence by an *alien* and fantastic being; so under the sway of egoistic need, he can only affirm himself and produce objects in practice by subordinating his products and his own activity to the domination of an alien entity, and by attributing to them the significance of that alien entity, money.[18]

If money could be but abolished, then so would the Jew be abolished; and the emancipation of humanity from its fetishes could begin.

Having made up his mind, Marx now resolved to buttress his thoughts with reading; and throughout the spring of 1844, in the apartment he shared with other German exiles in the Rue Vaneau, while Jenny and the baby Jennychen were visiting in Trier, Marx buried himself in the political economists: Smith, Ricardo, James Mill, McCulloch, Say, Sismondi. His co-editor of the *Annual*, Ruge, with whom he naturally quarrelled, left a description of this chaotic self-education in a letter to Feuerbach: 'He works with uncommon intensity, but finishes nothing, breaks off completely and plunges back into a limitless ocean of books. With his scholarly temperament he belongs wholly to the German world, but his revolutionary attitudes exclude him from it. . . . Irritable and bad-tempered, particularly when he works himself sick and has not been to bed for three, even four, nights on end.'[19] From them he derived not only a confirmation of his material view of history – as a battlefield not of incarnate ideas but of economic interests – but also a cynicism: not in the sense we find in Balzac, that lurking behind all action is a heap of coins, but in a radical scepticism about society that goes back to Diogenes and forward to the shattering novels of Dostoyevsky.

Marx was expelled from Paris, after pressure from the Prussian government, at the beginning of 1845, but not before he had gained from that city the third element of his personality: to German idealist philosophy and Anglo-Scots political economy he added French revolutionary socialism. Like many of his own and the generation before, Marx was haunted by the failure of the great French revolution; and later wrote, in the most beautiful passages in his masterpiece, *The Eighteenth Brumaire of Louis Bonaparte*, that all attempts to carry forward its programme had degenerated into mere play-acting. Certainly, the estates as legal social classes had been abolished and all Frenchmen were equal before the law; but distinctions of wealth remained as somehow *natural*, as the irreducible residue of inequality, like differences of height or strength or sex. The monetary terror of the *assignats* had failed as much as the Terror of the Place de la Révolution. The livre had been restored in the form of the Germinal franc as a symbol of property rights and the means of transferring them. Meanwhile, Paris, once the capital of revolution, had become the capital of reaction, symbolised in Guizot's cry to the French voters, '*Enrichissez-vous!*', and Balzac's gluttonous tales of financial skullduggery and whoredom.

The best French mind of the 1840s, Pierre-Joseph Proudhon, whom Marx recognised as a substantial rival (and attempted to demolish in a disagreeable pamphlet called *The Misery of Philosophy*), accepted the eighteenth-century principle that property, in the sense of the free disposal of the fruits of labour, was the essence of liberty: his quarrel was with the tax that owners of property, especially money, imposed on its users through interest, discount, rent, sinecures and so on. For Proudhon, the productivity of money was merely one of those layers, like subordination to the state, that came between human beings and reality, and its abolition would abolish all authority (except, as we have seen, of men over women). 'We've chased out our kings, but royalty still exists in its most material and abstract expression: the royalty of money.'[20] A more practical man than Marx, Proudhon was a delegate to the assembly in the June days of 1848, and sought to found a bank which would short-circuit money since it would exchange goods only for goods. The bank failed to raise its subscription.

Out of Marx's first Parisian residence, there survives a set of notes and excerpts, which were discovered in Holland and published in 1932 by the Soviet scholar David Ryazanov (who was shot by Stalin for his pains). Christened by the Soviet Institute of Marxism-Leninism *Economic and Philosophic Manuscripts of 1844*, the *Pariser Manuskripte* were widely read in Germany after the war and left a profound impression on the generation that reached its political maturity in Berlin and the West German cities in 1968. They are early drafts, of course, of the great compendium to out-Hegel Hegel that survives in its most lengthy form in *Capital*. Their focus is money rather than, as in the later works, its anterior or underlying reality which Marx thought of as alienated or stolen labour. Yet they preserve, in the freshest and most affectionate form, the kernel of Marx's view of society, which is close to that of Proudhon: that a social system that evaluated men and women in terms of money and made morality a function of credit was unworthy of the human being. Society is quite simply deranged:

Private property has made us so stupid and partial that an object is only *ours* when we have it, when it exists for us as capital or when it is directly eaten, drunk, worn, inhabited, etc., in short *utilised* in some way. . . . All the physical and intellectual senses have been replaced by . . . the sense of *having*.[21]

Or from the same manuscript, numbered 3 by the editors

Man becomes increasingly poor as a man; he has increasing need of *money* in order to take possession of a hostile nature; and the power of his *money* diminishes exactly in inverse proportion to the increase in production: in other words, *money* increases his neediness. The need for money is therefore the real need created by the modern economic system, and the only need which it creates. The *quantity* of money becomes increasingly its sole important attribute. Just as it reduces every entity to an abstraction, so it reduces itself in its own development to a *quantitative* entity. Excess and immoderation become its true standard. The expansion of production and of needs becomes an *ingenious* and always *calculating* subservience to inhuman, depraved, unnatural and *imaginary* appetites. Private property does not know how to change crude need into *human* need; its *idealism* is *fantasy*, *caprice* and *fancy*.[22]

In these manuscripts, one hears, not for the last time from Marx, the authentic voice of the *Quixote*: that the world of money is a phantasmagoria, and one must ride out to break lances with it, astride the bony charger of philosophy and helmed with political economy (though the helmet appears, to the philistines, to be a barber's basin).

For what else was a man to do: 'turn his back on human misery, look out for his own skin, turn into a beast?'[23] Draw a pension from Guizot like Heine, or milk the blood and sweat of one hundred and fifty serfs on his wife's estate in the Ukraine like Balzac? Marx's course was disastrous: eventually he withdrew into books, abandoned revolutionary activity, went on beer-crawls, watched his children die, screwed the help, chased legacies, and set an example of violence in debate that still haunts our century. For all the beauty of her nature, Jenny Marx gave in to a sour and angry old age. The girls made terrible marriages or liaisons and two of them committed suicide. And what was it all for? When Karl Marx tries to give us his utopia (which is, as we have seen, an ideal society without money), it is insipid; or rather does not pass beyond the comforts of a country gentleman, a sort of premature Tolstoy:

> In communist society, where nobody has one exclusive sphere of activity but each can become accomplished in any branch he wishes, society regulates the general production and thus makes it possible for me to do one thing today and another tomorrow, to hunt in the morning, fish in the afternoon, rear cattle in the evening, criticise after dinner, just as I have a mind, without ever becoming hunter, fisherman, herdsman or critic.[24]

Beside that, *Rob Roy* is sophistication itself.

At moments like those, one senses a great hole in Marx's personality: that he never succeeded, either in his life or in his writings, in stemming that wound to his nature that is commemorated for him by money. For the Marxians, Marx chose to be poor and his life is a nineteenth-century life of Christ: for only the poor, delivered without protection to the blasts of reality, can truly understand the world: others can only describe it. I am not sure. I would have loved Marx and Freud to have conversed, as later Freud and Mahler in a famous ambulatory psycho-analysis in the town of Leiden in Holland. For Freud was also shaped by the Hegelian tradition: he saw religion as a projection of the family relations of early childhood, but barely attempted to advance the analysis to religion's successor, money. Freud's thoughts on money are mere sketches. From his patients, dreams, folklore and fairy-tales, he rooted some attitudes to money in the early development of the child, in which money and bodily functions come to be entwined, sometimes inextricably so; but we long to learn more of the psychological process.[25]

With respect to Freud, I believe he became ensnared in that diabolical feature that money shares with religion: that it is both the game and the reward, the illness and the palliative. In a manual of 1913, *On Beginning the Treatment (Further Recommendations on the Technique of Psycho-Analysis)*, he reveals a level of self-awareness that would have been reprehensible in the stupidest Viennese bourgeois:

The next point that must be decided at the beginning of the treatment is the one of money, of the doctor's fee. An analyst does not dispute that money is to be regarded in the first instance as a medium for self-preservation and for obtaining power; but he maintains that, besides, powerful sexual factors are involved in the value set upon it. He can point out that money matters are treated by civilized people in the same way as sexual matters – with the same inconsistency, prudishness and hypocrisy. The analyst is therefore determined from the first not to fall in with this attitude, but, in his dealings with his patients, to treat of money matters with the same matter-of-course frankness to which he wishes to educate them in things relating to sexual life. . . . Ordinary good sense cautions him, furthermore, not to allow large sums of money to accumulate, but to ask for payment at fairly short regular intervals – monthly, perhaps.[26]

In other words, money must somehow be kept out of the arena in which analyst and patient conduct their struggle: for otherwise, *meine Damen und Herren*, we shall all starve! As a programme for life in Vienna and London, it was unimpeachable; and that is why the Freuds were happy and successful and the Marxes were not.

Marx was survived into our century by the Marxists, who made disastrous attempts to establish social systems on foundations other than money: by Lenin, Guevara at the Central Bank of Cuba and, if they can be called Marxists, the Khmer Rouge. He was also survived by a son. Henry Frederick Demuth, whose mother was not Jenny but her maid, Helene Demuth, was born in the most terrible period at Dean Street, in June 1851. He was quickly foisted onto Engels, but as that good man lay dying in 1895, he wrote down on a slate for Eleanor (Tussy) to read: Marx was the father. Freddy lived as an engineering worker in Hackney and Stoke Newington, and survived into the era of the Soviet Union and a powerful British socialist party. We have a photograph of him on a workmen's outing, and also a set of letters to him from Eleanor that even now still oppress the heart under their dead weight of suffering and kindness. Though only one of his letters survives, one senses in hers not just his generosity – he lent Tussy's worthless common-law husband, Edward Aveling, money from his wages – but his loyalty. But the

light is going out for her. 'I don't think you and I have been
particularly bad people – and yet, dear Freddy, it really seems as
though we are being punished.' Aveling needs expensive hospital
treatment, and Eleanor's spirit is running out with her money: on
February 10, 1898, she writes to Freddy in terms as clear as she
dares: 'It's all coming down to a single point where I must give out
even the little that remains to me. Dear Freddy, don't blame me.'
On March 31, 1898, she surrendered to the enemy that had killed
her whole family, drinking off a glass of prussic acid.[27]

★

Before we leave this fruitful epoch, let us consider one more
historical figure, whose relations with money were as disturbed as
Marx's, but whose tactics could not have been more different. We
are back, to our delight, in Paris, capital of the nineteenth century,
in 1844. While Marx is reading his economists, and Balzac is juggling
tarts and *rentes* in *Cousine Bette*, another man is pacing the hot streets,
in those last days before they are bust open by cod-imperial
Boulevards, seeking out poems that have been lost like dropped
coins. Baudelaire brings to the nineteenth-century city – that arena
of money where even time must be paid for – to the prostitutes and
businessmen and ragpickers, to the swirling crowds of shoppers and
clerks, the lyricism his predecessors had reserved for skylarks and
shepherdesses. Watteau's island of love is just an impotent dream of
money:

> *C'est Cythère,*
> *Nous dit on, un pays fameux dans les chansons,*
> *Eldorado banal de tous les vieux garçons.*[28]

[It's Cythera, they say, a land celebrated in song: the everyday Eldorado
of all the old farts.]

All the great writers of the nineteenth century address money.
For most of them, it is a device to disrupt or resolve the narrative,
often over great intervals of distance or time: the bill of exchange is
to the nineteenth-century novel what the foundling was to the
eighteenth. It is also used for social description, either as slang or
under the mistaken impression that money prices and values are

somehow eternal. The novels of Balzac, Zola and most of the English writers, even at times Kipling, are the counterpart of gold-standard economics: they reveal a child-like faith in money and fixed-interest investment. The worst example is the opening of *Père Goriot*, where Balzac tires of describing the furniture of the boarding-house by social category and merely gives its price in francs (which, of course, makes the passage utterly meaningless to us); the central section of Turgenev's *Fathers and Sons* likewise disappears. But the very greatest novels of the epoch – *Great Expectations, The Wings of the Dove, Oblomov,* certain volumes of Proust and *Crime and Punishment* – use money not as the contingent or unpredictable in the narrative machine but as the machine itself, the uncontrollable force that drives society in a headlong flight: or, to speak in terms of grammar for a moment, not as substantive and adjective, but as verb. Dostoyevsky, above all, had the Russian ability to follow an argument into the furthest reaches of delusion and pain. The question that Pushkin, Chateaubriand and Balzac merely toyed with – what if one killed a horrid and wicked old lady for her money? worthless sex, worthless person, valuable thing? – he answered in *Crime and Punishment* for all time. The answer is, by the way: don't even think of it!

Yet Baudelaire is in a class of his own. His poetic personality is unstable: cynic, bad boy, drunkard, satanist. He wrote some bad lines. Yet there are lines in his verse where he seems to break through the appearances of money to a sort of core reality, and one hears, for the last time, the authentic note of antiquity.

Baudelaire was himself infantilised by money. His stepfather charged him for his upbringing and he was so improvident that he was made a ward of the court. Baudelaire's allowance was doled out to him by a notary in Neuilly, M. Ancelle, a kind man whom he loathed. Baudelaire could, like Marx, have been a lawyer, but he chose instead to be a pauper so that he might for ever hang on his mother's apron-strings, punishing himself and her. A letter he wrote to her on December 26, 1853, reveals the nature of that reciprocal torment:

> I know how to stuff two shirts under my trousers and torn coat that lets in the wind, and I am so experienced in using straw or

even paper to plug up the holes in my shoes that moral suffering is almost the only suffering I perceive as suffering. However, I must admit that I have reached the point where I don't make any sudden movements or walk much because I fear that I might tear my clothes even more.[29]

His notebooks are littered with deranged flow-of-funds statements, in which the uses of cash are clear enough – *Moi 300 Maman 300 Jeanne 300* – but the sources are books that he must have known he could not write and probably couldn't be written. At one point, he makes a list of his friends. They are all prostitutes.

All critics have noted Baudelaire's incompetence with money. Proust, a very good critic indeed, noted something else: that there were, particularly in the *Tableaux de Paris*, phrases of time that belonged with the city but were somehow untouched by it. In them, it seems to me, time is not a money-value – a matter of monthly rent, annual interest, daily wage, hourly fee and so on – but an aspect or sample of eternity.

> *Le monde de Baudelaire est un étrange sectionnement du temps où seuls de rares jours notables apparaissent; ce qui explique les fréquentes expressions telles que 'si quelque soir . . .'*[30]

> [Baudelaire's world is a curious compartmentalisation of time where only rare and notable days make an appearance. That explains such frequent expressions as 'if one evening . . .']

Proust felt those poems were the swan song of the antique spirit, and it would be presumptuous for us to disagree. For in them, Baudelaire seems to have pierced the veil of money – in all its restlessness and relativity – to something permanent, which for want of a better word we would call beauty. Proust selected some lines from the poem 'Les Petites Vieilles' ('The Bag-Ladies') as marking the extreme outer limit of human expression: *il semble impossible d'aller au delà* (it seems impossible to go beyond this).[31] Beyond it, if we may extend Proust's argument by an appeal to Longinus, lies only the perfection of sublimity which is not words but silence: the silence of Ajax in the underworld.

In those lines from 'Les Petites Vieilles' are distilled phenomena, which are reborn in the verse as intense physical sensations. Dust and air, water, warmth, light, sound, colour, burst from the oompahing of a military band in a public garden. The question that so haunted his age – whatever happened to the heroism of 1789? – Baudelaire answers without effort. It is here, listening to the band in the square. Mirabeau and Valmy and Napoleon I, indeed the whole history of France, are just formalities of that beauty. For poetry, the perfection of language, has a special quality, which is this: it is beyond money and all its entanglements. It costs nothing to write or read and remember, belongs to everybody, can't be sold and lasts for ever: it is, in Gottfried Benn's lovely phrase, 'the unremunerated labour of the spirit.'[32]

> *un de ces concerts, riches de cuivre,*
> *Dont les soldats parfois inondent nos jardins,*
> *Et qui, dans ces soirs d'or où l'on se sent revivre*
> *Versent quelque héroïsme au coeur des citadins.*[33]

9

The Sheet of Glass

Buchan's . . . petition is perfectly hopeless.
Lord Deas

The crash of the City of Glasgow Bank, which closed its doors on
October 2, 1878, was the greatest bank failure in the history of the
United Kingdom, and destroyed more than a tenth of Scotland's
banking capital. A committee of investigators entered the bank's
premises in Virginia Street, Glasgow, and reported on October 19
that the bank's liabilities – what it owed – exceeded its assets – what
it owned – by the sum of £6,213,313 17s. It is not possible to
express that debt in the money of today. I can only say that in
October 1878 a cook in a Scots country household was fairly happy
to earn £14 a year, a steerage passage from Glasgow to New York
cost £6 6s and a bottle of vintage Bollinger champagne cost 5s: not
that much champagne was drunk that autumn and winter in the
Lowlands of Scotland.

In those days, a shareholder in almost all the British joint-stock
banks, even if he were merely trustee of the shares, was exposed
to unlimited liability: that is, he or she risked not just the value of
the shares but also – as at the Lloyd's insurance market in London
today – a proportional share of any losses made by the company up
to the limit of his or her wealth. The liquidators needed to find six
million pounds to make good the depositors and the holders of its
banknotes; and the only place for them to go was the 1,249
shareholders or partners, mostly small or middling people, in
Glasgow, Edinburgh, Aberdeen and the Borders. On October 25,
the liquidators made a first call on all shareholders of £500 per £100
nominal share.

There is in the town of Peebles, at the west end of the High Street by the bridge over the Eddleston Water, a house which is known to this day as Bank House. On the sealing-wax-red door, there is a brass plate, so polished with Brasso over the last hundred and thirty years that it is quite illegible; but according to my father, William Buchan, who saw it as a child in the 1920s, it used to read: *Mr Buchan, Writer*. That was John Buchan, grandfather of another writer, also John Buchan, and my great-great-grandfather. He was not a writer in the general sense – the only text I've discovered from his pen is a letter in the *Peebles Advertiser and County Newspaper* – but a writer to the signet, that is what the English call a solicitor. He was also a banker of sorts, and trustee of the estate of one Robert Gibson, late cooper of Peebles, and that estate owned £540 nominal in City Bank stock. On October 25, 1878, the unfortunate Mr Buchan received a demand from the liquidators of the bank for the sum, payable in two instalments, of £2,700: the equivalent, for example, of the price of six of the new semi-detached villas in a half-acre of garden then springing up round Peebles or five years' revenue of the Royal Burgh itself.

Mr Buchan sued the liquidators to have his name struck from the list of paying shareholders or contributories. His case, which seems even to me to have been rather hastily assembled, was heard in the First Division of the Court of Session at Edinburgh on January 23, 1879, and treated as little more than a nuisance. It was dismissed with costs. His appeal to the House of Lords, which was heard on May 20, fared scarcely better. Later that year, under the influence of 'Buchan's case' among others, Parliament reformed the law, permitting limited liability to banking companies other than the Bank of England: that had the perverse effect of making banks even more irresponsible and, now that their deposits are de jure or de facto guaranteed by the state, they have become, with a handful of exceptions, institutional imbeciles that lose their capital once in every cycle of cheap and dear money. Anyway, it was all too late for Mr Buchan.

Mr Buchan paid his contribution, but it used him up and he died, by all accounts, a broken man. What interests me is not the legal story, not even the criminal trial of the City Bank's directors, one of the longest, most intricate and most spectacular ever to take place in

Scotland. My concern is the effect of the crash on a set of people with my name, and particularly the novelist John Buchan, who was born in 1875 into this gathering monetary storm. The events made a profound impression on him, causing him to pursue money while at the same time to treat it with the utmost suspicion. In his memoirs, *Memory Hold-the-Door*, published posthumously in 1940, John Buchan makes no mention of his family disaster and the best accounts are those of his sister Anna, also a novelist, and that of his son, William Buchan, who assembled from a failing family memory an accurate narrative.[1] Neither supplied details and I have gathered those from the contemporary law reports and newspaper articles.

★

The besetting problem of Scotland, for most of its recorded history, has been a shortage of money. By that, I don't mean that individual Scots are short, though many of them are, sometimes desperately so, like Burns, who wrote a sonnet on the back of a 1780 guinea note: 'cursed leaf! . . . For lack o' thee I've lost my lass'; but that for centuries there was never enough money for the commercial ambitions of the Scots. Money in the form of coin was first minted in the twelfth century, in the reign of King David I, but it tended not to stay: Scotland usually imported more things from England and the Continent than it exported, and the difference had to be paid in coin.

In the seventeenth century, when English and European commerce was expanding by leaps and bounds, the best Scots minds felt acutely the shortage of money both for payment and for what we'd now call working capital; and Scots promoters were at the forefront of banking schemes in both London and Edinburgh, culminating in the foundation of the Bank of England in 1694 and the Bank of Scotland in 1695, both of which issued paper notes to supplement coin. They were followed in 1727 by the Royal Bank of Scotland, established by Law's friend Islay, who was Walpole's agent in Scotland, and the Coutts' banker who had been bankrupted by Law's bear operations in London, George Middleton. Their attempts to break the 'Old Bank,' as the Bank of Scotland was known, through insinuations of Jacobitism and concerted runs on its bank-notes, were not successful and Old and New Banks morosely settled down into a commercial Scotland that could just about support both of them. They were joined in 1746 by the British Linen Company, which gradually transformed itself into a bank, and three banks in Glasgow to finance the tobacco trade from Virginia.

In Scotland, there was no monopoly of note issue, as there was for the Bank of England in London and its suburbs. All the Scots banks issued notes, which competed for the public's patronage. That favour depended on their security, which could either be bullion or coin, or loans to the government by way of the funds or to good borrowers. It depended also on the actions of competitors, often malicious, as in the spectacular 'banknote wars' of the 1750s.[2]

This private and competitive money, since it was not subject to the ambitions of politicians and the monopolistic fallibilities of central banks, has long intrigued libertarian philosophers, notably Hayek. Adam Smith was more practical. He reckoned in *The Wealth of Nations*[3] that of two million sterling circulating in Scotland, three-quarters was in banknotes issued by the Scots banks, and he concluded, and Sir Walter Scott, who needed to please his bank creditors, concurred that the banks had been an unqualified benefit to a poor but vigorous country.[4]

At the time of Scott's essay, Scotland was still far from being a money society: in 1833, for example, the estate of the McNab at Glendochart in Perthshire, by no means the wildest Highlands, returned an income reckoned at £1,300, of which £500 came in cheeses, bolls of oatmeal, beasts and chickens.[5] But by the time of our story, there were some 790 bank branches in Scotland with banknotes, deposits and other liabilities of £92 million.

The City of Glasgow Bank was established in Virginia Street in 1839 by a group of merchants to finance their trade, particularly with the New World. The bank survived a heavy run with the failure of the Western Bank in 1857, and by the summer of 1878 appeared to be in a very prosperous condition. In the balance-sheet drawn up in June of that year, its 133 branches showed assets of £11,892,593 11s 8d. That the balance-sheet had not undergone an external audit was not considered significant. The bank's £100 shares had risen in price to £240, and the directors announced a net profit of £140,095 12s 10d and a dividend of 12 per cent nominal or 5 per cent on the appreciated shares.

Five per cent does not sound a lavish return, but in the 1870s in Scotland there was no inflation. In fact, many prices were falling as a result of the expansion of trade through Glasgow, and holders of the government stock of the period – the so-called Consols – appeared to be content with a dividend of under 3 per cent. Admittedly, the City Bank shares were riskier, for they were not backed by the faith and credit of the United Kingdom and their dividends could only be paid out of profits; but the directors of the bank – Potter, Stewart, Stronach, Salmond, Taylor, Inglis, Wright – appeared to be sound men, of a certain age, severe and whiskery of face and sober of dress, pillars of their kirks and Masonic lodges. The livelihoods of widows and orphans appeared to be safe in their hands.

I have seen the register of shareholders as of July 1878, and though there are some big Glasgow holdings, most of the partners are what Benjamin Franklin used to call the 'middling people.' Indeed, the register is a sort of snapshot of middle Scotland. There are ministers, farmers, tax men, bakers, feuars (tenant farmers), calico printers, collectors of customs, builders, drapers, artists, portioners, grocers, clothiers, tobacconists, overseers, yarn agents, shoemakers, commercial clerks, curriers, surgeons, dyers, inspectors of the poor, fleshers, carvers, tanners, cattle salesmen, cashiers, house factors. The *Peebles Advertiser* (October 12, 1878) later reckoned that among the shareholders were more than 200 spinsters, 154 married ladies, 98 executors and 76 trustees. In other words, almost half of the beneficial shareholders were women and children – classes that, in high Victorian social theory, were not supposed to be exposed to the risks and opportunities of the world of money.

Among those ladies was Janet Gibson, the widow of our Peebles cooper, Robert Gibson. Mr Gibson had died in 1854, and on November 2 of that year, John Bathgate, the trust's agent and town clerk of Peebles, wrote to the bank asking that the £540 in stock be transferred into the names of the three trustees, including Mr Buchan. Mr Buchan claimed in court that the transfer was done without his authority; but unfortunately there existed a minute of

1856, signed by him, and charging 8 shillings to the trust as fee for the transfer. The two other trustees died and, in 1872, Mr Buchan signed the trust's dividend warrant as 'sole surviving executor.' That was also presented in court.

What do I know of this man, the patriarch of my family? A locket in the possession of a relation contains tiny photographs thought to be of Mr and Mrs Buchan in early middle age. His shows a solid man with thick black hair and that look of frozen severity of most early photographic portraits. He was born in June 1811 near Stirling, and used to tell people in Peebles that his first memory was of the cannons fired to celebrate the victory at Waterloo. He was apprenticed to a Mr Monteith, a writer at Stirling, but in 1835 he came to Peebles as temporary clerk to the then Town Clerk, John Fotheringham, and stayed. When the City Bank opened its Peebles branch in 1840, he became its sub-agent under Walter Thorburn; and when it closed after the failure of the Western in 1857, he was successively agent of the Royal Bank and the Commercial Bank. He was also for some time procurator-fiscal (district attorney) and a member of the town council.

In 1844, he married Violet Henderson, and they had five children, starting with John, the father of the two novelists. This John, instead of following his father into business, was caught up in the religious revival sweeping Scotland at that time and became a minister of the Free Kirk. A virtuous and otherworldly man, though passionate in church politics, he was, I believe, the first in our family to publish a work of literature: a book of verse in the Wordsworthian tradition called *Tweedside Echoes and Moorland Musings*. His younger brother, Willie, did join his father, and the firm of J & W Buchan was founded in 1874. That firm is still in business, though no members of my family have been employed there since the death of great-uncle Walter at Bank House in 1953.

According to his obituarist in the *Peebles Advertiser*, Mr Buchan, writer, was remarkably quiet and retiring, very diligent, somewhat lacking in oratorical power, but nailing good with documents. 'He could prepare a deed,' the obituary said, 'in a manner which would have done credit to the most skilled conveyancer.'[6] He seems to have been a respectable man, perhaps a little narrow in outlook and not especially learned: his legal arguments, including an attempt to distinguish between his obligations as Gibson's executor and his trustee, were demolished in court. He may have been a little credulous, for one senses in his lawsuits a belief in justice, whereas what is treated in court is not justice but the law. In 1862, he had bought an estate in Midlothian, not realising the fragility of his prosperity. The Victorian novelists were fascinated by money's ability to telegraph, over immense distances, sudden prosperity or disaster. I now see why. For fifty miles away in Virginia Street in Glasgow, and nine thousand miles away in New Zealand, Providence was preparing Mr Buchan's destruction, a *Great Expectations* in reverse.

For though the City Bank paid its dividends and published its spanking balance-sheets each June, there actually wasn't anything there: the bank rested not on hard assets – holdings of bullion and coin, land, buildings, government stocks and loans on which interest was being paid – but on air. Its banknotes were among the most beautiful ever printed, always a warning signal: one thinks of the banknotes of nineteenth-century Bolivia. For in the course of the 1850s and 1860s, under Robert Salmond as managing director and then Alexander Stronach, the bank made large advances to the directors and also to three of their associates engaged in trade with India, Australia and New Zealand; and these loans were no longer paying interest. In 1865, when Robert Stronach took over from his brother as manager, he wrote to the board demanding that a committee be set up to run down these problem loans. Instead, hundreds of thousands of pounds more was lent in an attempt to refloat the businesses. Eventually, in despair, the bank took to speculating in pastoral property in the Antipodes, convinced that a quick rise in land values would extinguish the bad debts. By the summer of 1878, the City Bank had lent £5,379,000 to just three customers and those loans were posted in the balance-sheet not as non-performing loans but as 'government securities.' To keep itself in cash, it took to redeeming its bills with new bills, a money-market trick known to Baudelaire – that banker! – as 'battledore and shuttlecock.' What had begun probably as bad business judgement had degenerated into fraud.

In the course of 1878, rumours of the problems in Australia and New Zealand reached the City of London, and the City Bank found its bills were being refused, and was driven to desperate expedients to raise cash for the business. Eventually, on September 30, the directors finally faced reality and asked for funds from the Royal Bank of Scotland, which had helped when the Western failed in 1857. The Edinburgh banks demanded to see the books. On October 1, the directors resolved to stop trading. Just after 9 a.m. on October 2, Stronach sent out telegrams to the branches, one of which is preserved in the archive of the Bank of Scotland: 'Bank has stopped payment close your door at once & pay nothing whatever other banks will pay the notes.'[7]

As I've said, there was no longer a City Bank branch at Peebles, and the town had less anxiety for the depositors than for the shareholders, and particularly the trustees. According to an analysis by the *Peebles Advertiser*, the district had to find some £26,000 to meet the first call from the liquidators, and a fund was set up to aid them, with Mr Bathgate's brother as secretary.[8] By January, it had raised more than £700. As the scale of the disaster became apparent, there was rage at the directors of the bank. A magazine cartoon shows them carousing at the boardroom table, fishing into a great chest marked 'In Trust' which spills banknotes into the fetid air. Robert Bruce and John Knox, Scotland's national and ecclesiastical heroes, look on in stern despair. 'And has Scotland,' says the Bruce, leaning on his battle-axe, 'come to this after all our struggles and sufferings?' 'Fear not, my friend,' replies Knox, clasping his Bible, 'the Lord will yet judge them.'[9]

On October 13, a Sunday, while Mr Buchan was no doubt brooding on his misfortune in Peebles, a strange event occurred in the West Free Kirk at Pathhead, by Kirkcaldy in the Kingdom of Fife. The Rev. John Buchan stood up to preach his sermon. He chose as his text – and as I say this, I still can't quite believe it – the verse from St Matthew (6:19): 'Lay not up for yourselves treasures upon earth, where moth and rust doth corrupt, and where thieves break through and steal.' I quote from the sermon:

> No doubt money has a certain power. It can buy fine houses, rich raiment, dazzling equipages, luxuries, lands, and such like, adulation, cringing and flattery. But that is all it can do. What a man most needs money cannot buy. Not the love of one true human

friend, not peace of conscience, not a ray of God's sweet mercy, not a crumb of comfort in the hour of death. It cannot bring back our lost to us or robe our souls for the judgement seat. . . . Not to Israel alone but to Britain do these words apply. 'Oh this people have sinned a great sin and have made them gods of gold.' . . . Wealth is a perishable possession. . . . And what a melancholy proof we have had of this in the suspension of the City of Glasgow Bank. . . . Without warning multitudes awoke the other morning to find their treasure gone or rendered useless. On Monday the £100 shares sold at £236, on Tuesday the doors were closed. Can there be a more striking commentary on the perishable nature of wealth?

I cannot know how Mr Buchan responded to his son's homily when he read it, unctuously reproduced, in the newspaper.[10] Nor can I reconstruct their relationship. But I know it was the turning-point in a small-town family chronicle.

This was more than the sudden and irrevocable transfer of family authority across the generations. Something small and hard that day went out of my family, and something else, which, at a loss for words, I'll call fantastic, came in to replace it: the Rev. John standing still before the windows of town jewellers' shops, murmuring to his children: 'And the twelve gates were twelve pearls; every several gate was of one pearl, and the street of the city was pure gold, as it were transparent glass.'[11]

On Friday, January 31, 1879, at a quarter to six in the evening, after eleven days of gruelling evidence and Scotch hair-splitting, Potter and Stronach were found guilty as charged of fabricating balance-sheets; and the other five directors of uttering – that is, publishing – them. The prosecution had already made a tactical withdrawal from charges of embezzlement. You should not, the Lord Advocate, prosecuting, had told the jury in conclusion on the 28th, consider the seven dejected panels to be bad men. With a nice understanding of what we now call 'white-collar' crime, he said, 'I tell you that any offence such as this is impossible except to a man of good character. If a man is not of good repute . . . he would never be put in the important position of a director of a great bank.'[12] None the less, the sentences handed down on February 1 – eighteen months in gaol for Potter and Stronach, eight months for the others – were not well received in the West and the Borders. A person who signed himself 'Workingman' in the *Peebles Advertiser* recollected the recent case of a man invited to serve four months in prison for tossing a stone into the Tweed with the alleged intention of stunning a salmon.[13] There was, it seems, one law for the rich and one for the poor.

And another for the middling sort. Already on the 23rd, the First Division of the Court of Session at Edinburgh had thrown out 'Buchan's case:' Lord Deas described the petition as 'perfectly hopeless.'[14] At appeal before the House of Lords, on May 20, one of the learned lords, Lord Selborne, expressed sympathy for Mr Buchan's misfortune, for he had never enjoyed the income from the shares; but the law was the law and, as Lord Hatherley commented acidly: 'If he was not a shareholder, who could be?'[15] The Lord Chancellor, Lord Cairns, said Mr Buchan had had more than a quarter-century in which to sell the shares with their attendant risk. Outside, *The Economist* stepped ponderously to the lectern: 'The state of the law relating to trustees makes it gross imprudence for a man to be a trustee of shares in any enterprise of unlimited liability.'[16] Such was the judgement of the metropolis on a wee bit writer-body from Peebles.

Mr Buchan lived on, in poor health, for a while. Early on Monday morning, September 24, 1883, his son Willie entered his bedroom and thought at first that his father was asleep. 'Like many others,' the *Peebles Advertiser* wrote on the 29th, 'he was a sufferer from the collapse of the City of Glasgow Bank, and the failure of his health may fairly be ascribed to that calamity. His remains were conveyed to their last resting-place in Peebles Churchyard yesterday by a large company of mourners.'

For the effects of these events, we should consult not John Buchan's *Memory Hold-the-Door* but the reminiscences of his younger sister, Anna, who was born in 1877: for Anna's pre-occupations in *Unforgettable, Unforgotten* are domestic, while John's are of the open air; and in that they incorporate the division of artistic interest between the sexes in the small-town Scotland of that era. Anna says life at Pathhead and then in Glasgow was tight – 'indeed, after the failure of the Glasgow Bank there was little more than my father's modest stipend, but so well did Mother manage that the house was run with every comfort.'[17] The family employed, it seems, a cook and a nurse for the children, a domestic reinforcement we might all envy. Gradually, as John's earnings came into the household, the world Anna describes begins to expand.

There is something dizzying about the speed with which the Rev. John's children get down to work. John published his first book at the age of 18, and by the time he left Oxford University in 1899, he was a full-grown novelist and critic. He was called to the Bar and for a while concentrated on legal aspects of finance, commemorated in his pamphlet of 1905, *The Law Relating to the Taxation of Foreign Income*, a dry sort of title for what is now a book collector's Potosí; but for him everything, even income tax, was touched by the fantastical, the romantic and what the Scots used to call the 'canny' (supernatural). He wore all manner of professional disguises – colonial administrator, propagandist, spy, MP, viceroy, lord – without at any point inhabiting them; but from 1922 until 1936, every summer, John Buchan published a novel or a collection of stories. Anna, for all the inhibitions of her sex, was as energetic; and if he sold books in millions of copies, she sold them in hundreds of thousands. In their lives and emulation, one detects not just the traditional vigour of children 'born beneath the shadow of the steeple,' but the faint echo of the crash of the City of Glasgow bank.

For John, in particular, saw very clearly the imaginary foundations of his own and his country's prosperity. Civilisation was 'a line, a thread, a sheet of glass'; beyond it was the primordial bedlam.[18] His imperialism, like Kipling's, was a dream beginning to disintegrate into nightmare; and in his romances of the war years and after, his 'sheet of glass' caught the imagination of an anxious age. In time, it becomes a formula of masculine popular fiction in Britain, repeated by Fleming, le Carré and others right up to the later 1970s: what for John Buchan had been a call to arms, became a fantasy of victory and then a consolation for defeat. But for John Buchan, that fragile pane was not military and administrative, but moral: it is the Scotsmen advancing to their deaths at Loos, and also the phantom balance-sheets of the City of Glasgow Bank. In his last book, *Sick Heart River*, which was published after his death in 1940, in a story that begins on Wall Street and ends in the High Arctic, John gave his own version of his father's sermon on money at Pathhead.

And so, at last, this enterprise reveals its inner purpose. What began in Jeddah, Saudi Arabia, ends in southern Scotland. I step out from under the weight of all this money and claim my inheritance, which is the brass plaque on the sealing-wax-red door of a stone house in Peebles, Scotland. For it was that illegible plaque set me travelling through these countries and libraries and picture galleries: to find again the thread, frayed to a single twist, that connects me not only to my grandfather but to his father, the priest, and his father, the banker, and so on and on and back and back into the muddle of time and Scotland; to unravel the confusion of money and language; and to restore to that brass plaque the words worn away by one hundred and thirty years of polish and bad weather, so that they gleam for a year or two, as bright as money, in the precious sunshine of Scotland.

MR BUCHAN, WRITER.

10

S £ ¥ S £ ¥ S £ ¥ S £ ¥ S £ ¥ S £ ¥ S £ ¥ S £ ¥ S £ ¥ S £ ¥ S £ ¥ S £ ¥ S £ ¥ S £ ¥ S £ ¥ S £ ¥ S £ ¥

Mississippi Dreaming: Reprise

> Thus in the beginning all the World was AMERICA, and
> more so than that is now; for no such thing as MONEY
> was any where known.
>
> Locke

In Rock Creek Cemetery in Washington, D.C., in the deep shade
of an arch of holly trees, there is a tomb known as the Adams
Memorial. The monument is not well known outside the District
of Columbia, but for some time it was thought to be the masterpiece
of its sculptor, Augustus Saint Gaudens, and the greatest work of art
ever made in the United States: greater even than Saint Gaudens'
monument on Boston Common to the black soldiers bayoneted at
Fort Wagner in 1863 that Robert Lowell describes in *For the Union
Dead*. Galsworthy's Soames Forsyte thought the Adams Memorial
better than Niagara Falls.

It is a bronze figure of a veiled woman in shock, or intense misery
and was held at the time to be excessively enigmatic, despairing,
atheistical. Henry Adams, who commissioned it, finally saw it in
1892 on his return from the South Seas and was amused − if such a
sensation can be attributed to such a black temperament − by the
reactions of the American public:

> As Adams sat there, numbers of people came, for the figure
> seemed to have become a tourist fashion, and all wanted to know
> its meaning. Most took it for a portrait-statue, and the remnant
> were vacant-minded in the absence of a personal guide. None felt
> what would have been a nursery-instinct to a Hindu baby or a
> Japanese jinricksha-runner. The only exceptions were the clergy,

who taught a lesson even deeper. One after another brought companions there, and, apparently fascinated by their own reflection, broke out passionately against the expression they felt in the figure of despair, of atheism, of denial. Like the others, the priest saw only what he brought. Like all great artists, Saint Gaudens held up the mirror and no more. The American layman had lost sight of ideals; the American priest had lost sight of faith. Both were more American than the old, half-witted soldiers who denounced the wasting, on a mere grave, of money which should have been given for drink.[1]

True to himself, Adams gives no clue as to his intentions with the commission and spent much of his life obfuscating them. In *The Education of Henry Adams*, the finest autobiography ever written in the United States, the description above appears after an inexplicable break of twenty years in the narrative; and we are thrown back to the bronze, which we must now examine, stepping out of the scalding Washington sunshine into the cool green shade.

Seated before a blank stone slab, topped by an ornamental Greek cornice (which was supplied by Stanford White), the larger-than-life draped figure recalls not so much the calm women of the classical Attic grave-stones or stelae as the more perturbed images of further east: the pediment figures of the Hellenistic temples in Beirut, Baalbek, Palmyra, even the Indus Valley. The drapery is nightmarish in its massive, monotonous rhythm. The hand raised to the face suggests a residual quickness or animation which is instantly extinguished by the shrouded head and the eyes, which are neither closed nor open, but wholly self-absorbed: like the eyes of a singer about to go through the curtain or a tortured prisoner making his confession on TV. The concentrated stillness and gravity of the figure convey not calm or the acceptance that Adams evidently wanted but an uncontrollable anxiety: as if something authentic, powerful, sensitive, feminine, benign, had stepped back from the world for ever.[2]

Adams commissioned the piece as a monument to his wife but did not supervise it. She was Marian or Clover Hooper, the daughter of a well-known Cambridge, Massachusetts, family, whom he had married in 1872, just after the break in the narrative of the *Education*.

What we know of her comes mostly from her letters to her father and the letters of Henry James, who'd met her in the Cambridge of the 1860s and loved her deeply: in her wit, often at his expense, her intellectual grace, elegance, beauty, spirit and moral spontaneity, she was 'the incarnation of my native land.'[3] For her sake, James would even put up with the cynical and morbid Adams, who as the grandson of one United States President and great-grandson of another, found life in the post-bellum United States something of a disappointment. James even wrote a story about the Adamses in Washington, 'Pandora', in which Clover's charm shines through the uncertain setting. She was an early pioneer of photography. On December 6, 1885, on an impulse that cannot be recovered, she walked into her dark-room and drank a bottle of potassium cyanide.

Many of the best writers of the post-bellum United States thought that something valuable had been lost in the war and its aftermath: only Adams attempted to construct, from his shattered existence, a philosophy of history. Turning away from his wife's tomb, in inexpungible guilt and utter desolation:

> Landed, lost and forgotten, in the centre of this vast plain of self-content, Adams could see but one active interest, to which all others were subservient, and which absorbed the energies of some sixty million people to the exclusion of every other force, real or imaginary.[4]

In short, the world, after 1865, was 'a banker's world.'[5]

In Whitman, Howells and Twain, the simplicity, innocence and peace of America had been sacrificed on the altar of money. Where formerly, Twain wrote, 'the people had desired money,' now they 'fall down and worship it.' The American gospel was: 'Get money. Get it quickly. Get it in abundance. Get it in prodigious abundance. Get it dishonestly if you can, honestly if you must.' It was not simply that with slavery eradicated, the frontier more or less settled, the natives demoralised or extirpated, and the Hamiltonian Constitution enforced at the point of the bayonet, there was no other outlet for an energetic people than the pursuit of money. Twain's Mississippi novels, and particularly *Huckleberry Finn*, are acts of mourning for the passing of an America which seemed real to a degree that the present did not; a reality which is conveyed in the novel in powerful sensations of heat, light, dust, danger, sweetness, friendship, speech.

Adams has no time for regret: to himself, he is merely a mannikin on which a useless education had been hung. But he senses the American unreality. Outside the cemetery, he takes stock:

> Thus, in 1892, neither Hay, King nor Adams knew whether they had attained success, or how to estimate, or what to call it; and the American people seemed to have no clearer idea than they. Indeed, the American people had no idea at all; they were wandering in a wilderness much more sandy than the Hebrews had ever trodden about Sinai; they had neither serpents nor golden calves to worship. They had lost the sense of worship; for the idea that they worshipped money seemed a delusion. Worship of money was an old-world trait; a healthy appetite akin to worship of the Gods, or to worship of power in any concrete shape; but the American wasted money more recklessly than any one ever did before; he spent more to less purpose than any extravagant court aristocracy; he had no sense of relative values, and knew not what to do with his money when he got it, except use it to make more, or throw it away. Probably, since human society began, it had seen no such curious spectacle as the houses of the San Francisco millionaires on Nob Hill. Except for the railway system, the enormous wealth taken out of the ground since 1840, had disappeared. West of the Alleghenies, the whole country might have been swept clean, and could have been replaced in better form within one or two years. The American mind had less respect for money than the European or Asiatic mind, and bore its loss more easily; but it had been deflected by its pursuit till it could turn in no other direction. It shunned, distrusted, disliked, the dangerous attraction of ideals, and stood alone in history for its ignorance of the past.[6]

Lonely, and out of temper with his times, Adams took, like Onyegin, to travelling; and one day in 1900, in the great Gallery of Machines at the Paris Exposition, standing before the forty-foot dynamos, which filled the hall with their rhythmic purring, he suffered an epiphany which he recorded in the famous chapter in the *Education* called 'The Dynamo and the Virgin.' Counterposed against the weathered image in Rock Creek Cemetery – of a woman not as reflected desire, beauty, purity or taste as in so much Victorian plastic art, but as power, the power to combine the scattered wills of human beings, the power of the Virgin that had made the great cathedrals – is the manifold and alien power of the machine, dissipating human energy long before humanity could reach perfection; creating perpetual change without progress; an America which, swept clean, would be replaced in another form biennially.

★

For all visitors to the United States from other lands, there is some special quality of U.S. society that would seem to lie quite near the surface and to be definable. These visitors – say, de Tocqueville in 1835 or Moritz Bonn in the 1920s – saw that quality as restlessness or individualism or emulation, but none of those quite encapsulates that special U.S.-ness. Bouncing onto the Triborough Bridge, one turns and sees a heavenly city, quite different from any other. There is something frozen, shocked about the Manhattan skyline. It is petrified money. See – as you fumble in the ash-tray for eight quarters for the toll – the monuments of the Roaring Twenties: the Woolworth and Chrysler buildings and, above all, the Empire State, embodiments of interest at 3½ per cent and stocks at Irving Fisher's 'permanently high plateau,' frozen to death in the cold arms of the Depression. On March 25, 1931, while unemployed families were encamped in tent ghettoes in Central Park, *The New York Times* apostrophised the 'Everest on Fifth Avenue' with a determined American optimism:

> The dozens and scores of pinnacles that have pierced the skies over Manhattan in the last dozen years, towers for doing business in and towers for living in, are the permanent notation of a great surge of prosperity. The tide itself once so often recedes. The towers are there to testify to the vast energy that threw them upwards and that is certain to reassert itself after the necessary retirement. . . . For a while the receding tide leaves these ambitious monuments high and dry. Then the waves begin to lap forward again . . .

The Empty State Building, as it was called by the vaudeville artists on Forty-second Street, survived the 1930s by charging tourists to ride the elevators up one hundred and two floors to the viewing platform: it was advertised by stunts, notably its role in the film *King Kong* (1933). It had cost $41 million and the lives of fourteen of the 'sky boys' that built it. It finally repaid its investors in 1951.[7]

Here and there, one can make out the headquarters of banking corporations. Those with Ionic columns and massy pediments embody prudence and security: the promise to keep the customer's money intact, which is the oldest franchise in banking. They must be from the turn of the century, for these others, great slivers of air and glass, promising ease and fantasy, rest on foundations not of steel and stone or the wisdom of bank presidents but on the Union itself: for in 1933, and as a response to the bad banking practices that had helped cause the Depression, Congress enacted a law insuring bank deposits, replacing the crazy credit of the banks by the sovereign credit of the United States. In midtown, the pompous and facetious boxes of the 1980s boom, which look like chairs, or desks or ski-ramps or anything rather than houses for commercial bureaucracies, which is what they are, already carry that startled air as they, too, begin to petrify; and, if you have a real eye for money in architecture, you will descry, towering above the tangible and sensuous city, in the bitter blue air, phantom skyscrapers of computing power, as empty and transparent as the Empire State in its dog-days, from which the tide of money is, no doubt, already receding.

But we are now descending the ramp into Harlem. If you came this way, as I did sometimes, returning from the airport after a long flight from Mexico or Santiago de Chile, you would feel no displacement: as if on Lenox Avenue, where black men lounge on burst school chairs beside grilled liquor stores, slapping their thighs or staring without rudeness at the passing women, you had found the permanent America; and you would think, as I did, that you could live happily in this rustic city of weeds and empty lots, and while away your life among these people, poor as a rat, and sleep easily through the sirens and the jazz:

> But if she is clipping quickly down the big-city street in heels, swinging her purse, or sitting on a stoop with a cool beer in her hand, dangling her shoe from the toes of her foot, the man, reacting to her posture, to soft skin on stone, the weight of the

building stressing the delicate, dangling shoe, is captured. And he'd think it was the woman he wanted, and not some combination of curved stone, and a swinging, high-heeled shoe moving in and out of sunlight.[8]

But the stoplight changes, we are across the ditch of Ninety-sixth Street, and gliding along the tedious canyon of Park Avenue. Here all is bustle, movement, crowds under the dry cliffs of 1920s apartment buildings. What is this movement? What is it for? Not, surely, for the ease and comforts of life: for the apartments of the billionaires, which we shall eventually enter on business, with their low ceilings and evil proportions, would disgrace the agricultural workers of my childhood village. The restaurants are no more comfortable: for the maître d', whose brother we last saw, wall-eyed and drunk, outside the post office in Bagni di Lucca, is turning away trust funds of under $50 million.

Not for society, for New York society we shall soon learn, at all but the lowest levels, is ill-mannered, dull beyond description and so subordinate to paid labour that I have seen women trade securities by mobile telephone before the dessert has been served. Not for redemption, for how could Paradise be preferable to the United States? It is for money, which rears over Manhattan like a colossus, round whose base New Yorkers scuttle like beetles on the forest floor.

Undoubtedly, in this phantasmagoric city, in which money is in motion or petrified, being is subordinate to becoming. Every New Yorker is in the process of becoming another New Yorker. A real-estate broker is, in reality, an unacted Chekhov. A Korean vintner looks up, blinking, from Donald Trump's *The Art of the Deal*. In the Metropolitan Museum of Art, in front of a Zurbarán, one hears, from a lady admiring the fall of a monk's cassock, 'I'm there.' There is little of the old European sensation of location in place, family or social class: only the city address has some temporary social reality. In New York, there is a past, of sorts, accidentally petrified by depression or rising interest, but no present: only the imaginary future of undiscounted desire.

To the twentieth-century visitor, New York City is as Venice was to Goethe in 1786: a triumph of human artifice. More even than Venice, New York reveals the city as a place of pure consumption. Almost nothing is produced in Manhattan except trash, six tons per person per year, which is desposited on an infuriated continent or dumped, secretly, at sea. New Yorkers are almost wholly unaware of the capital sources of their sustenance: it is not simply that many have never seen a chicken, grown a tomato, caught a fish, but they are also far from clear whence comes their gasoline, steel or plastic. Money provides their whole existence: it is their soil and sun and water. Like most Americans, New Yorkers work hard, but their work is parasitic of more basic labour; and nowhere more so than on Wall Street, which draws the money of the continent into its maw, keeps some, and despatches the rest in new directions. (Though we must remember that Wall Street, unlike the City of London, is a social not a topographical entity: Michael Milken, who rose each morning at three o'clock, worked in New York time but Californian space.) The displacement of nature by money is most disorienting to the visitor; and even New Yorkers sometimes sense there is something deluded, or at least comical, about their existence. Tom Wolfe, who grew up in the southern tradition shattered but not destroyed at Appomattox Courthouse in 1865, attempts in *The Bonfire of the Vanities*[9] to pierce the comic veil and penetrate the delusion. He takes as his starting point the famous passage in Dickens' *Dombey and Son* (1848) in which a little boy confronts his merchant father with the question:

'Papa! what's money?'

and then, unsatisfied with gold, silver and copper, guineas, shillings and half-pence, and his father not trusting himself to explain circulating medium, currency, depreciation, paper, bullion and rates of exchange, the boy asks again,

'I mean what's money after all?'[10]

It is a dangerous model, because the counterposition of money and childhood, artifice and innocence, evokes powerful emotions that may needs be diluted on the page. But there is no sentimentality in Wolfe's version, which unfolds at a beach club on Long Island:

'Daddy. . . . What are bonds? What is deal?'

Now his mother began laughing. 'You've got to do better than that, Sherman!'

'Well, honey, bonds are – a bond is – well, let me see, what's the best way to explain it to you . . .'

'You build roads and hospitals, Daddy? That's what you do.'

'No, I don't actually build them, sweetheart. I handle the bonds, and the bonds are what makes it possible—'

'You *help* build them?'

'Well, in a way.'

'Which ones?'

. . . 'Well, not any one specifically.'

'The road to Maine?'[11]

The Master of the Universe ties himself in knots. For even poor Sherman has grasped the imperative, which is categorical enough to be worth repeating once a century: that even in great cities of finance, if you *cannot* explain your job to your child, you probably *shouldn't* be doing it. For the child, who does not use money, has a different conception of reality; and will think you a thief, or at best merely messing about: making misery like Dombey, Sr., or crumbs like Sherman McCoy.

★

It is rash of a foreigner to make general statements about New York, let alone a country with an extent of three thousand million square miles and two hundred and sixty million inhabitants, constantly replenished by birth and immigration. Yet, during a long residence in the United States in the 1980s, I began to hear the same sentences and witness similar events; and I thought to make out a pattern. All human beings arrange their reality by means of mental categories. Some of those American categories – categories of religion, hygiene, celebrity – do not concern us: those that do concern us are two.

The first is law. Americans hold man-made law in great respect, even when they break or manipulate it: Hamilton's Constitution, of course, and its amendments (excluding the Eighteenth, which banned liquor), but also city ordinances, building codes, driving and parking regulations. For Americans, law is not something alien and imposing – as, say, for the Germans waiting obediently at red pedestrian stoplights or, in the East, shooting illegal emigrants – but as embodying agreements of what is right and a right, and therefore supremely adaptable to circumstance. For a period I was president of a housing corporation in lower Manhattan and on its behalf prosecuted a lawsuit. The suit was conducted with intense passion, and much unnecessary stage business: I was for ever being led off by counsel to glass rooms, to curb my justified anger, though I wasn't angry, merely sleepy. There was much 'See you in court!,' a phrase I had longed to use but was now weary of; until at last, as dawn coloured the sky over the East River and the subway began to steam and roar, we reached a settlement that I could have negotiated in one and a half minutes in a telephone conversation with the opposing principal. For that labour of a day and night, counsel received a fee of $14,000 payable in three instalments; his famous adversary, and two women associates, some five times that sum in cash. It occurred to me that the palaver, the Chinese food and Diet Coke, the glassed-in meeting rooms and icy, legal insults ('a pattern of racketeering,' 'abusive and coercive conduct,' 'without merit') and the splendid fees *authorised* the settlement which would otherwise have appeared to my fellow-stockholders as arbitrary, footling, unacceptably Old World.

The second mental category is money. Americans, as Santayana noted, prefer to talk of quantities rather than qualities and are therefore apt to consider things and actions in terms of money quantities. The great diversion of United States life – and the force that runs through U.S. history, and makes it intelligible, as Moritz Bonn was the first to recognise – is speculation in real estate: that is, the conversion of Eden into money. It was the force behind the great movements westward, where pioneers sold out their homesteads at immense premiums to a timid second generation; then, when the coast was reached, there was money to be made in swampland in Florida in the 1920s, in subdivided farmland in the 1950s and 1960s and, in the 1980s, in shoreland reclaimed from the sea. Yet white Americans appeared to me curiously restive in their homes, which to them are dead money, which they are for ever tempted to revive by sale or multiple mortgage. To own an unmortgaged house, car, machine – to accumulate equity, as they say – is to them an offence. To admire a man's beach house on the

Connecticut coast or Lake Michigan, or his all-terrain vehicle, is to be told its replacement cost and its owner's equity, if any. In New York City even, where these habits of thought are most deeply entrenched, people feel that they themselves are capital, which must for ever seek its most remunerative employment; and that there is an opportunity cost – income forgone – in bidding you Good Day.

For a European, and especially an Englishman, educated to regard wealth as residing in real property, where since the sixteenth century the spoils of piracy, commerce and venal matrimony have sought social perpetuity in fields and woods, stone, brick, glass, these North American attitudes are peculiarly stimulating. Henry James, who wandered between the New and Old Worlds, made the opposed sensations of possession the theme of a very great novel called *The Wings of the Dove*. In the novel, his beloved Clover Adams and all the doomed heroines of his American youth are reborn as Milly Theale, as mysteriously mortal as Marie Duplessis, but an honest woman: 'an angel,' in the revealing formulation, 'with a thumping bank account.'[12]

Milly is contrasted with an Englishwoman, Maud Lowder, who disposes of girls in marriage by virtue of her money. Her surroundings are presented in all their ghastly English physicality:

> They . . . were furthermore conclusively British. They constituted an order and they abounded in rare material – precious woods, metals, stuffs, stones. He had never dreamed of anything so fringed and scalloped, so buttoned and corded, drawn everywhere so tight, and curled everywhere so thick. He had never dreamed of so much gilt and glass, so much satin and plush, so much rosewood and marble and malachite. But it was, above all, the solid forms, the wasted finish, the misguided cost, the general attestation of morality and money, a good conscience and a big balance. These things finally represented for him a portentous negation of his own world of thought – of which, for that matter, in the presence of them, he became as for the first time hopelessly aware. They revealed it to him by their merciless difference.[13]

Mrs Lowder's mind is done up in the same hideous high Victorian style:

Aunt Maud sat somehow in the midst of her money, founded on it and surrounded by it, even if with a clever high manner about it, her manner of looking, hard and bright, as if it weren't there. Milly about hers had no manner at all – which was possibly, from a point of view, a fault: she was at any rate far away on the edge of it, and you hadn't, as might be said, in order to get at her nature, to traverse, by whatever a piece of her property.[14]

The conflict of attitudes ends, by the way, in disaster all round: Milly dies and gives away her money, an action which the English simply cannot morally comprehend.

Every day, I was struck by the insubstantial nature of American property. Americans do not build to last. All over the northern states are the ruins of industrial plants destroyed by changes in technique, fashion or the rate of interest. Houses may be built in timber, not just because it is abundant but because builders have no interest in the hundred-year reversion, even when interest is low.[15] In the Connecticut woods, a lady broker described a house to me as 'pre-owned'; and that term from the automobile trade, that had replaced the older euphemisms 'used' and 'second-hand,' entranced me. The house as vehicle! (Life is a bridge, says the Persian motto on the Red Fort in Agra, pass over it, but build no house on it.) And American houses built after the Federal period do not last, for they are constructed of timber and sheetrock or from cedar kits delivered by flat-bed truck from Seattle.

For what impulses are gratified at home? Ever since the 1920s, when Moritz Bonn stood captivated before the soda fountains of Kansas City and the automatic cafés of Manhattan, simple desires have been conveyed and absolved by money away from home. Meanwhile, the household was opened to the outdoors through mechanical appliances and supermarket deliveries. News, amusement, companionship, sex come down the wires of money into the television or computer monitor. The notion that Americans are individualistic and self-reliant has always astonished me: apart from the poor, Americans seem to do almost nothing for themselves. Only competitive sport reveals that old individualism, and inspires the watching public to peaks of sentiment. Yet American gratifications, which appeared to me so bland and savourless, and so uniform because so corporate – so Babbitt-like, in short – were to Americans teeming with choice and sensation. Once, on a flight to Kingsport, Tennessee, which was delayed by a storm at Washington, the stewardess offered cold drinks by way of apology; and the business people in front, and to the side and across the aisle, deliberated carefully, before selecting, out of technically indistinguishable compositions of water, air and corn sugar, the registered trademark that best embodied the emotions of childhood. It was as if the sensations of Proust's glass of orangeade had become automatic.

The sense of possession is weaker in the United States than in Europe for this reason: all possession is in the form of money, which is mobile and indifferent both to its holder and to its form. For the white Americans I met, money was a living entity that must on no account be confined. Even the most inert and resistant entity had been converted into a security, priced and traded: industrial plant, land, rights to water, autumn crops, buildings and the air above them, the right to put an aircraft down at an airport, emissions of sulphur dioxide from a power plant, student loans, instalment payments on tractors or passenger cars or trailers, bank liabilities and Vacation Home Loans in Mexico. Debt, which in Europe is a threat to liberty – whether the Marshalsea, as for Dickens' Dorrit, or simply the poky flat or uncongenial job to which the repayments condemn you – is liberty in the United States: it buys present relief from actual or imaginary frustrations, and the future can take care of itself. Debt is the optimism of Americans, and when reality enters as default or bankruptcy, it imposes no professional penalty and leaves no social stigma. In 1989, I visited a colossal Baptist church that towered over its parking lot in the suburbs of Charlotte, North Carolina. It had been built by leveraging the collection plate at 15:1. It embodied not merely faith in Credit, but credit in Faith.

All people and entities in the United States aspire to the condition of zero net worth: that is, that one's assets, priced into money, are exactly matched by one's money liabilities. The most visionary U.S. financier, Michael Milken, went further: during his tenure as head of the Beverly Hills office of Drexel Burnham Lambert in the middle years of the 1980s, from a sleepless eyrie at the intersection of Wilshire and Rodeo boulevards, he saw that a corporation need have no book-keeper's value. Indeed, it could have an immense *negative* net worth – that its debts could vastly exceed its book assets – provided its income – his conception of profit was perhaps the broadest ever promulgated – could pay the interest on its immediate obligations. With the greatest brutality, he ripped the equity capital out of corporations as one might roe from a sturgeon, and tossed the body back into the predatory waters of American business. A large portion of the cash freed passed to Milken himself as a fee: he himself had little or no future interest in the entities he'd crippled. Not surprisingly, he made many enemies, and though the ninety-eight charges brought against him were technical in the extreme, he was obliged to serve a prison sentence in a minimum-security federal penitentiary.[16]

At first, Milken's corporations were capitalised for a permanent prosperity in which markets would for ever expand, product prices rise and interest fall. After the middle 1980s, they were not so much capitalised as primed to explode. The securities issued to buy them, and secured on their assets, had to offer such high rates of interest – up to 18 per cent a year – that they could not be serviced from revenues, only from liquidation, scattering their assets and employees to the four winds.

One would need to be a person of financial taste to do full justice to the style of those deals. They open in a sort of bloated classicism, but rapidly, under the pressures of competition from other invest-ment banks, a rising stock market and the encircling Feds, fall into a mannerism until by late 1987 – by which time Ivan Boesky had turned state's evidence and promised to deliver Milken to the authorities – they are pure bedlam. Their names play like fountains in my imagination: American Can, Uniroyal, Phillips Petroleum, Revlon, Metromedia, Union Carbide, Storer, Beatrice Foods, Unocal. By the end, the corporations were capitalised to liquidate in a matter of weeks in the hope that somehow the proceeds would pay the credulous bondholders their capital and interest. Eventually, as the stock market continued to inflate the cost of industrial properties, the debt instruments issued to buy the corporations from their stockholders no longer even made the pretence of paying interest: they were zero-coupon bonds, or various classes of preferred stock or adjustable-rate participating subordinated debentures or a security called a Pay-in-Kind which rolled its interest payments into

itself each year till it blew the corporation into the bankruptcy
courts.[17] So great was Milken's credit, as great perhaps as that of Law
or J. P. Morgan in their primes, that he could create money with a
single sentence: a note to the AP – Dow Jones newswire that Drexel
Burnham was 'highly confident' of raising funds to buy this or that
corporation was accepted on Wall Street as the equivalent of the
money itself.

Milken lived fairly modestly in the San Fernando Valley, in a blue
shingled house that had once been the guest-house of Clark Gable
and Carole Lombard. At weekends, he liked to shop at the Gelson
supermarket with his young family, staring into the trolleys at the
check-out to see what others were buying: not so much for reasons
of household economy as for his stock-market operations. In 1986,
according to the indictment filed against him on March 30, 1989,
he received a salary of $550 million. Capitalised at twenty times on
Sir William Petty's model, those wages gave Milken a theoretical
worth of $11 thousand million, more than anybody else at that era,
and unexampled for a mere employee. Fortunes made in finance do
not reward any risk to life, health or property and, because they are
in money, require little intelligence and energy to administer;
indeed, because money has no qualities, few financiers have any
character at all. Yet such fortunes inculcate in their holders, whether
on Wall Street or in the City or in Tokyo, an ineradicable sense of
election. Milken was no exception.

By 1989, when the Securities and Exchange Commission and the
U.S. Attorney for the Southern District of New York had surrounded his shingled homestead, Milken was raving. The hostile
takeovers he had made possible through his debt securities had, he
said, broken the hold of entrenched corporate bureaucracies and
returned the ownership of industrial assets to the people. Nothing
could have been less true, though for a while a number of individuals
black-balled by the Harmonie Club – respectable Jewish finance –
strutted through the pages of *Business Week* in garlands of Havana
smoke and the rich scents of new wives. In a late interview, Milken
took on the accents of Law, promising to refinance through his junk
securities the debts of the Latin American states: to become, in short,
sole creditor to a hemisphere. *Idiot savant!* Like Law, he was more

enamoured of his theories than his money, and like Law, he was hounded out of the financial markets.

As people and corporations, so the Union itself. As we saw in Chapter 7, the United States began its national existence as a debtor. It continued happily as such until the Great War of 1914–18 crippled its European competitors, forced up the price of raw materials (in which North America was so rich) and left the United States at the peace some $10 thousand million to the good with the European governments and all its private debts repaid. That process was repeated, on a much grander scale, in the 1939–45 world war, when a century and a half of British capital investment was sold off on Wall Street at ten cents on the dollar to help pay for generous U.S. military assistance to the old country. The United States was the world's creditor until 1987, when once again the country owed more abroad than it was owed: the great boom of the 1980s, the tremendous expansion of paid employment and the re-armament that demoralised and then destroyed the Soviet Union, was financed by the sale of Treasury obligations to the thrifty Japanese public, which were then destroyed – on the approved Franklin model – by a grand devaluation of the currency in which they were denominated.

The American delight in credit, anatomised by James Grant for the post-bellum United States, is a quite different sensation from that of Europe and Asia. In those old civilisations, debt is a residue of the past – a war, a bad harvest. In the United States, and most naturally in Milken's great last financings, it is a challenge to the future. The Americans I met believed that they would amortise their debts into equity – actually possess their possessions – but recognised they had to meet an important condition: they must work till they drop. Such an attitude replaces the pleasure principle in the higher reaches of U.S. society. I do not mean that the American bourgeois have less fun than their counterparts in London or Milan or Bombay: they merely do not talk about it. Pleasure is the American bourgeois tabu. I never met a New Yorker who admitted to taking a summer holiday, although for several weeks in the summer, these men and women were absent from their offices (though calling in each day for their messages). It is only on the way down that pleasure re-enters consciousness as a purpose, usually in the form of regret. Here, for example, is the greatest of all Americans down on his luck:

> When we arrived at Dover, New Jersey, we got a New York newspaper, and I called his attention to the quotation on General Electric. Mr Edison then asked: 'If I hadn't sold any of mine, what would it be worth today?' and after some figuring, I replied: 'Over four million dollars.' When Mr Edison is thinking seriously over a problem he is in the habit of pulling his right eyebrow, which he did now for fifteen or twenty seconds. Then his face lighted up, and he said: 'Well, it's all gone, but we had a hell of a good time spending it!'[18]

Here we see, as phantom or vestige, the legacy of New England Puritanism. American bourgeois life consists of a series of circularities, which deliver no public satisfaction. Work is for money, money is for display, display is for work. Life is for work, work is for emulation, emulation is for health, health is for life.

Of course, the American poor stand outside those gruelling circuits, for they are the privileged class for whom money will satisfy actual, mortal need or gratify instinctive wishes. Also, I heard no mention of such matters during a winter's residence in the pueblos of New Mexico; nor, for that matter, in Harlem. Toni Morrison, in her first and finest book, *The Bluest Eye*, went so far as to say that black history was not written in money, but in sensation, above all in music.

> Only they [jazz musicians] would know how to connect the heart of a red watermelon to the asafetida bag to the muscadine to the flashlight on his behind to the fists of money to the lemonade in a Mason jar to a man called Blue and come up with what all that meant in joy, in pain, in anger, in love, and give it its final and pervading ache of freedom.[19]

That hypothesis, if I have reproduced it correctly, would thus explain the extraordinary vigour and appeal of black American music: it is the shadow or counterpart of white American money, itself vigorous, and extraordinarily appealing to the world.

But I lived in a white milieu. Lost like poor Henry Adams in a phantasmagoria, in which desire is for ever disrupted and dissipated by money, I sought at first something firm underfoot. I was for ever making bold and sketchily financed offers for tracts of American land: a 250-acre ruined farm in upper New York State, a ranch outside Santa Fe, New Mexico, and, successfully, as it were, a thousand square feet of lower Manhattan. That apartment, on the top floor of a Federal brick townhouse on Eleventh Street at Sixth Avenue – or, to be precise, a paper security representing rights and obligations to that territory – I wanted to reserve for my American daughter so she could stay there as a student and learn to love the city as much as her father and mother had loved it. Three years elapsed, and in that time I became a New Yorker. I regretted the money sterilised in the brick and boards and immense sky-light and coughing heat-pipes, resented the steady drip of money into real-estate taxes and maintenance payments; also having to administer the corporation. So I sold it to a sculptor, and hedged the proceeds into sterling with some slow-witted bank downtown, and as the dollar fell and rose and fell, made a thumping turn and then another, and thought myself a fine fellow in the world of money. In reality, I had exchanged an intense sensation of happiness for its imaginary potential: that, eighteen years on, by means of thrift, a book a year, retained earnings, re-invested dividends and compounded interest, I would hand my daughter on her birthday . . . what? . . . the top floor of the Plaza Hotel.

For where does all this money lead? Americans look without blinking at death, which they attempt to defer as long as possible. At the end of their earning lives, many Americans, whose fortunes far outstrip their allotted years, take to travelling: as if to view that Eden they ignored so long. In state or national parks, one is always coming on older people in shopping-mall pastels or T-shirts with defiant retiree slogans – I FOUGHT THE LAWN AND THE LAWN WON – discussing carriage weight beside their Winnebagos or moving off at glacial pace on heavily laden Harley-Davidsons. Once, at Christmas-time in Elko, Nevada, I passed a casino parking-lot scattered with recreational vehicles. Intrigued by this encampment, I parked and introduced myself. They were retirees from hyperborean Chicago, exceptionally courteous and hospitable, who passed the days migrating through the desert in pursuit of paying slots, each one a Law or Marie Duplessis at retail.

Others give themselves over to the greatest generosity to causes they consider meritorious. (I hesitate to use the word 'charities': for some time, I was a benefactor of an entity whose charitable mission, as I later learned, was the dynamiting of dams on salmon and steelhead rivers in the Pacific drainage.) To these acts of generosity, many Americans bring that energy and system they deployed in accumulating the money in the first place:

> I resolved to stop accumulating and begin the infinitely more serious and difficult task of wise distribution. Our profits had reached forty millions of dollars per year and the prospect of increased earnings before us was amazing. Our successors, the United States Steel Corporation, soon after the purchase, netted sixty millions in one year. Had our company continued in business and adhered to our plans of extension, we figured that seventy millions in that year might have been earned.
>
> Steel had ascended the throne and was driving away all inferior material. It was clearly seen that there was a great future ahead; but so far as I was concerned I knew the task of distribution before me would tax me in my old age to the utmost.[20]

So diligently to reverse the mechanism of money, without at any point gratifying its condensed desire, is a feature even of the robber barons. Americans often do not like their heirs, who, they fear, will dissipate the money in lawyers' fees, foolish speculations, the entertainment industry or homosexual attachments: in other words, enjoy life. Gates, the modern Edison, though barely forty years old, has vowed he will not leave his fortune to his children. So, under the ineluctable shadow of death, the industrialist puts money to work in the service of immortality: not in the next world, of course, or abroad but in the imaginations of other Americans: for fame, a matter of history, is subordinate in the United States to celebrity, a matter of geography.

Thus we see that attempt to purchase distinction in the realm of painting so carefully exploited by Duveen at the turn of the century. For in Frick's picture gallery on upper Fifth Avenue, devouring the famous pictures among the hideous greenhouse flowers or resting, full-length, on the real lawn, one forgets the Homestead strike and the Pinkerton agents and the bullets slicing into the Monongahela, forgets even that great river as it loops northwards toward Pittsburgh and leaves behind, on the inside of each great loop, the rotting corpse of an abandoned steelworks.[21] Pontormo's handsome Cosimo Medici, Ingres' Comtesse d'Haussonville, the frolicsome nudes of Boucher and Fragonard: what company for the old brute as he paddles slowly through eternity! To conquer, in one stroke, justified infamy, brats, death and the Internal Revenue Service!

Yet for Frick, as for so many other Americans, such pictures are merely securities. Duveen at length showed him Velásquez' portrait of Philip IV of Spain:

> Learning that Philip IV had paid Velásquez the equivalent of six hundred dollars for it, Frick made an elaborate computation to find out what six hundred dollars at six-per-cent interest compounded semi-annually from 1645 to 1910 would come to, and found, to his joy, that he had got the picture for less than nothing.[22]

My friends on Wall Street in the later 1980s were shocked that the pictures they had bought for so much, at evening sales at Sotheby's auction rooms on York Avenue, in their black ties and tuxedoes, for everyone to see, communicating their bids to young women who looked like Grace Kelly or Jacqueline Onassis – and no other ladies of past times – in socially lucrative display, between the New York close and the Tokyo opening; that those pictures were suddenly worthless in money – even, goddamnit, the Warhol piss paintings! They didn't complain, because Americans don't: they go to law or the rifle, depending on their socialisation. My friends were stunned that what goes up in money may also come down in money. Americans, who seem at first so expert in money and its behaviour, are in reality astonishingly trusting.

★

That American credulity arises in a number of illusions about money, which are as entrenched, in their way, as those of the English. Americans believe that money conveys knowledge and that the price of a commodity, or a security or even a market index, such as the Dow Jones Industrial Average or the Chicago Board of Trade averages, gives an accurate picture of reality. That belief has been organised into a body of doctrine, known as the efficient-markets theory. In its strong form – it has weak and middling forms – the theory holds that markets condense all knowledge relating to their constituents and are by definition 'correct' or justified: if the price or index changes, it is because there has been some increment to knowledge relative to the commodity or security, such as a rise in interest, a frost in Florida or a suicide in the executive suite.

The theory cannot withstand even a moment's thought. You buy or sell a security, say the common stock of Netscape Inc., not because you *know* it will go up or come down or stay the same, but because you *want* it to do one of those things. What is condensed in a price is the residue not of knowledge but of embattled desire, which may respond to new information and may not. At the time of writing, Netscape is priced in the stock market at 270 years' profits, a multiple that implies a 50 per cent rise in its reported net earnings every year for eternity: such a price belongs outside the realm of knowledge. The efficient-markets doctrine is merely another attempt to apply rational laws to an arena that is self-evidently irrational. A market cannot operate by laws, for the laws would be discovered, and it would cease to be a market. That is also the reason why business people never actually understand their products or services: if they found their secrets, so would others, and knock them off. The most successful commercial products are ineffable: Coca-Cola is the example that springs to mind.

This illusion has profound emotional consequences. If a market price contains all human knowledge, those investors that exit the market at the top and with their capital gains intact must, by definition, be superhuman and are fêted like gods. Men such as Baruch in 1929 and Goldsmith in 1987 were consulted as oracles even on matters on which they were obviously inexpert, such as government; till they missed the next market turn or the next but one and were forgotten as if they had never lived. In fact, of course, as we have repeatedly shown, markets condense not knowledge but desire; and to predict their indices requires not intelligence but a peculiar concentrated stupidity, such as one admires in a woman we remember wearing this year's fashions last year: the ability to wish the wishes of the last addition to a mob. R. C. Leffingwell, a former Treasury official who became a partner of J. P. Morgan & Co., explained the process in his testimony at the Senate hearings on the causes of the Depression in 1933:

> The people of this world in that regrettable period were like marionettes dancing on an invisible wire, subtly influenced by the excessive volume of cheap money. Irresistibly, farmers, merchants, business men and bankers respond to it, unreasoningly, as they would to a drug.[23]

For money to serve you, you must believe in it; if you doubt it a moment, it vanishes, like a ghost. What happened at the turn of the 1930s was that Americans lost faith in money. People stopped borrowing and bankers stopped lending: loans outstanding for business and real estate were, in December 1932, just $8.8 billion, scarcely more than half what they had been in June 1929. With each loan called or not renewed, the banker also wiped out a deposit on his balance-sheet: he destroyed money. In this wholesale liquidation, Andrew Mellon, Secretary of the Treasury, saw the work of an avenging angel:

> Liquidate labour, liquidate stocks, liquidate the farmers, liquidate real estate. . . . It will purge the rottenness of the system. People will work harder, live a more moral life. Values will be adjusted and enterprising people will pick up the wreck from less competent people.[24]

Few Americans could afford such sentiments. Most felt quite helpless. Because they had believed that markets of the 1920s were real, when those broke it seemed to Americans that reality had been turned upside down: that the snow of the 1929 winter, in Fitzgerald's formulation, was somehow of a different order because it was wet and cold and nobody swept it away; because, in short, money couldn't make it vanish.

Reality was suddenly transformed, not just in the market indices but in the hard, sensuous world that had been forgotten, which was now a world of street corners and ruined family farms and busted banks and men walking from town to town shooting vermin for food. In that transfiguration – the moment so prized by the Greek tragedians in which the hero *recognises* he has been made mad – things stood out in hard, unyielding concreteness. Corporations emerged from behind their stock symbols as cold furnaces and shuttered gates; bank presidents made grovelling fools of themselves before congressional committees; crowds dissipated into lonely, struggling individuals. In certain of Hopper's paintings of that period Americans are shown in a cold, mute isolation, squatters in their own civilisation. A little drawing I saw in a gallery on Madison Avenue, two zeroes to represent the tops of gasoline pumps, three undulating lines to show the telephone wires loping away into infinity, a squiggle that suggests the open bonnet of a Ford, still fills me with the sensation of desperate, pointless flight. It is the definition for me of the antique conception of panic. Walking in the state parks of New York or Tennessee, I would sometimes come on field-stone walls overtopped by second-growth timber; and sometimes a rusty harrow and a blackened chimney and a heap of jumbled stones where a house had fallen into its cellar-hole; or sometimes, among the strippy sugar maples or hickories, a single flowering apple-tree, badly in need of pruning, as sole memorial of a farming family that one day in 1932 simply got up from the table and walked out, leaving the dishes unwashed and the back door open.

The photographs of the American 1930s reveal an intense engagement with individual physiognomy; just as some of the federally funded publications are fascinated by individual speech, as here among the blacks of the Georgia Sea Islands:

> Hab yuh heahd uh duh man wut wuz put in prison in Springfield? He jis flied away from duh jail and wuz nebuh caught agen. Yes, ma'am, I know wut yuh hab tuh hav in awduh tuh fly aw vanish away, but it is mighty hahd tuh git. It's duh bone ub a black cat.[25]

In those artefacts of the Depression, Americans are attempting to rebuild their image of society, not from money, but from its fundamental components, human beings.

So formidable was the reality of the Depression, so intensely *real*, that Americans, half a century later, have still not quite shaken it off. It was as if behind the reality of money was another, permanent and subterranean, like the mycelium of a fungus; which would sprout horrible forms at unpredictable moments. Marx's famous comment of the 1840s – that every city has within it a little Ireland of diseased potatoes and death by famine – seemed to apply even to the United

States. The Dow Jones Industrial Average recorded its twentieth-century low of 41.22 on July 8, 1932 – only a fraction of a point above its starting level in 1896 – but nobody recognised that it was an epoch. The war revived business, and the Dow passed its 1929 level on November 23, 1954, thus seeming to wipe the Depression from the archive; but throughout the United States that my mother and father knew in the 1950s was a deep anxiety that somehow once again demand would collapse, people would cease to want things or want them enough to part with money, and the United States would slide unstoppably back into the Hoover Administration. I recollect in the spring of 1987, in Macon, Georgia, a lady describing shyly to me the extent of her clothes closet; not out of boastfulness at her own or her husband's riches; but rather as she spoke of her work at her local church; to show that even she, a poor provincial, was doing her level bit to sustain the word of God/consumer demand. Hence that uninterrupted shopping that is so wearisome in the United States, those thousand million transactions every day, those stores full of imports and malls full of tat, which seems so utterly purposeless, in reality expresses a deep and patriotic motivation: to banish reality for ever, to prevent the Depression ever happening again.

11

§ £ ¥ § £ ¥ § £ ¥ § £ ¥ § £ ¥ § £ ¥ § £ ¥ § £ ¥ § £ ¥ § £ ¥ § £ ¥ § £ ¥ § £ ¥ § £ ¥ § £ ¥ § £ ¥

The Sinews of War

'*M. Ouvrard, me dit-il, vous avez abaissé la royauté au niveau du commerce.*'

'*Sire, le commerce est le génie des Etats; il se passe tres-bien de la royauté, et la royauté ne saurait se passer de lui.*'

'*Sottises que tout cela . . . Eh bien! J'irai à Madrid; avec cinq cent mille hommes on fait ce qu'on veut.*'

Ouvrard[1]

'Mr Ouvrard, you've dragged kingship down to the level of trade.'

'Trade is the spirit of the State, Sire. Trade can do without kingship but kingship can't do without trade.'

'What balls! . . . I'll go to Madrid. With half a million men, one can do what one likes.'

Money, as we have seen, replaces violence in human intercourse. The chains of vendetta in the *Iliad* and the *Oresteia*, among the German and Frankish tribes and even, in my times, with the villagers of Mount Lebanon can now be interrupted by payments in money: which, as general consolation, comes to seem preferable to mere vengeance for a murdered brother, a stolen piece of property or a severed hand. The ancient Teuton word for such compensations, *Wergild* – which clusters, according to the etymologists, meanings for 'man' and 'yield/money' – became in time the basis of systems of civilian law, and much of criminal law. The process has reached a point of great refinement in the United States: the class actions against the tobacco manufacturers have sought, though unsuccessfully up to now, to make good through arbitrary sums of money not only the agonies of lung cancer but also the discomforts and pleasures of addiction to generations of smokers and the inconvenience to their lawyers.

Yet that displacement of violence by money, long held to be a mark of civilisation, has unexpected exceptions, or what Vico in the eighteenth century called *ricorsi*, or refluxes. Money is itself the chief object of violence, for, as Montesquieu well noted, it has a special charm to the criminal. While it would be rash to murder your neighbour and cart off his property to your house for the authorities to discover, you can steal his money because as soon as you have it it is no longer his, but yours: money belongs only to its holder.[2] Any project to label money as to its legally prescribed holder is doomed by the nature of money; and hampers commerce and infringes the privacy not only of criminals but of the law-abiding. Crime, in the age of money, is as hard to regulate as finance.

Over time, besides, money has become the handmaid of that legalised crime we call warfare. Warfare predates money, as the *Iliad* proves; but in the course of antiquity money was seen to play a special role in the prosecution of war. By the second half of the fourth century B.C., if we are to believe Plutarch, the notion has reached even the Immortal Gods: the oracle of the god Apollo at Delphi advised Philip of Macedon to look to his 'silver shafts'; and the thought was made proverbial for us by Cicero in his attacks on Mark Antony's conduct in Gaul:[3] *Pecunia nervi belli*, or money is the sinews of war.

The notion naturally fell into abeyance in Europe during the feudal era: military services by a heavily armed caste of feudatories were the very raison d'être of feudal society, but they were rewarded not with money but counter-services. But it was dusted off as feudal practices began to disintegrate in the later Middle Ages and men became more and more interested in classical wisdom and experience. The coins circulating in Europe permitted more systematic taxation or tribute in money which could then buy military services or the goodwill of the enemy or, in the case of the later Danegelds, both: according to the *Anglo-Saxon Chronicle*, the English king paid 82,800 pounds (that is, of silver pennies) in tribute to the Danes in 1018 and about 5,000 pounds to maintain an army of Scandinavian mercenaries. (The coin hoards of Norway, Sweden and Denmark are full of English pennies.) Soldiering became a profession and then, with the increased use of cannon and muskets, a business that few princes could afford. The cities could fortify themselves against princely depredation, and did so; but their chief weapon was their money, or rather their credit. They could actually pay their Switzers rather than leave them to take payment in kind (robbery, murder, rape).

The problem was that money, which is in itself purposeless, is easily diverted to ends the payer does not intend. Pericles used the money tribute from the Delian League not to build warships to defend the islands against the Persians but to make the greatest monuments of antiquity, the Parthenon, Propylaeon and Erechtheon on the Acropolis of Athens. The money Danegelds no doubt merely inflamed the arrogance of the Norsemen. With the feudal system in ruins, there arose a spirited debate in the most advanced city in Europe, Florence, as to what actually constituted strength in the state: money or men. Machiavelli argued that anybody with soldiers could obtain money.[4] He was contradicted flatly by his friend Francesco Guicciardini[5] whose nephew, Lodovico, helped make proverbial a comment of the *condottiere* Gian Giacomo di Trivulzio: asked by Louis XII in 1499 what was needed to capture Milan, the great mercenary said: Money, money and once again money.

The dispute was, in reality, a first attempt to come to grips with the oppositions of capital and labour in the department then of greatest interest to states, the strategic. The Guicciardinian view became one of the buttresses of bullionism as a national purpose, and then of the Dutch approach to policy, so admired by Sir William Petty: 'The *Hollanders* do rid their hands of two Trades, which are of the greatest turmoil and danger, and yet of least profit; the first whereof is that of a common and private Soldier, for such they hire from *England* and *Scotland*, and *Germany*, to venture their lives for *Six* pence a day, whilst themselves safely and quietly follow trades, whereby the meanest of them gain six times as much, and withal by this entertaining of Strangers for Soldiers.'[6] The Machiavellian line was upheld by Bonaparte, who was for ever tormenting his chief financier, Ouvrard, or tossing him into gaol or invading other countries. Yet after his return from Elba, when Ouvrard was raising for him two million francs a day in the European capital markets,

Bonaparte had somewhat changed his mind; and, after Waterloo, he asked Ouvrard for a loan of fourteen million francs (secured on some *rentes* in his possession), payable, naturally enough, in North America![7] Hitler had no interest in money, except as a mechanism for separating the German public from its wealth. In our times, Machiavelli seems to have been routed: Saddam Hussein, the dictator of Iraq, used the threat of his forces to extract money from the weak Gulf monarchies and then, when he had an army of 40 divisions, extracted a lot more; but those same monarchies still had purses deep enough to finance an international expedition to cut that army down to a local scale.

To say that warfare has become more expensive is merely to recognise that money has required time to colonise this activity. Law's first editor in 1790, General Senovert, complained that now France had established a standing army, all Europe had to follow suit; and it now cost 20,000 livres to destroy or incapacitate a German.[8] At that price, he thought, enemies should be bought off; and indeed the strategic development of recent years has been to replace violence as much as possible by money. The Cold War, at least in the metropolitan countries and among their allies in Europe, was a war almost without violence. The United States ended up in occupation of the battlefield because it was able to outspend the Soviet Union in developing weapons so terrible they were detonated only in the imagination: thermonuclear bombs, the ballistic and cruise missiles and aircraft to deliver them, and the electronic counter-measures to disable them. The United States was able to do so because of its better credit.

The Gulf War of 1990 and 1991 seemed to be exemplary. The purpose of the war was to reassure the Saudi monarchy, which disposes of much of the world's known reserves of crude oil and, not certainly but very probably, all its unknown reserves. That was not perhaps the most stirring call to allied arms, and offered no very patriotic death. Meanwhile, the Saudis and their Arab allies believed that the Iraqi public had been railroaded into war. Strategy therefore sought to restrict casualties, on the allied side to the usual attrition of a large manoeuvre with live ammunition, and on the enemy's side to the supporters of the regime. The result was a campaign against the enemy's war capital: missiles, ammunition, nuclear plants, factories that might be used for making chemical or biological weapons, centres for command, control and communication, airfields, roads and bridges. Here was warfare at its most attenuated: truly, Saudi money fighting Saudi money. It had its limits: aircrews risked their lives several times a day to bomb airfields that were not being used by Iraqi aircraft; while the roster of capital targets eventually included, by poor intelligence or excessive enthusiasm, a civilian shelter in the Baghdad suburbs. None the less, the tape and film of the U.S. bombing, conveyed by television, profoundly demoralised the Arabs, even those fighting for Kuwaiti independence and the Saudi monarchy: they were like the pepper crunching under Pepys' heels that day at Erith on the Thames, the physical embodiment of an overbearing and intelligent wealth.

The cost in money of the allied expeditions known as Desert Shield and Desert Storm should, to the conscientious accountant, include some charge for the construction of the air bases and military cities built in Saudi Arabia in the 1970s and 1980s as platforms for just such expeditions and some portion of the Pentagon and Whitehall overheads; but if we consider merely the payments made to the allies by the Saudi and Kuwaiti governments, some $10 thousand million, we come on a figure for each dead Iraqi soldier of a million dollars: ten thousand dead millionaires.[9]

Such a sum is obviously not a commercial value. For war disrupts not only human existence and notions of good conduct, but also the purposes of commerce measured in money. Shakespeare was fascinated by that last aspect of war, and gives us this conversation between Hamlet and the Norwegian captain:

Captain: We go to gain a little patch of ground
        That hath in it no profit but the name.
        To pay five ducats – five – I would not farm it;

                                            [farm: lease]

        Nor will it yield to Norway or the Pole
        A ranker rate should it be sold in fee.

                           [ranker: richer / fee: freehold]

Hamlet: Why the Polack never will defend it.
Captain: Yes, it is already garrison'd.
Hamlet: Two thousand souls and twenty thousand ducats

Will not debate the question of this straw!
> [i.e., not be adequate to resolve]
This is th'imposture of much wealth and peace . . .[10]
> [imposture: abscess]

In peacetime, money is created by order – either of princes at their mints or by banks with their loans – and soon takes actual, sensuous form within the life of a community: in buildings and factories, improved land, houses, gardens, automobiles and computers or sometimes, when such things appear too much trouble, in rising prices for securities. The money created gives the impression of wealth created and of nature tamed or ruined, depending on your point of view. In wartime, money is created by government order for another purpose. The counterparts of the new banknotes or bills are not the Empire State Building, but a field littered with craters and sobbing wounded and roads churned to mud by refugees. Paper money is deadly confetti: the Union greenbacks and the bonds of the Confederacy revealed their purpose in the peach orchard at Shiloh in 1862, as Johnston's men fell dead to bright pink petals, each one conveyed by a bullet.[11]

It is important to recognise that these processes do not, at first, destroy money. It remains money lining the pockets of the manufacturers of munitions and other war supplies, profiteers such as Ouvrard or the British parliament of 1919, who seemed to Baldwin merely 'a lot of hard-faced men who look as if they had done very well out of the war.'[12] Also their suppliers and employees. But as a war progresses in duration and violence, the liabilities created in money – which have no earning counterpart, as we have said, for they are life and wealth destroyed, not made – become intolerable and must be extinguished: by war reparations from the enemy, if victorious, and by default or by inflation, if defeated or otherwise unsuccessful.

In the Middle Ages, reparations generally took the form of ransom: for example, the 100,000 Cologne marks or 23 tonnes of silver exacted from England for the person of Richard I in 1194. But it was the Hundred Years War that made an epoch in war finance. When Edward III of England failed to conquer France in his campaign of the 1330s, he had no means of repaying his 1,365,000

florins in Florentine loans, and thus ruined not only the Bardi and
the Peruzzi families but their creditors in the city: Florence did not
recover as a market for capital for almost a century.[13] His adversaries,
Philip VI and John II, taxed their subjects by inflating the French
coinage: the *gros tournois* was debased from sixty per mark weight of
silver in 1336 to four hundred and eighty in 1355, and thus provoked
Oresme's great diatribe. Indeed, war in the age of money will
generally be attended by an inflation: money destroys life and
territory and then itself.

That can be shown, in particularly lurid form, in the financing of
total war in 1939–45. In England, under the practical genius of
Keynes, inflation was recognised as a useful tool of war finance, for
it is by means of higher prices that a state at war can capture the
work and products of its people from their private purposes; but
inflation, as we have seen and Keynes well knew, is devilishly hard
to direct and control.[14] At home, the 1941 budget set out a mixture
of forced loans, forced savings and sharp increases in taxation.
Income tax was increased to ten shillings in the pound (50 per cent)
for the standard rate and surtax to 19/6*d* (97.5 per cent). A reduction
in allowances created four million new taxpayers. In paying for
munitions and supplies from overseas, Britain soon ran out of gold –
reserves were only £60 million in the spring of 1941, or about one
week's war expenditure – but the spectre of defeat had been
dissipated by Roosevelt's re-election to a third term as President
and, that March, by the open-ended U.S. credit known as Lend-
Lease. In the Middle East and particularly in India, the base for the
war against Japan, Britain simply ran up debts in sterling. By the end
of 1943, and even after the sale of £1 billion (thousand million) in
investments in the United States, Britain owed abroad the quite
unprecedented sum of £6 billion, only half of that covered by Lend-
Lease and Canadian Mutual Aid. On September 13, 1945, in the
board room of the Federal Reserve in Washington, Keynes spoke
for two and a half hours to the assembled U.S. officials, stressing in
equal measure Britain's unique contribution to the war and her
devastated international balance-sheet. The next afternoon, he spoke
for three hours. In the end, the United States proved as generous as
ever: a new loan of $3,750 million and the cancellation of the Lend-
Lease debt, which was $30 billion in gross and about $21 billion net

of British counter-services. But, as Keynes himself recognised, it was not enough: he had returned from Washington with less than half a loaf.

The British war effort brought hyperinflation to Egypt, Iran and India and a catastrophic famine to Bengal; but at home, the official cost of living index was scarcely higher in January 1945 than it had been in March 1941: what our parents remembered from the war was not rising prices but empty shops and endless queues.[15] The inflation came after Keynes' death in 1946. Shorn of the captive markets of empire and her dollar-earning international commercial estate, her economy more fitted for war than any but that of the Soviet Union, Britain yet wanted to taste the sweets of what appeared to be victory. Her debts were not just monetary but moral: for the sacrifices of the public – Churchill's 'blood, toil, tears and sweat' – there seemed no recompense but full employment, rising wages, a national health service, pensions, free education and all the other New Jerusalems in Britain, and independence for India. The result was an inflation without parallel in British history. My life began in rationing and proceeded, step by step, with the devaluation of sterling, which now buys less than a fifteenth of those things it bought in the year of my birth. The inflation was not tamed until the early 1990s, after the Thatcher governments had at last dismantled the wartime economy.

Staring out from his window at the Bank of England in 1996, one of the bank's directors, Mervyn King, had a vision of the inflation as a deluge: if the price level in London could be compared to the height of water in the Thames, then this inflationary river, which was at eight feet in 1800 and ten feet in 1945, had risen by 1996 to 200 feet, 'enough to swamp any craft that did not anticipate' it.[16] From our vantage at the west end of town, with a half-century of British history spread out below us, we can see that what was happening in those years, so baffling at the time, was a process of history that should have been evident to a child: that the devaluations and lowered flags, even the pop music and football riots, were joined by a thread of history which was the gradual liquidation of the debts of war. While the conduct of war and peace has altered greatly since the eighteenth century, I cannot hope to improve on Abbé Galiani's analysis of the French devaluations of 1718:

War is the luxury of monarchies and in peace it is impossible to get rid of the effects of war except by economy and frugality. On the other hand the French may be pardoned for their outcry against augmentations [devaluations] for the sick man always shouts and screams when he takes medicine, but not when he is catching his sickness by living too recklessly; that is why war is full of joyous songs and celebrations and gaiety, while monetary changes are lugubrious and sad. But there is no question that they are the medicine not the disorder or disease.[17]

For half a lifetime, my generation mistook the cure for the disease. Now on the threshold of middle age, we are cured, but shaken to the core of our natures and prone to suspicion and melancholy. We envy our parents, for their courage in war, and our children, for their lightness of heart, their easy commercial ways and their astonishing prosperity. Our consolation is philosophy or rather Galiani's resignation: 'anyway nobody has anything else to propose.'

Britain's chief adversary in the war, the German Reich, followed a radically different course. Having no rich nephew across the Atlantic, and reluctant to tax the population, the Reich resorted to subterfuges that still astonish by their cynicism, brutality, elegance and success. Even now, after long study of work by German scholars, I am not sure I have fully understood the mechanism or am qualified to describe it in English. For the Theresienstadt *Ghettokronen* that so haunted me when I saw them that day in Hampstead were but the tip of a great money fraud, surely the greatest ever perpetrated, that reveals better than any other the delusive character of money. The fraud was wholly successful in the sense that the Reich's money survived as long as its armies, which is all that Hitler ever wanted.

The subterfuge arose not simply in the restrictions placed on the German economy and armed forces by the 1919 Peace, the inflationary psychology of the early 1920s and the Depression of the 1930s, but also in Hitler's violent and romantic nature. He did not think in categories of money: territorial expansion and anti-Semitism were his sole economic policies. The section of his political testament, *Mein Kampf* (*My Struggle*), that purports to explain the economic theories of the National Socialists does nothing of the sort: as he explains, the slogans of the Weimar era, such as the 'breaking of the bondage of interest' (*Brechung der Zinsknecht-schaft*), were not ends but means: 'For me and all true National Socialists there is only one doctrine: People and Fatherland. *For our struggle is to secure our existence, augment our race and our people, feed our children and keep pure their blood.*'[18] In truth, in those passages, Hitler is in revolt against the history of money: cities, finance, joint-stock ownership, the stock and bond markets, peaceful commercial competition, the 'economisation of the nation' and the 'dominion of money' have destroyed the will and vigour of the Germans. Four hundred years of history will be resolved in a single combat: a pure-blood race rooted in its own soil confronts the Jews and their money.[19]

In May 1933, two months after Hitler had come to power by election, a shell company known as the Metallische Forschungsge-sellschaft m.b.H – the Metallurgical Research Co. Ltd. – usually abbreviated to Mefo, was founded with Siemens, GHH, Krupp and Rheinstahl as partners. The firm's capital was just one million Reichsmarks, for it wasn't going to do any research: its sole function was to create a form of money: it issued three-month bills to army suppliers and munitions manufacturers which could then be discounted – cashed – at commercial banks against a guarantee of acceptance at the end of the quarter by the Reichsbank. These bills were known under the general 1930s euphemism of 'job-creation measures' but persisted long after the Reich had reached full employment in 1936: in reality, they were merely instruments to finance re-armament and civil works with military use – autobahns, shipyards and so on – off the state's budget. The banks took them up because they had little other use for their deposits: mortgage lending, for example, was banned by law in 1938.

In his Reichstag speech of September 1, 1939, Hitler said the Reich had spent some 90 billion Reichsmarks on re-armament. Hjalmar Schacht, the president of the Reichsbank in the 1930s, gave a figure of 34 billion at the Nuremberg trials. The difference may arise merely in the definition of what constitutes armament. Anyway, by 1936, more than half of the government's expenditure was on military preparations of one sort or other, half of it financed through the budget, half of it through the Mefo.[20] Two years later, with the new demands of integrating Austria and the Sudetenland into the

Reich, and the construction of the defences known as the *Westwall*, the state's finances were at the point of breaking. Taxes, which are statements about the legitimacy of any regime, were not in question. Schacht was now warning of the severe inflationary consequences of the paper being issued in such profusion: he evidently thought that the Reichsbank guarantee on the Mefo bills gave him a weapon. He also threatened to resign if any more bills were issued in 1938.

Schacht overplayed his hand. On January 7, 1939, he and all his fellow directors signed a letter to Hitler, warning that spending had brought state finances to 'the brink of collapse' and demanding that all Reich projects be financed by taxation or long-term loans, and be approved by the finance ministry. I must here stress that the directors voiced no objections to the goals of Hitler's foreign policy: their concern is not with 'a military build-up that has made possible a foreign policy that has forced the world to take notice' – Nazi German is very hard to translate – but to avoid its inflationary consequences from which 'nothing material can be gained.' The 'two great foreign policy initiatives in the East Mark and the Sudetenland' – that is, the occupation of Danzig and Czechoslovakia – 'were bound to lead to a rise in public spending, but since their completion there is no sign of a contraction in spending policy, but rather evidence of plans for a *further increase*, to the consequences of which for the currency it is our categorical duty to draw attention.' On the front of the letter, Dr Lammers, the head of the Reichs Chancellery, noted in ink:

1) Submitted to the Führer today
2) Führer's decision is contained in enc. Führer's Edict of Today and the Discharge and Appointment Documents of 20.1.39[21]

In short, they were all fired.

One of the sacked directors, Karl Blessing, became governor of the Reichsbank's successor, the German Bundesbank, in 1958 and served with great devotion until 1969. The Reichsbank itself, by the law of June 15, 1939, lost its independence. When war broke out in September, Hitler already had in place the instruments to finance it and, in Walter Funk as bank president, a suitable yes-man.

Expenditure, which rose to a peak of 171 billion Reichsmarks in the last year of the war, vastly exceeded the yield from taxes (37 billion) and even the forced contributions from occupied countries, such as the Netherlands (24 billion). The armies and their equipment were paid for by the sale of paper obligations of the Reich to the public, amounting to around 380 billion Reichsmarks by the end of the war or about thirty times the debt at the time Hitler took power.[22]

The terms used to describe this financing in the secret documents are indescribably sinister: the goal was a 'noiseless,' 'invisible,' 'frictionless' process. It was a closed system sealed without chink against reality. The state's debts were converted into banknotes: the currency in circulation rose from about 11 billion Reichsmarks at the outbreak of war to about 70 billion at the fall of Berlin. The Germans, all employed, all earning, received wages in banknotes that they couldn't spend; so they deposited the money at the banks; but the banks couldn't lend it, except to the government; so they bought the government's paper; which was converted into more banknotes; and round and round and round. Prices and wages were tightly fixed, so that inflation at first simply did not manifest itself, except at the edges: the sharp rise in the Frankfurt stock market in 1941 was one such inflationary symptom, and tells one something about the ability of stock-market indices to predict events! But by 1944, public confidence in money was evaporating, and there was a flight into things, led by the portly figure of Göring, who was amassing by confiscation and murder a nice collection of pictures. Any free buying and selling occurred in the black market. Yet the finance ministry went on compiling its insane statistics right to the very last days of the war. At Hitler's death, the Germans possessed 70 billion Reichsmarks in worthless coins and banknotes and 380 billion in obligations of a regime which no longer existed. Put another way, the expenditure on the war roughly equalled the cumulative national product of Germany since the mid-1920s. Germany had been converted into money and destroyed. Zero.

Of course, there was much more to the Third Reich than its financial statistics. I have devoted space to these technicalities to remind you that money, generally considered the guarantor of liberty, will just as happily serve a tyranny; and will permit, to use eighteenth-century language, a Lacedaemonian system to masquerade as an Athenian. Hitler could have used other means to rob the

Germans of their property, vigour and lives and did so; but he also used money, which gave his enterprise, at least until the war turned against him, a specious air of order and sense. The Germans thought they were working to preserve themselves but, in reality, they were doing the opposite: they were destroying themselves. A whole nation fell prey to the monetary delusion in its most extreme form. Let us now address that delusion in a particular case.

★

The fortress in Bohemia known in Czech as Terezin and in German as Theresienstadt was founded by Emperor Joseph II and named after his mother, Maria Theresa, a woman who has left her mark elsewhere in the history of money. A paragon of late eighteenth-century military architecture, Theresienstadt was declared a closed city on September 22, 1784, passed through the nineteenth century as an insignificant garrison town and first enters history in the winter of 1941. In the star-shaped fortress with its six towers, in a space just seven hundred yards long by five hundred broad, the builders had crammed a garrison church, a water tower, a hospital where the assassin Gavrilo Princip died of TB, an officers' mess, three small parks, a brewery, a bakery, 150 houses, 40 huts and, against the city walls, eleven massive red-brick barrack buildings in the style of the Austrian late baroque. From November 1941 until the end of the war, this space served as a prison for some 155,000 Jews from the so-called Protectorate of Bohemia and Moravia, Austria, Germany, Denmark, the Netherlands, Slovakia, Hungary and Poland, with a peak population of nearly 60,000 in September 1942. Of these people, some 25,000 were still living when the town was taken over by the International Committee of the Red Cross on May 5, 1945. Of the remainder, 35,000 had died in the town of disease, violence, hunger or suicide, while a further 88,000 were transported by train to extermination camps at Lublin, Riga, Treblinka, Minsk and above all Auschwitz-Birkenau, of which number some 3,500 survived.

The story represented by those numbers has been told in one of the very greatest works of dispassionate history, H. C. Adler's *Theresienstadt 1941–1945*, published at Tübingen in 1955. We shall confine ourselves to the money of Terezin. The Third Reich was such a chaotic regime, riven by bureaucratic faction and caprice and contradictory policies, that the Nazis were never wholly clear about the prison's purpose: an apartheid New Jerusalem, as some of the Prague Jews themselves wanted, which could be put on show to visiting neutrals; or a holding camp for a programme of extermination. At the Wannsee Conference of January 20, 1942, Heydrich spoke of an 'old-people's ghetto,' and for a while the SS ran a business selling retirement homes in Theresienstadt to elderly German Jews. It became the place to send what the SS called *Prominenten*: German and Austrian officers with high military decorations, scholars and artists of international renown, superannuated quislings, and high Danish or Dutch officials. To this murderous ambiguity, the money of Theresienstadt was suited: for its purpose, more than any other money in this book, was to give *the impression of normality* in a world gone screaming mad. It served, like the 'post office,' 'shops,' 'café,' and the orchestral 'concerts' in the main square, not just as a sadistic SS joke but as a screen or euphemism to the Germans and their allies and a consolation to a terrified people under the shadow of annihilation.

In September 1942, in the midst of the brutal and chaotic arrangements for the so-called *Alterstransporte* – the despatch of 10,000 old people from Germany and Austria to death at Trostinetz, near Minsk in Belarus – the SS announced that the town would soon move onto a money economy. The purpose, according to a manuscript account written by a member of the Jewish administration in Theresienstadt, was to 'facilitate the exchange of goods ... increase labour productivity through a gradation of wages ... procure additional provisions and essential commodities and direct them through the channels of commerce.'[23]

According to another Theresienstadt manuscript, abandoned by the architect and civil engineer Otto Zucker when he was sent in September 1944 to head a 'new camp in the Dresden area,' or rather to be murdered at Auschwitz, wages were introduced in November 1942. Each ghetto inhabitant was to be paid, according to six grades for both men and women, with those not working placed in the lowest grades. Each was to receive both cash, which could be spent but only under an unwieldy system of rationing, and payments into blocked accounts in a new Bank of the Jewish Autonomous Administration, sumptuously established in the old Town Hall on the square. The notes, in denominations of 1, 2, 5, 10, 20, 50 and 100 crowns, were designed, according to Adler, in the camp and show Moses with the Ten Commandments and the signature of Jakob Edelstein, the Chief Elder. Again according to Adler, some anti-Semitic caricature was introduced by the engraver in Berlin: a beaked nose, ringlets and long fingernails. My examples, which may not be contemporary but rather forged from the original plates in the 1960s, are dated January 1, 1943, but Otto Zucker says that the bank did not start making payments until May 12 of that year.

Already, some shops had been opened. There were eight at first: groceries; gentlemen's clothing; ladies' clothing; lingerie; shoes; household goods; gifts, perfume and stationery; luggage. The shops contained a mixture of knick-knacks stolen from the luggage of the German Jews in the camp – brooches, chains and other trinkets – which in some cases the owners managed to buy back with their *Ghettogeld*, and a few objects such as wooden shoes and overalls made in the camp. The luggage, which everybody needed to store their things in because there were no cupboards, often carried the name and *Transportnummer* of a previous owner. Goods re-appeared when their temporary owners were deported.

A butcher's and a dispensary were opened, but the entry from the street was barred: the choice cuts of meat and fat sausages, and the medicines, were not in fact for sale. There were also some workshops – clock, pen and spectacles repair – barber's shops and a lending library. An orchestra was assembled with instruments that had been confiscated from the Jews of Prague. For a while, in December 1942, the Prague newspaper *Der Neue Tag* could be had, until it carried the news of Stalingrad. The final step was the cleaning up of a pre-war pub on the south-east side of the square, which had been used as a dormitory, and its opening as a 100-seat café. Engineer Zucker wrote in his diary: 'In these months the Ghetto lost its camp-like character.'[24]

The problem was that there was nothing to buy. According to Zucker, the bank received from the SS 53 million crowns on April 21, 1943. Five million crowns were issued, but of those only two million returned to the bank. The remainder was hoarded, thrown away or used as chips for card games: the Jews, it seems, preferred their own games to those of the SS. One old German lady hoarded hers, for she thought she'd have to pay reparations to the other European Jews when the war was lost.[25] To increase the circulation of the notes, the Jewish administration started charging 50 crowns a month for so-called 'leisure activities' and up to 50 crowns to collect a postal package. At the café, a cup of ersatz coffee or tea with a piece of sugar cost two crowns, but one was permitted only one cup a day. In September 1943, the transports to Auschwitz began again and those selected to go generally gave their money away, as people do before they die.

Soon afterwards, the inmates began to hear the word *Stadtverschönerung*: City Beautiful! In the spring of 1944, the people of Theresienstadt transformed their town. They swept the streets, weeded the main square and planted it with twelve hundred rose bushes. They built a bandstand across from the café. In the northeast bastion, they made a playground with swings and roundabouts and a kindergarten. They painted and plastered buildings out and in, draped curtains over windows, hung pictures (stolen from the Prague Jews), decked tables with vases of flowers. The bank was done up in the best Berlin style: the 'director' received a vast partner's desk and a suite of leather club chairs. The problem of overcrowding was solved by three transports north on May 15, 16 and 18, comprising 7,503 people (385 survivors). Those left behind had an idea that a commission of some sort was coming, to do with the International Red Cross, Danes, or Swedes or maybe Swiss. As May turned into June, excitement mounted to a pitch. The Jewish officials tinkered day and night with details of the programme.

June 23, 1944, was a beautiful fine day in Theresienstadt. The commission, as it rolled up in three cars before the Jewish Autonomous Administration building, consisted of senior SS officers in civilian dress and two Danes and a Swiss: Frantz Hvass, chief of the political department of the Danish foreign ministry, Dr Juel Hennigsen, of the interior ministry, and Dr Rossell, of the International Red Cross. They were greeted by Paul Eppstein, Chief Elder after Edelstein's murder, in a frock coat and top hat, but with a black eye from a recent blow from Commandant Rahm. In his introductory presentation, Eppstein gave various vital statistics – numbers of inmates, nationalities, ages, calorie intake and so on, most of them false – spoke of agriculture, crafts, industry, retailing and the bank, and then the tour began. The visitors saw a game of football, a distant view of farm girls with their rakes, the laundry, bakery and pharmacy, the bank and post office, the butcher's shop, the firehouse, a dormitory, the hospital and even the psychiatric ward (whose sickest patients had been sent to Bergen-Belsen on March 20). Dr Rossell took a number of photographs. It was, all in all, a success, though naturally there could have been some improvements. On July 9, the Jewish central secretariat sent out a circular:

> The designations 'Ghetto money' and 'Ghetto crowns' are not to be employed, effective immediately. In their place stands the designation 'Theresienstadt crowns' (abbreviation: Th. Cr.).[26]

In August, a film crew arrived to record for posterity the City Beautiful. It completed filming half-way through September, and with its departure, the comedy was over. On the 27th, Eppstein was executed. On the 28th, Zucker was deported in a group of 2,500 (371 survivors). On the 29th, a further 1,500 left (76 survivors), and, on October 1, 1,500 more, including Mrs Zucker with eight suitcases: as she was helped aboard, Rahm told the transport director, 'Frau Zucker lies in her husband's arms tonight or there'll be hell to pay'; but her husband was already burned (293 survivors).[27] In the course of that October, 13,500 Theresienstadters went to their deaths.

Back in Copenhagen, Hvass wrote up his notes:

> To round off this report, I cannot forgo expressing the admiration one must feel for the Jews who have succeeded in creating, by their outstanding commitment and within the framework of the Autonomous Adminstration, such relatively good external conditions for their co-religionists and imbuing them with the courage and strength to go on living. Whether they can preserve their will to live will evidently depend not inconsiderably – as we witnessed during our visit to the town – on the population's belief that their accommodation in Theresienstadt has merely a temporary character.[28]

★

The Greeks measured their history from the first Olympic Games, the Romans from the foundation of the city by Romulus and Remus, the Christians from the birth of Christ, the Muslims from

Mohammed's displacement from Mecca to Medina, the Chinese from the Hsia Dynasty. German history begins on May 8, 1945, zero hour, *die Stunde Null.*

The first moneys of this new era were suitably primitive. In the districts of U.S. military occupation, notably Frankfurt on the Main, the Germans used cartons of American cigarettes. It was a money well suited to its environment, for, as the official history of the German Bundesbank correctly records, it did not inflate: if there was nothing to buy, the money was simply smoked. In the Soviet zone of occupation, a money was introduced but it did not circulate outside the zone: on departure, the visitor was obliged to surrender his Ost-marks for a ridiculous handful of foreign coins. Even so, the German communists, building on old Prussian bureaucratic virtues and the remains of electrical and optical industries, created a state of sorts. The treasured mementoes of my German residence, the *Aufbau* editions of the classics and the recordings of Kurt Masur and Peter Schreier, were all bought for Ost-marks in the Alexanderplatz.

In the west, the D-mark was introduced over the weekend of June 19–20, 1948. On the Monday, its exchange was quoted at 13 marks and 43 pfennigs to the pound sterling. As I write this, the exchange is 2 marks and 71 pfennigs.

The rise in the exchange attempts to reflect the different experience of inflation in West Germany and Britain, and to predict future inflation. As the actual and moral debts of the war began to appear unpayable, so sterling weakened: against services and commodities at home and those priced in foreign currencies, including the D-mark. Lenders of sterling to the British government, corporations and public demanded higher interest to compensate them against loss in the purchasing power of their funds. Profits had to be that much higher to cover interest charges. Investment slowed down. Business stagnated. Britain's share of trade in the world drained away, like sand in an hour-glass, by one percentage point each year. In West Germany, in contrast, with its inflation behind it, interest was low and business boomed: the monetary measures of business grew by 5 per cent a year in the 1950s and 1960s, and 4 per cent in the 1970s. With reconstruction complete in the 1980s, the economy stopped growing, but then the Berlin Wall came down, offering a challenging new field for commercial exploitation.

In this cautionary comparison, all observers, British and German, agreed on the singular role of one institution. It was the West Germans' great good fortune to have imposed on them a central bank, modelled not on the Reichsbank of Schacht and Funk but the U.S. Federal Reserve: a bank that would be more insulated even than its model from the demands of politicians and public opinion; and one whose institutional goal was not that of prosperity or social peace but 'of safeguarding the currency.'[29] The Germans found able and crafty public servants – Blessing, Klasen, Emminger, Pöhl, Schlesinger, Tietmeyer – to run it; and they supported it when it put out the inflationary fires of 1950, 1956, 1974, 1981 and 1992. For Germans had had it with inflation.

The Bundesbank sits in its own small park in Frankfurt, the barbed wire on its high steel fence hidden in the tops of flowering trees. Inside, there is that quiet economy of effort that is the essence of the German bureaucratic genius: short hours under cloudy skies, frequent and nourishing meals, formal manners, apple-pie files, suppressed gallantry, a distaste for the telephone. These old working habits are its only history: everything else fell in the war. If, as Eugen Böhm-Bawerk thought, interest is the measure of a country's cultural sophistication, then here, between a sports stadium and a thundering highway, is Germany's Opera and Conservatory.[30]

In the course of the 1980s, Europeans of both East and West began to envy the Federal Republic and its bank. Alarmed, the Soviets took to the crudest bullying; but when, in 1983, they failed to foment a civil war in West Germany over the U.S. nuclear forces in the country, they withdrew, sulking, and revealed to their allies their strategic bankruptcy. One by one, the Eastern European regimes began to crumble: first Poland, then Hungary and Czecho-slovakia, then, in 1989, the German Democratic Republic. In the West, an envious France had been experimenting with a novelty, *un franc fort*. Italy, with its love of gesture, promoted its central bank governor to prime minister. Ireland, Portugal, Spain and Greece were drenched in money, raised from the rich German public in high taxes and interest-paying bonds.

The European Community, which had prospered since the 1950s through a series of timid steps, regulating first iron and coal, then agriculture, then tariffs and state subventions, then labels on consumer products, then diplomacy and processes of law, now dreamed of a great leap: it would capture the bank! A European Central Bank, sited perhaps in Frankfurt, whose single goal would be sound money! Low interest for everybody for ever and ever! As these thoughts took bureaucratic shape in Brussels, Paris and Bonn in the second half of the 1980s, certain consequences of political logic became evident: that the bank, and the power it alone disposed of to make and unmake money, would cut the European parliaments down to rumps and disenfranchise their electorates; that all countries must be in the bank, for one could not have one country devaluing every year and stealing markets from the others; that a central bank without a central government was something of a democratic novelty; and that therefore such a regime demanded a federal union of truly American type. For without a devaluation to cheapen its land and products and activities, a state in depression has no choice but to ship out its workers to more prosperous districts; and that has always happened in the United States, most brutally in the migrations to California of the 1930s. That the United States was a federation of one language and little local variation in law and custom – a far cry from the Europe of the 1980s – was forgotten in the general enthusiasm.

As in the United States in 1787, the federalists attempted a coup d'état. In the course of 1992 and 1993, several electorates were asked to vote on closer union. The Danes, sick of being bullied by their southern neighbour, voted against: they were warned, in vague but terrible terms, of the penalties of their recalcitrance. The Norwegians also voted no, but they were few and very rich and a long way away. The French voted yes, by a small handful, and with that *petit oui* – a phrase from sexual manners – Paris boasted that it had a mandate for a single money and a federal state. Even the Swiss, who had kept themselves insulated from continental schemes for nearly five centuries, wavered a little; before remembering they had absolutely nothing to gain, and rather a lot to lose. The Mediterranean countries, modernising economies restrained by years of fascism, indeed had nothing to lose. Italy had long recognised that it was essentially ungovernable. In the breathing-space that followed the end of the Cold War, the magistracy had attempted to reform Italian public life, but their investigations soon dissipated in that conspiracy of silence known in that country as *omertà*, manliness. In such circumstances, national sovereignty merely meant corruption and was best dispensed with. The Spanish and the Portuguese sensed they could go on doing what they had always done, at somewhat lower rates of interest.

In this drama, Britain, like Rhode Island at the Constitutional Convention, kept herself aloof. As the only country in Europe that could look at its recent history without flinching, Britain wondered why there was such hurry. The British sensed, as an old commercial power, that there was more to life than lower interest; and that the displacement of politics onto the field of money revealed how shallow were the democratic traditions of the continentals. Keynes was still a name in England. The learned recollected that by taking sterling off the gold standard in 1931, Keynes and others had saved the country from the Depression. A flirtation with fixed exchange-rates between 1990 and 1992 had not been a success. The Bundesbank was administering its hardest medicine, to stamp out the inflation that had attended the unification of the Germanys and to warn the federal government never to flout the bank's authority again. Suspecting that the British government and public had no attachment to hard money, on September 16, 1992, the speculators in the capital markets drove sterling out of the European Exchange-Rate Mechanism.

That event, attended by the direst warnings from the Continent, inaugurated a period of prosperity such as Britain had not enjoyed since the 1960s. Prices stayed where they were, interest fell, sterling eventually rose, exports and living standards rose, employment rose, the stock market rose. Of course, Britain was no longer in the first rank of Europe either in power or in prosperity; but she was a lot more prosperous than in 1945 or even 1985; and her armed forces had performed as well as ever in the Gulf. For reasons that baffled even the British, but probably had to do with the skill of its young working people, the country was attracting substantially all the Asian investment in Europe. Awash with the revenues from oil in the North Sea, and the dividends of industries restored to profit in the 1980s, the City bought back the U.S. industrial estate sold off in the war: for a country living off foreign dividends, devaluation carried no fears. The world in 1996 was in a deflationary phase, even before the Internet had begun to reveal its power to drive down prices. With twenty million people seeking work in Europe and not finding it – nearly five million in Germany alone – it might be that the Continent needed more money, not less. In such conditions, the last person Europe needed at the helm was Tietmeyer.

To the British, trade was good, solid, palpable. Barriers to trade were bad. But political union was just a contraption, and the bureaucratic rhetoric of Brussels did not translate into English. The British felt threatened in their sense of specialness: *they* were not going to abandon their ancient culture, like the Irish and the Portuguese, for superfluous motorways paid for by the German taxpayer. And they wondered why, if union was so good, the benefits of joining were not enumerated. Where were the European *Federalist Papers*? Why were the penalties of not joining so luridly portrayed? Why, as the unfortunate Danes had discovered, were there merely threats? Not far from the surface was the old suspicion of Germany. The Germans had failed to gain continental supremacy through arms, but were now achieving it through money; truly, the triumph of the Guicciardinian strategy.

The fear was unfounded, as fears often are. The old German racial nationalism of forests and pigtails had brought only disaster. It was sentimental, rather than passionate, and had been displaced by a civic nationalism, no less sentimental; which, because the European project was coeval with the Federal Republic, had a pronounced Community tinge. Yet the Germans still felt haunted by a Romantic ghost: the wanderer between two worlds, sometimes turning to the East, sometimes to the West, perpetually unsatisfied. To the British, it all sounded too clever by half. The notion in Bonn that Germany must bind herself to Western Europe as once Odysseus to the mast, lest she be sent mad by the Siren songs of hegemony, sounded in London plain daft. When Helmut Kohl, in early 1996, threw the word 'war' into the discussion, the British felt confirmed in their worst suspicions. The Chancellor, inasmuch as he meant anything, meant nothing more profound than that there used to be wars in Western Europe, but since the founding of the European Coal and Steel Community, there hadn't been any, and that was something, wasn't it? But it was poor diplomacy. The Tory government in London took to quarrelling with Bonn. Quarrelling with Germany became its *point d'honneur*. The continentals progressed from threats against Britain to actual discrimination against, of all things, her beef: here was a savage delight for the British patriot! Meanwhile, the financial deadlines of the Maastricht Treaty took on the character of ultimatums.

A storm had blown up out of a blue sky. There was no urgency to union. The military threat to the Continent, which had seemed so palpable at the time of the U.S. missile deployments in Germany in 1983, had vanished. Business conditions weren't bad. A world free-trade treaty, known as the GATT, had been ratified in 1995. The old European policy of small steps, though wearisome beyond description, had functioned for two generations and seemed likely to go on doing so. In attempting to force union, for reasons of bureaucratic inertia, damp ideology and personal ambition, the continental politicians, notably Delors, had provoked disunion and revealed the deep distinctions in tradition and mentality that the old policy had concealed and contained. The Tories in Britain conducted affairs with a childish frivolity. Together, they behaved more irresponsibly than the orators of South Carolina and New England in the gathering storm of the late 1850s.

The continentals misunderstood the nature of money. They thought it was a sort of high road, flat and clear of emotional traffic, that would skirt the bogs of politics and custom; but as Law had found, and the British politicians showed in their language, however puerile, it was as encumbered by passions and fears as any monument of national self-esteem, whether it be the House of Westminster, the bullfight, the Purity Decree of German beer or the Great British Sausage.

Since the late Middle Ages, as we have seen, states had been governed in several important departments by the markets for capital. Central banks could influence those markets by their prestige or by certain crude operations in the market, but not control them. Divine-right and elected governments had but two weapons at their disposal against those markets, violence and inflation. In renouncing such weapons beforehand, the continentals held out the possibility of a Europe alienated to the *rentiers*, its past and future subordinated to the rate of interest; or rather, since that was unpalatable to their personal ambitions, of an overweaning federal government that would ride as hard over the *amour-propre* of the states as Sherman in Georgia in the winter of 1864. The future held that among its infinite possibilities; but it was not a future that the British, in 1996, were prepared to entertain.

12

Money: A Valediction

Tant'oro ci ha in terra, tante cose, tant'uomini, tanti bisogni . . .
Davanzati[1]

There is on Earth just so much Gold, so many Things, so many
Men, so many Desires.

This essay draws to its close. It has been a pleasure and a labour, and
I can think of no happier fate for it than that it be found wanting by
the experts, and yet survive for a while as a sort of by-way of the
study of money, like an alley one enters to escape the blinding,
crowded street. If I have laid too much stress on money's disservices
to humanity, I ask for understanding: for money has no lack of
professional devotees.

From the masterpieces of literature and art I have assembled for
you, let me now distil what we have learned.

We have learned that money, far from existing for all eternity like
Melchizedek in the Bible, has a history. For from obscure beginnings, money has spread out to colonise the world, both in its forms
as coin or banknote or book entry and as a notion of happiness
penetrating the minds of men and women. Money was probably not
invented in a particular place and at a particular era, but came into
manifold being, for manifold purposes. Money permitted human
beings to expand not only their possessions but their wishes beyond
limits held ultimate by predecessors. By now, money has become a
system, which we understood, by way of the simile of the railway
shunting yard, as gathering the wishes of the most estranged and
scattered populations and despatching them to unimagined destinations. We also saw that money became indifferent to its physical

form, and whether human beings revert to gold or cattle as money of account and payment, or pass into a realm of pure electricity, is a matter of indifference also to us.

Money is one of those human creations that make concrete a sensation, in this case the sensation of wanting, as a clock does the sensation of passing time. It is that double aspect of money, airy and substantial, that has fascinated all civilisations. Human beings have never quite been able to decide whether money is a universal come down to earth or a daily thing for ever aspiring to perfection. It seems to have a wandering or frontier reality, like a ghost or a sailor who, to the ancient Greeks, seemed not wholly of the living or of the dead. We saw, however, that quite early in its history, money revealed other dualities – as currency and capital, action and potential, means and end; and passed from being a mere conveyance of desire to the object of all desire, Schopenhauer's *Glückseligkeit in abstracto*.

The relations of human beings, both to one another and to the world of things, took on some of the character of money. They became fluid, temporary, indifferent, unstable. Reality, which men and women had been at first content to name and then to legislate, was priced. Sir William Petty's dream of finding an equation to link all phenomena became actual in the algebra of money. Earth, air, fire and water were priced. The idea of the common fell away. A veil of money was draped over the world. Men lost sight of the natural sources of their existence. The past became mere penury, barbarism or folklore: men ceased to understand their scripture and their annals.

We saw that the desire incarnate in money offered a reward to the imagination, as between two lovers; and that reward seemed at first to be guaranteed by rare and beautiful metals, of whose inner nature and capacity men could only dream. In time, that guarantee was unveiled as only the projected authority of a community: first of princes, who put their faces or emblems on progressively lighter coins; then of merchants in the credit of their signatures on bills of exchange; and then of public banks, which embodied even in their architecture the wisdom and restraint of free cities, states and then unions of states. It was the community that authorised the wishes expressed in money or frustrated them. To use money was to submit to the state, and when states disintegrated their moneys vanished as completely as their laws. Yet we know also that money's abstraction and republicanism, which to most people seem timeless and self-evident, are neither and may be disrupted or reversed; and we gave examples of certain exotic currencies of wartime and the aftermath of war. At the moment, it does appear that money is losing it stateliness and that extraterritorial markets for money or debts expressed in money are more powerful masters of human destiny than states. And yes, no doubt, we will all return, for a while, to gold.

Money also attracted ethical sensations. For some time, and in many places, money was thought to be bad, but it is now thought, on the whole, to be good. That inversion is the greatest to have occurred in the moral sentiments of the West. Desires that resisted incorporation into money turned pale and lost their power to convince: disinterested friendship, love and philanthropy became as suspect as the goals of once passionate wishes, honour and salvation. Miserliness, which places potential above actual gratification, had once seemed the disease of money, as short sight is the disease of books; gradually, it lost its pathology and became the condition of moral health.

Because money reveals nothing of its history in use, and belongs to its holder, it promotes both theft and fraud: for, as we noted with Montesquieu, you are unwise to keep goods stolen from your neighbour in your house, but you can keep his money because it's no longer his. Professions that in earlier ages seemed barely legit-imate, let alone honourable – stockbroking, consumer credit, futures trading, risk arbitrage, all types of parasitic commission business, kiss-and-tell – are now celebrated as manly and ladylike. Money wealth, though it is as colourless as celebrity, appears to many to be good. Actions are good that bring money. Moral choices are thus simply bought out; rather as to a teenage whore or burglar, the garbled memories of moral instruction dissolve in the imperatives of smack.

From classical antiquity, we learned in Chapter 1 that money is a great civiliser, indeed will promote the division of labour, the foundation of civil existence. But it is for ever threatening to conceal the virtue of an object in its price and the propriety of an action in its profit. It is therefore noxious to reason as it was then understood.

We learned from the Middle Ages in Europe that money is fatal to Christianity, and also to any timeless or cherished pattern for society. From the book-keepers, we learned that money can be written or rather forged into a written language which can express reality after a fashion; but at the price of a compulsion and the ludicrous, almost grotesque, restriction of the personality. We learned from the economists that money is an avenue to both choice and prosperity, now redefined in civil language; that men and women chase money as energetically as one another; and money thus opens a window on the mechanism of society and drops certain clues as to its future. But we rejected their assertion that money makes men's affairs predictable, let alone rational, just as we doubted their monetary anthropology. Their liberty, as merely differential rights to property, seemed to us like bourgeois avarice with its face washed.

The Romantics reminded us of the evil of money: how the habit of calculating and making comparisons in money diminishes much that is strange and precious in creation, indeed abolishes quality itself as a mental category by which to understand reality; displaces trust in people by trust in money, and thus poisons the relations between human beings and atomises society; and submerges being in possessing. But we rejected their violence and bitterness, their indiscriminate nostalgia and their crackpot monetary experiments; for we have stood, as it were, in drifts of worthless banknotes outside the Cambodian Central Bank in Phnom Penh, and the burned child fears the fire. From psycho-analysis, we learned that men and women never quite slough off the forgotten sensations of childhood and will project onto their creations, money as earlier God, a cruel or benign paternity.

In the course of this history, I disinterred from the deposit of past times certain men and women and placed them on plinths for your inspection: the person or persons called Longinus, Jesus Christ, Friar Pacioli, Columbus; Cervantes, Rembrandt, Petty, Saikaku, Law; the Marxes, Proudhon and Baudelaire; Marie Duplessis and Clover Adams; Carnegie, Frick and Milken; even, with apologies for a family story, John Buchan, sr. I did that for our guidance, lest we lose ourselves in a waste of stony abstractions or in the mangled and perilous remains of exploded monetary systems; and also because I

believe men and women make their own history, if not always quite
as they intend. I now introduce the last of these monetary heroes,
the embodiment and, as it were, culmination of an English civilisation in whose ruins I had the honour and misfortune to grow up:
John Maynard Keynes.

Keynes, who was born into a university family in Cambridge,
England, in 1883, seemed to himself and to his age to be the last or
seal of the economists: there is something emblematic in his childless
homosexuality. Already in October 1905, Alfred Marshall, the
professor of political economy at the university, was using to him
the language of a latter-day John the Baptist:

> This is a very powerful answer.
> I trust that your future career may be one in wh. you will not
> cease to be an economist.
> I should be glad if it could be that of economist.
> I shall be compelled in lecture to say a good many things wh.
> you know already.[2]

Keynes' early theoretical work, both on probability and on the
money of India – a long-running headache in imperial Britain and
commemorated in a famous joke in Wilde's *The Importance of Being
Earnest* – is brilliant beyond description. Yet as a homosexual,
cruising the London streets in the shadow cast by Wilde's trial and
incarceration,[3] Keynes was naturally at something of an angle to the
British Empire. Amid the pompous and insecure monuments of
Edwardian London, he sought refuge in a demanding social and
topographical bohemia known as Bloomsbury. He was a conscientious objector in the First World War, and bravely defended his
pacificism before a tribunal. In 1919, he published an article on the
Versailles peace negotiations, 'The Economic Consequences of the
Peace,' which tolled the death-knell of the old imperial system just
as in 'The Economic Consequences of Mr Churchill' six years later
he demolished the foundations of the International Gold Standard.
Yet, as Keynes aged, he made his peace with imperial England,
married a woman (a ballerina, actually) and entered government
service, where, in the second war of his lifetime, he assumed the
mantle of the economist-saviour more comprehensively than any
man since Necker. As he sailed to New York in August 1945 to

negotiate the U.S. loan to refloat the empire, his troopship passed HMS *Onslough*, which signalled: 'Best of luck to you and your distinguished passenger.'[4] It was as if he was Aristotle before Alexander, the antique philosopher sent out beyond the gates to sue mercy from the arrogant young conqueror. At the close of the Bretton Woods conference, which was called to devise the post-war monetary regime, the delegates stood up and sang: 'For he's a jolly good fellow . . .'

Yet in the midst of that happy and successful life, showered with the fruits of the Old World and the New, Keynes was uneasy about money: not for his own needs, for after a poor start he was a successful stock-market speculator, but for society. He wrote two philosophical treatises on money, which add somewhat to our understanding, and they are the last works of political economy written in English. They are called *A Treatise on Money*, published in 1930, and *The General Theory of Employment, Interest and Money* of 1936. We shall discuss the second or more complete of these.

Keynes' first concern in the *General Theory* is to distinguish money from other remunerative property or capital, such as land or machines. He saw money, in the form of cash or what he called liquidity, as a sort of distillation of the uncertainty of life. Writing as he was in the mid-1930s, he expresses the anxieties of his age: the suitcase stuffed with banknotes against the hard rap on the door. We hold our property in money when we lose faith in the possibilities of the Ordinary shares of Amalgamated British Misery, in the credit of Consols and even the rural Bloomsbury at Charleston in Sussex and the path Keynes weeded each Saturday with his own hand, while his friends, no doubt, said spiteful things to his upraised bottom.

Like all the economists, Keynes disbelieved in the past and his ignorance of history was proverbial: like his predecessors, Keynes thought a curtain came down after each step, and the only value of an object or institution was the cost in money to replace it. The future, he thought, could be embodied in money. 'The importance of money essentially flows from its being a link between the present and the future.'[5] Money is God's guarantee to Noah, the rainbow over the receding waters: the promise that whatever disaster lies in store, something will be saved from the wreck: in short, that we will still be able to buy and sell things. Keynes believed that such thoughts, in highly abbreviated form, lay behind every decision of spending and investment.

Many doctrines carry in them the seeds of their own refutation. We cannot know the future. All we can do is have wishes about it, which we embody in property, including money, and we are rarely, if ever, confirmed in our choices by events except by chance. Anybody in England who held his property in money through the Keynesian era would have starved. Keynesianism, which was founded, however shakily, on such works as the *General Theory*, in seeking to combine work for all with profits for all, and thus buy social peace, almost destroyed sterling money. In England between 1948 and 1996, the pound sterling – up to then by far the most reliable currency over the long run – lost five-sixths of its power to buy things priced in a currency that was itself devaluing, the mark of one of the German successor states, the Federal Republic. Against many classes of property, it lost more than 95 per cent of its purchasing power. In this inflation of money, the most spectacular since the *assignats* or even the sixteenth century, Keynes' social class came bitterly to grief. In the United States, in early 1966, the unemployed were only 4 per cent of the potential workforce, interest was 1½ per cent a year and it seemed the kingdom of heaven was at hand: at which point, naturally enough, markets for money and debts expressed in money promptly fell to bits and did not pick themselves up for a generation. If money is any protection from uncertainty or guarantee of our social future, it is so only in appearance, like the drunken guard on the Moscow subway.

His other thought of interest to us is this. Like Aristotle, the Muslims, the medieval Schoolmen and Proudhon, Keynes disapproved of the productivity of money: he believed that interest rewarded no genuine sacrifice on the part of the lender, any more than the rent of land on the part of the lord.[6] The money lent or fields rented out are, by definition, surplus to all his needs, except his wish for money. Keynes saw usury not as some piece of antique claptrap, fusty medievalism or totalitarian sloganeering, but the key to the nature of money and of modern society. Like Proudhon, whom I'm sure he never read, he saw the rent of money as a charge on humanity, and he tried to imagine a world in which money did not charge for its use. He did that not through prescription, which would have brought him ridicule or the penitentiary, but by prophecy: he said that money would abolish itself. He believed that as the volume of capital, including money, increased, so its rate of reward or interest would fall and what he called the functionless investor would no longer receive a bonus. People would still use money, but they would be like Marty Siegel, a corrupt Wall Street investment banker of the 1980s, who kept his bribes in banknotes at home to pay the help, or, in Keynes' example which I have not been able to verify, like the father of the poet Alexander Pope, who retired from business with a chest of money for his old-age pension. Somewhat deterred from saving – from fearing or willing the future – people will live in the present: they will spend more, and more people will be employed. The field of choice will be extended, and with it the variety of life. History, so weary-making in the age of money, will dissolve into happiness.

To describe his prophecy, Keynes used a very odd phrase: the euthanasia of the *rentier*. Since he was writing in the mid-1930s, when euthanasia was a euphemism in Germany for the murder of sick children, the phrase indicates not just bad taste but strong feeling. We also sense, through veils of Greek and old French, a catastrophic self-disgust. For without the charge on money, there would be no Clive and Vanessa, Virginia and Leonard; no Charleston, and no King's College, Cambridge, whose financial affairs Keynes managed with such skill; and nothing of that leisure class, engaged in love affairs and philosophical speculation, of which Keynes was such a glorious embodiment. There would be no J. M. Keynes.

But let us give the Keynesian suicide note in its author's words:

On such assumptions I should guess that a properly run community equipped with modern technical resources, of which the population is not increasing rapidly, ought to be able to bring down the marginal efficiency of capital in equilibrium [its profit] approximately to zero within a single generation; so that we should attain the condition of a quasi-stationary community where change and progress would result only from changes in technique, taste, population and institutions, with the products of capital selling at a price proportioned to the labour, etc., embodied in them. . . . A little reflection will show what enormous social changes would result from a gradual disappearance of a rate of return on accumulated wealth. A man would still be free to accumulate his earned income with a view to spending it at a later date. But his accumulation would not grow. He would simply be in the position of Pope's father, who, when he retired from business, carried a chest of guineas with him to his villa at Twickenham and met his household expenses from it as required. . . . It would mean the euthanasia of the rentier, and, consequently, the euthanasia of the cumulative oppressive power of the capitalist to exploit the scarcity of capital.[7]

There is much that is attractive about the argument and the way it is expressed. Rates of interest on money have been falling since the epoch of Hammurabi. There have been sharp and protracted rises, but the *tendency* has been downward, and would appear to aim towards zero as an arrow its target. The amalgamation of computer science and telephony known as the Internet, though now just a collection of electronic club-rooms, may soon break down the Chinese Walls surrounding national markets and make them instantaneous; render warehousing as superfluous as branch banking; and thus redistribute working capital and reduce the rate of interest and the rate of profit.

Yet a moment's thought reveals that Keynes is dreaming; for his exclusions are so oceanic that they swamp the argument. Keynes, the most worldly of the economists since Ricardo, nevertheless fell into Robinsonade: the notion that society is a desert island, timeless, and inhabited only by himself. Technique, taste, population, institutions: surely Keynes, in 1936, must have seen that those were not minor variables? They are the ordinary variables of social existence; are themselves made and shaped by money; and changes in these variables are forever destroying capital and making it scarce and desirable.

In 1945, as we saw in Chapter 11, the capital stock of the Third Reich and its money were worth zero. The same was the case of one of its successor states, the German Democratic Republic, in 1990. In early 1996, Russian industry was priced to liquidate within one year. Thanks in part to money, the population of the world has doubled since the war, and these additional people on the Chinese mainland, in India and elsewhere in Asia are baying for money. A single prototype CD and its player halved the money value of all the world's stock of vinyl discs in an instant; and somewhere in the world are warehouses of flared trousers, superannuated toys, seaplanes and armoured trains, mainframe computing power and so on that cost labour, ingenuity and seas of money to make and are now worthless in money. For the world, as we have said, is a battlefield of wishes, which are limitless and cannot be satisfied except for a moment. Money expresses man's permanent dissatisfaction, which is the spring of his activity, his achievements, and his profound unhappiness. Like desire itself, money is destroyed only to be reborn, like the lovely nymph in Forough Farrokhzad's last poem:

> Dying each night with a kiss
> To come alive with a kiss in the morning.[8]

Far from removing the features of capitalism that Keynes found distasteful – unemployment and the arbitrary distribution of wealth – money removes them only to replace them, and truly its history is that mad bacchanal I saw in a vision in Arabia in 1979 and later found, confirmed, as it were, in Hegel. Above all, it stamps its image on the world: for though, as Keynes thought, it appears to increase the variety of life by extending the field of personal choice, those choices come robed in money. You can have your automobile in any colour, provided it is black. You can convey any desire, provided it can be bought and you have the money to buy it.

I doubt Keynes was sincere in either of those passages I quoted. A true economist, he saw nothing to the human being but a short and purposeless existence, in which filling disused mineshafts with bottles of banknotes is as valuable an activity as any other; no past, no future; no community or posterity; no idea. '*In the long run*, we are all dead.'[9] The phrase is remembered not for its flippancy but for its severity. It is a bleak statement, which was to become typical of the 1930s. For it is the creed of the appeaser. For we have duties not only to ourselves but to our forebears and our children; just as Keynes himself, who gave his life to fight the fascists to defeat in the 1940s, fulfilled his duties to his forebears and to us. We cannot detach a portion of our nature and worship it, without diminishing the human being that remains; and it is the entire human being, not merely its self-regarding wishes, that must be thrown into the battle as the shades of summer darkness come down.

For money is not omnipotent. The Age of Money, which came after the Age of Faith – the God of the Seventeenth Century that dislodged the God of the Middle Ages – has plunged the world into the most perilous instability. There are more than five thousand million people in the world, huddled into cities that survive only by virtue of money, which transmits their desires to a hinterland the size of the earth and returns with the momentary satisfaction of those desires. But money is to us as the potato was to the cottagers of the County Mayo of the 1840s: sustaining as nothing else but liable, like all things, to failure. If money fails in its function, those cities – Cairo, Tokyo, Peking, São Paulo, Delhi, Lima, London, Tehran – those cities will starve; as Marx foresaw, every city has a little Ireland in it.[10] Famines in history have generally occurred from a shortage of food, rather than money: but in Eastern Europe in the 1920s and Bengal in the 1940s, people starved because nobody would accept money, and in the United States in the 1930s, because nobody could be persuaded to part with it. The catastrophe I'm describing may not occur. But it can occur, and it would be well to imagine it.

Yet even without such an apocalypse, the future is not promising. Money, far from being the harmless arena of human emulation as its apologists hold, is a great destroyer. Because money is eminent desire, there is no satisfaction in the external world unless it is conveyed in money, until the world is *possessed* in monetary garb – like an Indian bride in her finery, hair reeking of attar of roses, eyes stinging with *kohl* – ; because money is all power and potential, the external world is a poor thing and may be altered and exploited without compunction.

El mundo es poco. Columbus sucked a thousand years of gold from the Caribbean in two or three, and then extinguished all its human life. The Conquest he not so much inaugurated as carried to the New World now rages all over the globe, including its polar regions. Woods are paved, mountains mined, seas eaten, species annihilated. All the large land and sea animals of the earth, and most of its birds, are under sentence of extinction. They are being killed not by the rifle, but by a more lethal invention, money. Money is no longer, as Adam Smith thought in an excitable passage, 'a waggon-way through the air' that leaves the earth free for men;[11] but is actually destroying it, in the sense of extirpating its most intimate and precious nature, as the cattle-money of the Masai is destroying the grasslands of East Africa. To say that human beings must accept those losses, and live among their parasites – learn to love sparrows and magpies and no other birds, hold cockroaches to be the only insects – in a world of perfect artifice is the final idolatry: that money is our ineluctable destiny, not merely our life, but our death as well. Schopenhauer watched the old men of his age barricade themselves behind money against the siege engines of death.[12] Now all people do that. Humanity itself is transforming into the dragon of the Nibelungen, squatting in a filthy cave amid heaps of dusty treasure. The Ego is satisfied at last, surrounded by annihilating possessions.

Amid thoughts like these, we return to Chapter 2 and marvel at the prophecies of St Matthew: that the agony of Jesus on the cross was not at his own death but at the death of his doctrine; and that as he closed his eyes, he saw, first dimly and then with great clarity, the thirty tetradrachms. I make that point not to revive religion, least of all the Christian religion, but in recognition of the heart of our problem, which now reveals itself with equal clarity. It is that we did not make the world which exists, truly exists, independent of our possession of it: independent, to revive the language of Aristotle, of human valuation, what use or money we make of it. The world exists for itself, but human beings, like the lords and princes of Germany at the time of Thomas Müntzer, 'transform every creature into property – the fishes in the water, the birds of the air, the plants of the earth: everything has to be *theirs*.'[13] It is time to halt the Conquest and sit down, as once Columbus on his blazing Jamaican beach, and consider the scale of our folly.

You will say: but don't these billions of people, brought and to be brought to birth through the midwifery of money, have they not the right to the existence that we love? Does not each one of them, to use an old-fashioned formulation, have a soul as immortal as yours and mine; or, in atheistic language, the equal right to see the sun and breathe the air? Certainly! And that is precisely why the untrammelled pursuit of money is imprudent: one does not issue

hand-guns to the inmates of overcrowded prisons. It was merely
money speaking, as drink speaks in the body of the boozer and gear
in the junkie, deathly and swaggering. We are at war; and as we
showed in Chapter 11, the wartime counterpart of money created is
life, actual life, and wealth, actual wealth, destroyed. We need to
break the compulsory nature of money and make possible a future
in which we are not at permanent war with nature and one another.

For that we must seek values, not in any moralistic or censorious
sets of meanings, let alone as the Russian dolls of the economists;
but values that cannot fit on the money scale: that record objects
and sensations that are priceless in the sense of both precious and
beyond a price in money; that are set above the yapping jaws of
money like a pie left to cool on a high kitchen shelf. Those values
have nothing to do with either utility or price. We need to dispense
with economics and book-keeping or rather restore them to their
places in the hierarchy of organised thought (which for us might be,
as once for Aristotle, below poetry, good conduct, politics and the
management of the household). Religious belief offers such non-
money values, and no doubt religion will be restored in the West in
some other guise; but such a restoration is not in fact necessary.
Merely to state that something is precious but not for sale or
mortgage is not metaphysical nonsense, except to the economists.
For value is mere sensation and we feel a generous action is precious,
and a sudden view of mountains and a handsome face, and such
sensations of non-money value have survived as painful residues,
even in England.

But that, the economist cries, is the grossest subjectivity. Granted
even that large numbers of people agree on such values, how are
they to be allocated among the teeming billions unless by money?
By birth or beauty? By force? Or arbitrarily? For it is precisely from
those injustices – aristocracy, violence, chance – that money sought
to deliver us in Chapters 5, 6 and 7. Human beings are not born
equal, nor can rulers, even in the United States, provide them with
equal chances at the fruits of life. Money, at least, mobilises the
delights of existence and ensures, through its spasmodic behaviour,
its cycles of inflation and deflation, and its belligerence, that nobody
holds on to them for very long: at different epochs it chooses
its Law or Keynes to be its own assassin and irrigates the future

with its own blood. Over time, as Hume put it, the passengers in the coaches will swap places with the servants on the box in front.[14] That is the nearest thing to justice in the world.

I fail to see why those values need to be allocated. It is again a monetary thought, for we have seen already that money must always be poised or in motion and must always be in somebody's possession, lest its moneyness evaporate: whereas the eagle remains the eagle whatever its activity or domicile. It is real as a father's kiss is real, precisely because it is not priced. I suspect that as the unowned elements of nature become more scarce, they will become not expensive but literally priceless; and will pass, like exhausted Old Masters, into communal ownership, which is no ownership at all. They will dissipate, to revive the language of Chapter 3, into mortmain, immobile and inalienable, the image not merely, as the monks thought, of God's kingdom made actual property here on earth but of our belated recognition of earthly reality.

Money will no longer be productive, not, as Keynes thought, because of its superabundance in quantity but because of its perniciousness of quality. It may even, like plutonium, be a charge on its holder. People will not accumulate it, because it will not bring them the fruits of existence but rather will destroy them; because it does not create true wealth but destroys it. As interest and profit fall away, human beings will be last recognise the nature of their wishes and at last be able to satisfy them. They will cease to injure the objects of their desire. Humanity will be at peace in the world: at home, as it were, at home.

I know you are weary of communism, of the lullaby of Calvary and Dean Street, but it will be heard as long as there is money; like the Sibyl's books, it is offered to every age, and always at a higher price in money. To reject it is to persist in a delusion so complete that human beings exult in their irreparable losses; and, like Hazlitt's misers, 'are not sorry when they die, to think they shall no longer be an expense to themselves.'[15]

One day, who knows, the human race might stir. My heroes and heroines wake from their sleep and rub their eyes. Honour pushes credit away with an indescribable grimace of disgust, charity runs shrieking from the Charity Ball and virtue and solvency discuss a separation, which becomes permanent. Liberty puts down her shopping-bag and rests her bunioned feet. The Owl of Minerva opens one eye, then the other, and extends her tattered wings for flight. And as these dreams dissolve, the Age of Money, which came after the Age of Faith, will itself draw, as all things under the sun, to an end.

Notes

I wish to thank Tariq Ali, Robin Blackburn, Count Capponi, Joseph Cribb, Fram Dinshaw, Michael Hofmann, Lord Normanby, Anna Pavord, Lord Stewartby, Jeremy Stone, Martin Taylor, Susan Watkins and Ursula Wide.

Introduction

1. *An Inquiry into the Nature and Causes of the Wealth of Nations*, II, iii, 28.
2. Op. cit., Chap. XI, Harmondsworth, 1969, p. 108.

1. Mineral Stones

1. Abd al-Rahman ibn Muhammad ibn Khaldun, *The Muqaddimah: An Introduction to History*, trans. F. Rosenthal, London, 1958, Vol. II, p. 313.
2. At the turn of 1871, Stanley was at Zanzibar, thinking about money. He had been commissioned by the *New York Herald* to find the Scots missionary explorer David Livingstone, who had been lost to European and American publicity for two years; and travel in the African interior was expensive in money. One sort of money Stanley had in abundance. At the commissioning meeting in Paris the previous October, the newspaper's young managing editor, James Gordon Bennett, Jr., explained how Stanley was to pay for his expedition: 'Draw a thousand pounds now; and when you have gone through that, draw another thousand, and when that is spent, draw another thousand, and when you have finished

that, draw another thousand, and so on; but FIND LIVING-STONE.' (*How I Found Livingstone*, London, 1874, p. 2.) Stanley's difficulty was that en route to Lake Tanganyika, where he expected to have news of Livingstone, the chief coins that represented sterling money – gold sovereigns – weren't esteemed; and 'moneys' accepted in one place were not a few miles away. 'One tribe,' he wrote later, 'preferred white to black beads, brown to yellow, red to green, green to white and so on. Thus, in Unganwezi, red (samu-samu) beads would readily be taken, where all other kinds would be refused.' (Ibid., p. 22.) The skill, evidently, was to take precisely that amount of currency that would carry the party through one currency district and later back through it, and no more; for these moneys were heavy and the more carried, the more men to carry them, the more food needed to feed the men and the more money needed to buy the food and so on *ad infinitum*. After consulting the Arabs who traded in slaves at Zanzibar, Stanley – an orphaned Welshman brought up in New Orleans – carried 29,200 yards of assorted Indian and American cloths, 22 sacks of 11 varieties of beads and 350 pounds of No. 5 and No. 6 brass wire. These moneys, Stanley wrote in *How I Found Livingstone*, corresponded to the copper, silver and gold of Europe and the United States. In addition, he took a great deal of ammunition, and that proved useful, when money failed, for slaughtering men and animals. The expedition that set off in five caravans from Baganogo on February 18, 1871, consisted of 192 men carrying rather over 11,000 pounds of goods.

Stanley duly found Livingstone at Ujiji and put him in funds – 992 pounds of beads and all the wire, which had found no takers – so the Scotsman could continue his own exploration of the interior, where he died two years later.

3. *Aucun puisse ne doit faire doute, que à Nous et à Nostre Majesté royal n'appartiengne seulement & pour le tout . . . de faire monnoier teles monnoyes, & donner tel cours, pour tel prix comme il Nous plaist . . . en usant de nostre droit.* Letres adressés au Seneschal de Beaucaire . . . touchant le cours des Monoyes, 16, Janvier 1346 [i.e. 1347] in *Ordonnances des Roys de France*, ed. E.-J. de Laurière, Paris, 1729, Vol II, p. 254.

4. 'No doubt it was the same thin and narrow face that we saw, Robert and I. But we had arrived at it by two opposite ways,

between which there was no communication, and we should never both see it from the same side.' Trans. C. K. Scott Moncrieff, London, 1967, p. 213.

5. *Style*, Part II in *Essays on Style, Rhetoric and Language*, ed. F. N. Scott, Boston, 1893, p. 43.

6. *Cambodian Witness: The Autobiography of Someth May*, London, 1986, pp. 245 and 255–6.

7. *Kitab al-ishara ila nahasin al-tijara*, ed. H. Ritter, in *Der Islam*, Vol. 7, 1917, p. 49.

8. *Politica*, 1. 9. 1257a, trans. B. Jowett, Oxford, 1921.

9. 'The Honourable Archivist said, "When the way of exchange had been opened between agriculturalists, artisans and merchants, then the monetary values of tortoise shells and cowry shells, metals, spades and knives, and hempen and grass cloths arose from it. The origin was long ago and far away."' *Shih chi*, Chapter 30. Chapter 129 quotes Lao Tzu on the virtues of self-sufficiency, but says that since at least the Hsia, men had hankered after music, women, grass- and grain-fed meat, pleasures, luxuries, power and display, and the authorities simply had to accept that. 'West of the mountains abounds in timber, bamboo, paper mulberry and ramie, yak tails, jade and stones. East of the mountains there is plenty of fish, salt, lacquer, silk, musicians and beauties ... Each [man] applies himself to his productive occupation, [and] enjoys his work. Like water running downward, day and night ceaselessly, [the objects of desire listed] are not summoned and yet they come of themselves; they are not sought and yet the people produce them. Is it not [in conformity with] the *Tao* and does it not give evidence of spontaneity?' Trans. R. C. Blue, 'The Argumentation of the *Shih-huo chih* Chapters of the Han, Wei and Sui Dynastic Histories,' *Harvard Journal of Asiatic Studies*, Vol 11, 1948, pp. 12 and 121–3.

10. Genesis, 37:28.

11. *The Decipherment of Linear B*, Cambridge, 1970, p. 101.

12. *Documents in Mycenaean Greek*, Cambridge, 1956, p. 113.

13. Ibid., p. 198.

14. *The Wealth of Nations*, I, ii, 1.

15. *Iliad*, VI, 234–236.

16. *Dionysii Longini de Sublimitate*, Sect. IX, 7.

17. *Iliad*, ix, 632–636.

18. *Dionysii Longini de Sublimitate*, Sect. IX, 15.

19. *Historiae*, I, 29.
20. Ibid., I, 93.
21. Ibid., I, 94.
22. H. Diels, *Die Fragmente der Vorsokratiker*, Berlin, 1922, Vol. I, p. 58.
23. 'Thus I dare boldly affirm. That the same *Rule of Propriety*, (*viz.*) that every Man should have as much as he could make use of, would hold still in the World, without straitning any body, since there is land enough in the World to suffice double the Inhabitants, had not the *Invention of Money* . . . introduced (by Consent) larger possessions . . . Where there is not something both lasting and scarce, and so valuable as to be hoarded up, there Men will not be apt to enlarge their *Possessions of Land*, were it never so rich, never so free for men to take.' *Second Treatise of Government*, 48 and 50.
24. *De Republica Lacedaemoniorum*, VII.
25. *An Inquiry into the Principles of Political Oeconomy*, Edinburgh, 1966, II, XIII, p. 217.
26. *Politica*, 1. 9. 1257b 14.
27. *Aphorismen zur Lebensweisheit*, Chap. III in *Sämtliche Werke*, ed. W. Frhr. von Lohneysen, Darmstadt, 1968, Vol. IV. pp. 414–15; and *Vereinzelte, jedoch systematisch geordnete Gedanken*, 320, in ibid., Vol. V, p. 691
28. *Politica*, 1. 9. 1258a 10.
29. *Politica*, 1. 10. 1258b 2.
30. *Inferno*, XI, 50 and 103–111.
31. *Ethica Nicomachea*, 1133a.19–31.
32. cf. K. Marx, *Capital*, I, 3, 3. 'The secret of the expression of value, namely, that all kinds of labour are equal and equivalent . . . cannot be deciphered, until the notion of human equality has already acquired the fixity of a popular prejudice.'
33. *Dionysii Longini de Sublimitate*, Sect. XLIV, 6.

2. Thirty Pieces of Silver

1. 'Das Geldevangelium,' MS Lübeck, 15th century, in *Parodistische Texte: Beispiele zur lateinischen Parodie im Mittelalter*, ed. P. Lehmann, Munich, 1923, p. 11.
2. 'The Overseer of the Poor' in *The Synagogue: or, the Shadow of the*

Temple. Sacred Poems and Private Ejaculations in Imitation of Mr George Herbert, ninth edition, London, 1709.

3. *Regula Fratrum Minorum*, I, Chapter VIII in *Opuscula Sancti Patris Francisci Assisiensis*, Quaracchi near Florence, 1904, p. 35.
4. Koran, 2:198.
5. Quoted in Ritter, *Ein arabisches Handbuch der Handelswissenschaft* in *Der Islam*, Vol. 7, 1917, p. 32.
6. Provide neither gold, nor silver, nor brass in your purses. Matthew 10:9.
7. *The Works of Flavius Josephus*, ed. W. Whiston, London, 1825, Vol. 1, p. 551.
8. Ibid., Vol. 2, p. 288.
9. Matthew 20:2.
10. Matthew 22:19.
11. Exodus 20:4.
12. Matthew 22:20–21.
13. Exodus 30:13.
14. Matthew 17:24–26.
15. The other is Matthew 27:51–54.
16. Ibid., 17:27.
17. Ibid., 26:4.
18. Ibid., 26:7.
19. Ibid., 26:9.
20. Ibid., 26:11–13.
21. Ibid., 26:14–16.
22. *Works*, Vol. II, p. 475.
23. Ibid., p. 500.
24. Zech. 11:12–13.
25. 'Of persons one would wish to have seen', *New Monthly Magazine*, January 1826, in *Selected Essays of William Hazlitt 1788–1830*, ed. G. Keynes, London, 1970, pp. 538–9.
26. Op. cit., Vol. 1, 1625–1631, p. 177.
27. Ms K.A. XLVIII, fol. 817 ro.
28. Translated from the French of the Abbé Martin, *Zeitschrift der deutschen morgenländischen Gesellschaft*, 29, 1895, pp. 107–47.

3. An Idea of Order in Borgo Sansepolcro

1. *L'Argent*, Paris, 1897, p. 79.
2. One such bill in the British Museum, drawn on the Yin Cao Heaven Bank for $50,000 [1996–2–17–2477] reads on the back: 'When you get this note, go to any place in heaven, have a wonderful time there, and use it for anything you like.'
3. *Thrand of Gotu: Two Icelandic Sagas from the Flat Island Book*, Chapter 45, trans. G. Johnston, Erin, Ont. 1994, pp. 106–7.
4. F. Poey d'Avant, *Monnaies Féodales de France*, Paris, 1858–1860, Vol. II, p. 289.
5. *Der Islam*, Vol. 7, 1917, p. 84.
6. P. Spufford, *Money and Its Use in Medieval Europe*, Cambridge, 1988, p. 68.
7. . . . *cioè di carta gialla coniata della bolla del detto signore*, ie the Emperor. *La Pratica della Mercatura*, ed. A. Evans, Cambridge, Massachusetts, 1936, p. 23.
8. Spufford, op. cit., pp. 205 and 390.
9. *Le Grant Testament*, 60.
10. The sources for this event are given in E. Gibbon, *The History of the Decline and Fall of the Roman Empire*, Chapter LXI; Le Nain de Tillemont, *Vie de Saint Louis*, Paris, 1847, Vol. 1, pp. 337–9; and G. Zanetti, *Dell'origine e della antichità della moneta Viniziana ragionamento*, Venice, 1750, p. 21.
11. *The Wealth of Nations*, III, iv, 8.
12. W. Sombart, *Liebe, Luxus und Kapitalismus*, Berlin, 1983, p. 120.
13. G. Simmel, *The Philosophy of Money*, London and New York, 1990, p. 286.
14. *L'Histoire de Guillaume le Maréchal, comte de Striguil et de Pembroke*, ed. Paul Meyer, Paris, 1891, Vol. 1, lines 1692 and 1876–1882.
15. Simmel, op. cit., pp. 285–6.
16. Pseudomisus, pseud., *Considerations concerning Common Fields, and Inclosures, dialoguewise*, London, 1653, p. 21.
17. *De l'Esprit des Lois*, 1748, VII. 1.
18. G. Luzzatto, *Studi di storia economica veneziana*, Padua, 1954, pp. 81–7.
19. *Le Côté de Guermantes*, I, Chapter 1; trans. C. K. Scott Moncrieff, London, 1967, p. 19.

20. *The Vision of William concerning Piers the Plowman*, Passus IV, 391–392; V, 191–194; both in C text.

21. P. Lehmann, *Parodistische Texte*, Munich, 1923, p. 9.

22. *The* De Moneta *of Nicholas Oresme*, ed. C. Johnston, London, 1956, Chapter VII, p. 11; Chapter XXVI, p. 47, etc.

23. *E s'egli avvenisse (che col tempo in ogni modo avverrà) che S. GIOR-GIO tutta quella città occupasse, sarebbe quella una Repubblica più che la VINEZIANA memorabile. Le Historie Fiorentine*, Lib. 8, ed. G.–B. Niccolini, Florence, 1843, p. 388.

24. *Economic and Philosophic Manuscripts of 1844*, Moscow, 1959, p. 60.

25. *Bibliotheca Sanctorum*, Rome, 1964, Vol. 5, pp. 1168–9.

26. John Pope-Hennessy, *The Portrait in the Renaissance*, New York, 1966, p. 269.

27. *E servaremo i esso el mō de vinegia; qle certamēte fra glialtri e molto da cōmēdare.* R. G. Brown and K. S. Johnston, *Paciolo on Accounting*, New York, 1963, p. 118.

28. R. E. Taylor, *Luca Pacioli*, in A. C. Littleton and B. S. Yamey, *Studies in the History of Accounting*, London, 1956, p. 176.

29. Ibid., p. 189.

30. Large gold coins, weighing $3\frac{1}{2}$ grams, known as *ducati d' oro* or *zecchini*, first minted at Venice in 1284 and current till the 1840s. They were imitated as far away as India. Ibid, p. 182.

31. *Wilhelm Meisters Lehrjahre*, Chapter 10, in *Werke*, Berlin and Weimar, 1981, Vol. 6, pp. 36–7.

32. *Debtor and Creditor Made Easie*, 1682, in Littleton and Yamey, p. 8.

33. *Der moderne Kapitalismus*, Munich and Leipzig, 1916, Vol. 2, p. 119.

34. Brown and Johnston, *Paciolo on Accounting*, p. 133.

35. Ibid., p. 118.

36. Ibid., p. 138.

37. Sombart, op. cit., p. 118.

38. *The Complete English Tradesman in Familiar Letters*, Letter XX, London, 1726, p. 344.

39. Sombart, op. cit., p. 120.

40. Ibid., p. 123.

41. Op. cit., pp. 345–6.

42. Brown and Johnston, op. cit., p. 124.

4. A Disease of the Heart

1. Log entry for Saturday, October 13, 1492, in Cristóbal Colón, *Textos y documentos completos*, ed. C. Varela, Madrid, 1982, p. 32.
2. Printed in Martín Fernández de Navarrete, *Collección de los viajes y descubrimientos*, Madrid, 1825, Vol. I, p. 307.
3. BUS MS 2327 printed in *Textos*, p. 302.
4. Martín Fernández de Navarrete, op. cit., Vol. 1, p. 301n.
5. *Textos*, pp. 300–2.
6. Ibid., p. 295.
7. Ibid., p. 293.
8. Ibid., pp. 304–5.
9. MS Vitr. 6, *Textos* pp. 15–16.
10. *Textos*, p. 295.
11. *A History of Gold and Money*, London, 1976, p. 45.
12. *Textos*, p. 142.
13. Pierre Chaunu, *Séville et l'Atlantique*, Paris, 1958, Vol. 8 (I), p. 510.
14. Bernal Díaz del Castillo, *Historia verdadera de la Conquista de la Nueva-España*, Madrid, 1632, Chapter CVIII, folio 86.
15. *Oeuvres Complètes*, Paris, 1962, p. 892.
16. Francisco López de Gómara, *Cronica de la Nueva España*, Chapter XXVI, in A. Gonzalez Barcía, *Historiadores Primitivos de las Indias Occidentales*, Madrid, 1749, Vol. 2, p. 27.
17. *A View of the Coasts, Countries and Islands Within the Limits of the South-Sea Company*, London, 1711, p. 55.
18. Luis Capoche, *Relación general de la Villa Imperial de Potosí*, ed. Lewis Hanke, Madrid, 1959, p. 158.
19. Bartolomé Arzáns de Orsúa y Vela, *Historia de la Villa Imperial de Potosí*, ed. Lewis Hanke and Gunnar Mendoza, Providence, 1965, passim.
20. *Le premier fruit que les Espagnols recuellirent de cette conquête du nouveau monde fut la vérole, elle se repandit plus promptement que l'argent . . .* Voltaire, *L'Homme aux Quarante Ecus*, Geneva, 1768, p. 46.
21. *The Theory and Practice of Commerce and Maritime Affairs*, London, 1751, pp. 11–13.
22. *Paradiso*, XIX, pp. 118–19.
23. *Memorial de la política necesaria y útil restauración de la república de España*, Valladolid, 1600, p. 29, quoted in Vilar, 'The Age of Don Quixote', *New Left Review*, London, 68, 1971, pp. 59–71.

24. *Summa de trato y contratos*, Seville, 1571, folio 90, quoted in Vilar, *A History*, p. 79.

25. Don Diego Saavedra Faxardo, *The Royal Politician Represented in One Hundred Emblems*, London, 1700, p. 173.

26. Richard Cantillon, *Essai sur la Nature du Commerce en général*, ed. Henry Higgs, London, 1931, pp. 164–5.

27. Ibid., pp. 184–5.

28. Arzáns, op. cit., Vol. II, pp. 322–3.

29. Miguel de Cervantes, *Don Quijote de la Mancha*, Madrid, 1994, Vol. 1, p. 35.

30. Karl Marx, *Economic and Philosophic Manuscripts*, Moscow, 1959, p. 84.

31. *Don Quijote*, p. 49.

32. Ibid., pp. 42–3.

33. Ibid., pp. 248–9.

34. In fact, it reads 150,000 but J. G. van Dillen has shown the inscriptionist made a mistake. 'Isaac Le Maire et le Commerce des Actions de la Compagnie des Indes Orientales,' in *Revue d'Histoire moderne*, Vol. X, 1935, p. 137.

35. Act I, Scene iii, 135.

36. *De officiis*, 1, xlii.

37. Act I, Scene i, 32–5.

38. *Capital*, Vol. 1, Chapter IV.

39. Act I, Scene ii, 45–6.

40. Act II, Scene vii, 15.

41. Act III, Scene v, 24–7.

42. Act III, Scene ii, 155–60.

43. Act IV, Scene i, 40–3.

44. Act III, Scene iii, 30–1.

45. *Thornbrough* v. *Baker* (1676), I Ch. Case 284, quoted – with 'Land' substituted for 'Pound of Flesh' – in R. W. Turner, *The Equity of Redemption*, Cambridge 1931, p. 59.

46. *Instructions to his Sonne and to Posterity*, fourth ed., London, 1633, pp. 63 and 66.

47. *The Idea of Usury*, Chicago, 1949.

48. *The Principles of Moral and Political Philosophy*, Book III, Part II, Chapter I, London, 1785, p. 192.

49. *Treatise of Human Nature*, Book III, Part II, §1.

50. *The Wealth of Nations*, I, ii, 2.

51. Act V, Scene iv, 72–3.
52. Act IV, Scene iii, 28–44.
53. Act IV, Scene iii, 389–91.

5. The Floating World

1. *Canz.* xxviii.
2. *Siècle de Louis XIV*, Nouvelle Edition, 1768, Vol. 1, pp. 404–7; translation based on Martyn Pollack, *The Age of Louis XIV*, London and Toronto, 1926, pp. 100–1.
3. *Durch die Wiederholung wird das, was im Anfang nur als zufällig und möglich erschien, zu einem Wirlkichen und Bestätigten.* Hegel, *Vorlesungen über die Philosophie der Weltgeschichte,* ed. Georg Lasson, Hamburg, 1968, Vol. III, p. 712.
4. Herodotus, *Historiae*, VII, 143 ff. and Aeschylus, *Persae*, 238 ff.
5. Edward Forde, op. cit., p. 4.
6. W. S. Jevons, *Money and the Mechanism of Exchange*, London, 1896, p. 222.
7. G. J. D. Schotel, *Het Oud-Hollandsch Huisgezin der Zeventiende Eeuw*, Haarlem, 1868, p. 51.
8. *Considerations of the Lowering of Interest and Raising the Value of Money*, London, 1695, in *Works*, fifth ed., London, 1751, Vol II, p. 12.
9. 'About twenty years after the Fire; and in even that time . . . as the gay humour came on.' *The Complete English Tradesman*, fourth ed., London, 1738, Vol. II, p. 332.
10. 'To my Dear and Loving Husband' in *Several Poems . . . by a Gentlewoman in New-England*, Boston, 1678, p. 240.
11. Entry for November 16, 1665, *The Diary of Samuel Pepys*, ed. Robert Latham and William Matthews, London, 1972, Vol. VI, p. 300.
12. *Political Arithmetick*, in *The Economic Writings of Sir William Petty*, ed. C. H. Hull, New York, 1963, Vol. I, pp. 261–6.
13. Op. cit., ed. Latham, Vol. VII, p. 252.
14. S. W. Shelton, 'The Goldsmith Banker' in A. C. Littleton and B. S. Yamey, *Studies in the History of Accounting*, London, 1956, pp. 248–9.
15. *A Discourse of Money*, London, 1696, p. 136.

16. *The Diary of John Evelyn*, ed. E. S. de Beer, Oxford, 1955, Vol. IV, pp. 57–60, entry for March 24, 1675.
17. *Political Arithmetick* in *The Economic Writings of Sir William Petty*, Vol. I, p. 267.
18. James Hodges, *The Present State of England as to Coin and Publick Charges*, London, 1697, p. 147.
19. *A Discourse Concerning Coining the New Money Lighter*, 1696, p. 43.
20. Op. cit., p. 63.
21. Op. cit., ed. Hull, Vol. 1, p. 181; also *A Treatise of Taxes & Contributions*, London, 1662, pp. 25–26.
22. Ibid., ed. Hull, Vol. I, p. 129.
23. Evelyn, loc. cit.
24. *Political Arithmetick*, Preface in op. cit., ed. Hull, Vol. I, p. 244.
25. *The Wealth of Nations*, I, ii, 1–2.
26. *Eutaxia tou Agrou or A Vindication of a Regulated Enclosure*, 1656, pp. 20 and 22.
27. P. M. Garber, 'Tulipmania', in *Journal of Political Economy*, Chicago, 1989, Vol. 97, No. 3, pp. 535–560.
28. *Still Life with Bridle*, trans. J. and B. Carpenter, Hopewell, N.J., 1991, p. 47.
29. Based on English translation in N. W. Postumus, 'The Tulip Mania in Holland in the Years 1636 and 1637', *Journal of Economic and Business History*, May 1929, Vol. 1, No. 3.
30. Ibid., p. 454.
31. Ibid., p. 459.
32. . . . *si totallement nous defendons les usures nous estraignons les consciences dun lien plus estroict que Dieu mesme. Ioannis Calvini Opera quae Supersunt*, ed. Baum et al., Brunswick, 1871, Vol. X, I, p. 246.
33. 43 Eliz. c. 12 in Violet Barbour, 'Marine Risks and Insurance in the Seventeenth Century,' *JEBH*, , 1929, Vol. 1, No. 4, p. 574.
34. D. Browne et al. *A short Account of some approved Methods already settled to make Provision for Posterity*, October 11, 1712.
35. *A Proposal for a Subscription to Raise one hundred thousand pounds for . . . a Land-Bank*.
36. Dalby Thomas, *Propositions for General Land-Banks*, n.d.
37. John Asgill, *Several Assertions Proved in order to Create another Species of Money than Gold and Silver*, London, 1696, p. 21.
38. 'Of the Balance of Trade,' in *Political Essays*, ed. K. Haakonssen, Cambridge, 1994, p. 144.

39. G. Martin, *La Grande Industrie sous le Règne de Louis XIV*, Paris, 1899, p. 290.
40. R. Campbell, Esq., *The London Tradesman*, 1747, pp. 148 and 194.
41. *Du Dandysme et de G. Brummell*, Caen, 1845, p. 87.
42. T. A. J. Burnett, *The Rise and Fall of a Regency Dandy: The Life and Times of Scrope Berdmore Davies*, London, 1981, pp. 52–3.
43. *Du Dandysme*, pp. 107–8.
44. *Memoirs of the Lives of the Gamesters*, London, 1714; in *Games and Gamesters of the Restoration*, ed. C. H. Hartmann, London, 1930, p. 231.
45. *The Compleat Gamester*, 1674; in op. cit., ed. C. H. Hartmann, 1930, p. 84.
46. 'Why art thou poor, O King? Imbezling C—t,/ That widemouth'd greedy monster, that has done't.' 'An Essay of Scandal' in *A Collection of Choice Poems*, British Library Harley MS. 7319, p. 133.
47. Defoe, op. cit., Vol. II, p. 207.
48. James Boswell, *Life of Johnson*, Oxford, 1953, p. 681.
49. *Economic and Philosophic Manuscripts*, Moscow, 1959, p. 59.
50. Ihara Saikaku, 'Riding to success on a lucky horse' in *The Japanese Family Storehouse*, I, I.
51. Paraphrased in Howard Hibbett, *The Floating World in Japanese Fiction*, London, 1959, p. 11.
52. Saikaku, *The Life of an Amorous Woman and Other Writings*, trans. I. Morris, London, 1963, p. 10.
53. Ibid., p. 194.
54. *The Japanese Family Storehouse*, trans. G. W. Sargent, Cambridge 1959, VI, 5 at p. 144.
55. *The Life of an Amorous Woman*, p. 211.
56. Hibbett, op. cit., p. 45.
57. Shugo Asano, and Timothy Clark, *The Passionate Art of Kitagawa Utamaro*, London, 1995, passim.
58. *Saikaku's Last Fabrics*, published posthumously in 1694, in *The Life of an Amorous Woman*, p. 28.
59. Ezra Pound, *Personae: Collected Shorter Poems of Ezra Pound*, London, 1952, p. 128.
60. *The Life of an Amorous Woman*, p. 19.

6. *Mississippi Dreaming: On the Fame of John Law*

1. Louis Blanc, *Histoire de la Révolution française*, Paris, 1847, Vol. 1, pp. 271–2.

2. *Man hört von nichts, als Millionen, sprechen,* the Regent's mother wrote in exasperation to her sister on December 7, 1719. *Briefe der Herzogin Elisabeth Charlotte von Orléans aus dem Jahre 1719,* ed. W. L. Holland, Stuttgart, 1877, p. 322. cf. L.–S. Mercier, *Tableau de Paris,* Nouvelle Edition, Amsterdam, 1783, Vol. V, Chapter CCCXCII.

3. . . . *d'ailleurs, plus amoureux des ses idées que de son argent. Voyages de Montesquieu,* ed. A. de Montesquieu, Bordeaux, 1894, Vol. 1, p. 64.

4. See G. Brice, *Nouvelle Description de la ville de Paris,* Paris, 1725, Vol. 1, pp. 312 and 343; and J. P. Wood, *Memoirs of the Life of John Law of Lauriston,* Edinburgh, 1824, p. 162.

5. Defoe considered £80,000 a great fortune. *The Complete English Tradesman,* Vol. II, Chapter XLI.

6. *La folie du système des finances contribua, plus qu'on ne croit, à rendre la paix a l'église. Le public se jetta avec tant de fureur dans le commerce des actions . . . que ceux qui parlèrent de jansénisme & de bulle, ne trouvèrent personne qui les écoutat . . . Les fortunes rapides & incroyables qu'on faisait alors, le luxe & la volupté portés au dernier excès, imposèrent silence aux disputes ecclésiastiques; & le plaisir fit ce que* Louis XIV *n'avait pu faire.* Voltaire, *Précis du Siècle de Louis XV,* in *Siècle de Louis XIV,* 1768, Vol. III, p. 207.

7. Zanetti, *Della Pittura Veneziana,* Venice, 1792, p. 446.

8. *Disegni e dipinti di Giovanni Antonio Pellegrini,* ed. Alessandro Bettagno, Venezia, 1959.

9. Comte de Caylus, *Vie de François le Moyne* in Lépicié, *Vies des premiers-peintres du Roi, depuis M. Le Brun, jusqu'à présent,* Paris, 1752, pp. 122–7.

10. No. 21, 1962, pp. 75–93.

11. Edmund Burke, *Reflections on the Revolution in France,* Harmondsworth, 1969, p. 369.

12. *Mémoires de Saint-Simon,* Paris, 1958, Vol. V, p. 659.

13. *Lectures on Jurisprudence,* ed. R. L. Meek et al., Oxford, 1978, p. 519.

14. *The Journal of Sir Walter Scott, 1829–1832,* Edinburgh, 1946, p. 112. Entry for June 12, 1830.

15. *Capital*, ed. Engels, New York, 1967, Vol. 3, p. 441.
16. *History of Money and Credit from John Law to the Present Day*, trans. Jane Degras, 1940, p. 58.
17. 'John Law of Lauriston', *American Economic Review*, LVII, 2, 1967, p. 275.
18. Pierre Vilar, *Oro y Moneda en la Historia (1450–1920)*, Barcelona, 1969; in English as *A History of Gold and Money, 1450–1920*, trans. Judith White, London, 1976.
19. Paris, 1977.
20. Wood, op. cit., pp. 55–56.
21. Op cit., ed. Hull, 1963, p. 267.
22. Op. cit., ed. Beer, V, p. 175.
23. Since the introduction of progressive personal income tax, in England in 1909 and the U.S. in 1913, the entire resources of a country have been placed at a government's theoretical disposal. Paper money, a liability of the central bank, is secured not just on loans to the state but what guarantees that debt, which is the state's power to extinguish it by requisitioning through taxes the private wealth of the country's citizens.
24. Law, op. cit., p. 100.
25. BM 1642, 1688.
26. *Mémoires*, Vol. VI, p. 659.
27. *Mémoires et Avantures d'un homme de qualité qui s'est retiré du monde*, Amsterdam, 1732, Vol. VI, p. 5.
28. *Mémoire de Law au duc de Bourbon du 15 Octobre 1724* in Paul Harsin, ed. *John Law: Oeuvres Complètes*, Paris, 1934, Vol. III, p. 280.
29. Not printed, unsurprisingly, by Holland. In G. Scott Stevenson, *The Letters of Madame*, London, 1924, Vol. I, p. 226.
30. *Oeuvres*, ed. Harsin, II, p. 123.
31. *Briefe*, ed. Holland, p. 329.
32. *Lettre au Régent*, in *Oeuvres*, ed. Harsin, II, pp. 265–8.
33. *Histoire des finances pendant la Régence*, in *Oeuvres*, ed. Harsin, III, p. 310.
34. *Mercure de France*, mars 1720, in *Oeuvres*, ed. Harsin, III, p. 104. English translation in *The Present State of the French Revenues and Trade*, London, 1720, p. 44.
35. Mercier, *Tableau de Paris*, Vol. I, Chapter LXXVI.
36. *Réflexions politiques sur les Finances et le commerce* in E. Daire,

Économistes-financiers du XVIII Siècle, Paris, 1843, Vol. I, pp. 914 and 990.

37. Dutot, op. cit., Vol. I, p. 923; *Mémoire justicatif*, May 1723, in *Oeuvres*, ed. Harsin, III, p. 213.

38. Price, op. cit., Ann Arbor, 1973, p. 357.

39. B. Burrough and J. Helyar, *Barbarians at the Gate*, London, 1990, p. 218.

40. *The Man of Forty Crowns*, trans. Voltaire, London, 1768, p. 2.

41. *He bien Mons' pisses pourveüe que vous nous Escoutties. Er that Es undt sie blieben bei ihm stehen.* In *Briefe*, ed. Holland, p. 322.

42. *Mémoire sur le Denier royal*, in *Oeuvres*, ed. Harsin, III, p. 45.

43. *Oeuvres de J. Law*, Paris, 1790, p. xlviii.

44. 'Prices and Wages under John Law's System', *Quarterly Journal of Economics*, Cambridge, Massachusetts, 1937, Vol. 4.

45. *Briefe*, ed. Holland, p. 358.

46. Larry Neal, 'For God's Sake, Remitt Me!: The Adventures of John Law's Goldsmith-Banker in London, 1712–1729' in *Business and Economic History*, 23:2 (1994), pp. 27–60.

47. 'There is nothing worse for a gambler than an unstable situation on his home ground. All this wrecked his capacity to survive as a gambler. He lost a bit of his nerve and ability.' John Aspinall on Lord Lucan, *The Sunday Times Magazine*, February 9, 1997, p. 26.

48. *Mémoires*, VI, p. 659.

49. *Lettre au sujet de l'arrêt du Conseil d'Etat du 22 mai 1720*, in *Oeuvres*, ed. Harsin, III pp. 159–162.

50. Steuart, *An Inquiry into the Principles of Political Oeconomy*, Edinburgh, 1966, Vol. 2, p. 554.

51. *coperta dall'alto al basso di libri di biglietti. Diario degli Anni MDCCXX e MDCCXXI scritto di propria mano in Parigi*, Venice, 1865.

52. *Précis du Siècle de Louis XV*, in ed. cit., Vol. III, p. 269.

53. *Oeuvres*, ed. Harsin, III, p. 311.

54. *The Gentleman's Magazine*, Vol. 95, Jan–June 1825, p. 101.

55. E. Levasseur, *Recherches Historiques sur le Système de Law*, Paris, 1854, p. 317.

56. I cannot verify this quotation, which is in E. Montgomery Hyde, *John Law: The History of an Honest Adventurer*, London, 1969, p. 193.

57. The odds are 46,656:1. In his treatise *Uytreekening der Kansen in het speelen* of 1716, the mathematician Nicolaas Struyck examined the

mathematics in two of Law's games. In one, Law wagered 1,000 pistoles against his opponents throwing six sixes, but they had to pay him two pistoles if he threw four or more sixes. 'One can make with the dice 375 casts of four sixes, 30 of five sixes and one of six sixes, which makes 406 throws and, multiplied by six, 2,436 in all. Of those throws, there is just a single one that wins the 1,000 pistoles, but there are 2,435 that lose the two pistoles, from which it can be seen that MR LAW would have a considerable advantage.' *Les Oeuvres de Nicolas Struyck 1687–1769*, tran. J. S. Vollgraff, Amsterdam, 1912, p. 19.

58. E. and J. Goncourt, *Journal*, Vol. 1, pp. 246–9, etc.
59. Quoted in Hyde, op. cit., p. 215.
60. Op. cit., II, p. 557.
61. *éclaira les esprits, comme les guerres civiles aiguisent les courages. Précis*, Vol. III, p. 263.
62. In Vol. VI of his *Memoires et Avantures d'un homme de qualité qui s'est retiré du monde*, a libertine novella set in the Regency and printed at Amsterdam in 1731, Prévost gives a biography of Law which is unsupported in other sources: it is, in fact, a first sketch of Des Grieux's adventures. These became Vol. VII, now usually published separately as *Manon Lescaut*.

7. Coined Liberty: His and Hers

1. *House of the Dead*, 1862, Chapter 1.
2. *The Theory of Moral Sentiments*, I, III, III, I, ed. D. D. Raphael and A. L. Macfie, Oxford, 1976, p. 61.
3. *The Federalist Papers*, X, ed. I. Kramnick, London, 1987, p. 124.
4. Op. cit., Vol. II, XLI, p. 210.
5. Montesquieu, *De l'Esprit des Lois*, II, 4 in *Oeuvres Complètes*, Paris, 1951, Vol. II, p. 248.
6. To Samuel Cooper, April 22, 1779, *The Writings of Benjamin Franklin*, ed. A. H. Smyth, 1905–1907, VII, pp. 293–4.
7. *The Papers of James Madison*, ed. W. T. Hutchinson et al., Chicago, 1962, IX, p. 154.
8. Ibid., p. 161.
9. The Constitution of the United States of America, Article One, Section 10.

10. *The Federalist Papers*, ed. Kramnick, No. X, p. 128.

11. VI, XXI, XXV, XXVIII, XLIII, LXXIV.

12. No. XXX, p. 212.

13. No. XII, p. 134.

14. J. Boswell, *Life of Johnson*, London, 1953, p. 597, entry for March 27, 1775.

15. *The Federalist Papers*, No. X, p. 124.

16. *The Debates in the Several State Conventions on the Adoption of the Federal Constitution, as Recommended by the General Convention at Philadelphia in 1787*, ed. J. Elliot, Washington, 1836, III, pp. 80 and 587.

17. *Reflections on the Revolution in France*, pub. Nov. 1790, Harmondsworth, 1969, p. 225.

18. Quoted in M. Marion, *Histoire financière de la France depuis 1715*, Paris, 1921, Vol. III, pp. 420–1.

19. *Discours et Réplique sur les Assignats-Monnoie prononcées par M. Mirabeau l'aîné dans l'Assemblée nationale*, Paris, 1791, p. 102.

20. Ibid., p. 43.

21. Jean Morini-Comby, *Les Assignats: Révolution et Inflation*, Paris, 1925, p. 31.

22. Ibid., p. 60.

23. *Reflections on the Revolution in France*, p. 364.

24. Morini-Comby, op. cit., p. 129.

25. Burke, op. cit., p. 126.

26. Ibid., p. 170.

27. Marion, op. cit., III, p. 200.

28. G.-J. Ouvrard, *Mémoires sur sa vie et ses diverses opérations financières*, Paris, 1826, Vol. 1, p. 205.

29. Burke, op. cit., p. 313.

30. *Money of the Mind*, New York, 1992, p. 72.

31. *Cumulative World Production and Distribution of Gold*, CPM Group, New York, 1995; Keynes, *Essays in Persuasion*, London, 1951, p. 182.

32. *Essays in Persuasion*, London, 1951, p. 183.

33. *Wee Willie Winkie and Other Stories*, Macmillan, 1910, pp. 3–4.

34. *Conversations on Political Economy*, London, 1816, p. 102.

35. *Divan*, ed. M. Mosaffa, Tehran, 1957, p. 704.

36. *De pulchritudine foeminarum* in *Laurentii Vallae de voluptate ac vero bono*, Book I, Chapter XXII, Basle, 1519.

37. *Eugene Onegin*, Chapter 8, VI, trans. C. Johnston, London, 1977, p. 208.
38. 'Les plaintes d'un Icare'.
39. Mercier, op. cit., Vol. VII, Chapter DLV, p. 81.
40. December 2, 1995.
41. No. 295.
42. Pierre Dufour, pseud., 8 vols, Brussels, 1861.
43. *Mlle Marie Duplessis*, in A. Dumas *fils*, *La Dame aux Camélias*, Paris, 1852, pp. vii–viii.
44. Ibid., p. xiii.
45. *La Traviata*, Act II, No. 6.
46. Woolf, op. cit., Harmondsworth, 1963, p. 6.
47. Ibid., p. 40.
48. Ibid., p. 65.
49. London, 1945, p. 102.
50. Letter of August 24, 1845, in *Karl Marx–Friedrich Engels Gesamtausgabe*, 3, I, pp. 479–80.
51. *The Wealth of Nations*, IV, ix, 51.
52. 'I wished to set an example and burnt them all. I will not advise you to examine either your own or Mrs Eden's apparel or household furniture, least you be brought into a scrape of the same kind.' *The Correspondence of Adam Smith*, ed. E. C. Mossner and I. S. Ross, Oxford, 1977, No. 203, p. 246: to Sir Wm Eden.
53. *The Wealth of Nations*, I, iv, 2.
54. *The Wealth of Nations*, IV, i, 19.
55. J. Bonar, *A Catalogue of the Library of Adam Smith*, London, 1932.
56. *The Fable of the Bees*, third ed., London, 1724, p. 10.
57. London, 1989, p. 251.
58. 'Fire burns, and water refreshes; heavy bodies descend, and lighter substances fly upwards, by the necessity of their own nature; nor was the invisible hand of Jupiter ever apprehended to be employed in those matters.' *The Principles which lead and direct Philosophical Enquiries illustrated by the History of Astronomy*, III, 2, in *Essays on Philosophical Subjects* ed. W. P. D. Wightman and J. C. Bryce, Oxford, 1980, p. 49.
59. Op. cit., IV, i, 10 in ed. D. D. Raphael and A. L. Macfie, Oxford, 1976, pp. 184–5. cf. Steuart, op. cit., II, XXII, p. 281: 'Modern luxury is *systematical*: it cannot make one step but at the expense of

an adequate equivalent, acquired by those who stand the most in need of the protection and assistance of their fellow-citizens.'

60. *The Wealth of Nations*, IV, ii, 9.
61. Hugh Paton ed., *A Series of Original Portraits and Character Etchings by the late John Kay*, Edinburgh, 1838, Vol. I, p. 75.
62. *Economic Philosophy*, Harmondsworth, 1964, p. 53.
63. In his early work, Smith recognised the perils of metaphor. 'And even we, while we have been endeavouring to represent all philosophical systems as mere inventions of the imagination ... have insensibly been drawn in, to make use of language expressing the connecting principles ... as if they were the real chains which Nature makes use of to bind together her several operations.' *Essays*, IV. 76.
64. Printed as appendix to *Correspondence*, p. 337.
65. *Absolute Value and Exchangeable Value: A Rough Draft, 1823* in *The Works and Correspondence of David Ricardo*, ed. P. Sraffa, with collaboration of M. H. Dobb, Cambridge, 1951, Vol. IV, pp. 361 and 396.
66. Alfred Marshall, *Principles of Economics: An Introductory Volume*, eighth ed., London 1930, p. 14.
67. M. F. Le Play, *Les Ouvriers européens: Etudes sur les travaux, la vie domestique et la condition morale des populations ouvrières de l'Europe*, Paris, 1855, p. 275.
68. *Principles of Political Economy*, London, 1909, pp. 487–8.
69. Marshall, op. cit., p. 22
70. *The Nation and Athenaeum*, October 18, 1930.
71. *Essays in Persuasion*, London, 1951, p. 369.
72. Ibid., p. 320.
73. *Crime and Punishment*, trans. D. Magarshack, Harmondsworth, 1966, p. 166.

8. Death in Dean St.

1. *Rob Roy*, Edinburgh, 1880, p. 22.
2. 'The Life of Works of John Home' in *Essays on Chivalry, Romance and the Drama*, London, 1888, p. 388.
3. 'Honour is a homicide and a bloodspiller, that gangs about making frays in the street; but Credit is a decent, honest man, that sits at

hame and makes the pat play . . . But touching Robin, I am of opinion he will befriend this young man if it is in his power. He has a good heart, puir Robin; and though I lost a matter o' twa hunder punds wi' his former engagements, and haena muckle expectation ever to see back my thousand pund Scots that he promises me e'enow, yet I will never say but what Robin means fair by a' men.' *Rob Roy*, Edinburgh, 1880, pp. 187–8.

4. *English Bards and Scotch Reviewers*, line 181.
5. Quoted in J. G. Lockhart, *Life of Sir Walter Scott*, London and New York, 1871, pp. 482 and 485.
6. *Werke*, Berlin and Weimar, 1981, Vol. 1, 105–6.
7. KF Edition, Vol. 10, Decca CD 433 477–2.
8. *The Philosophy of Money*, trans. T. Bottomore and D. Frisby, London and New York, 1990, p. 478.
9. *Karl Marx: Interviews and Recollections*, ed. D. McLellan, London and Basingstoke, 1981, p. 25.
10. *Karl Marx-Friedrich Engels Werke*, Berlin 1973 (hereafter *MEW*), 32, p. 75.
11. *Religion and the Rise of Capitalism*, London, 1990, p. 48.
12. *1848: Briefe von und an Herwegh*, ed. M. Herwegh, second ed., Munich, 1896, p. 328. In fact, this description was paraphrased by Marcel Herwegh out of his parents' letters.
13. 15: 1–14.
14. *Marx-Engels Gesamtausgabe*, Berlin 1975 (hereafter *MEGA*), 1, 1, p. 450.
15. Op. cit., Munich, 1967, pp. 91 and 92.
16. *MEGA* 1, 2, p. 164.
17. *MEGA*, ibid., p. 166.
18. *MEGA*, ibid., p. 168.
19. A. Ruge, *Briefwechsel und Tagebuchblätter aus den Jahren 1825–1880*, Berlin, 1886, Vol. 1, pp. 343–4.
20. *Organisation du Crédit et de la Circulation et Solution du Problème social*, Paris, 1849, p. 23.
21. *MEGA* 1, 2, pp. 268–9 and 392–3.
22. *MEGA*, ibid., pp. 279 and 419.
23. *MEW*, 31, p. 542.
24. *The German Ideology*, Moscow, 1976, p. 53.
25. 'We have learnt, then, that after a person's own faeces, his excrement, has lost its value for him, this instinctual interest derived

from the anal source passes over on to objects that can be presented as *gifts*. And this is rightly so, for faeces were the first gift that an infant could make, something he could part with out of love for whoever was looking after him. After this . . . this ancient interest in faeces is transferred into the high valuation of *gold* and *money*.' Sigmund Freud, *New Introductory Lectures, XXXII: Anxiety and Instinctual Life* in *Complete Works*, trans. James Strachey and Anna Freud, London, 1964, Vol. XXII, p. 100.

26. 'Zur Einleitung der Behandlung,' *Int. Z. Psychoanal*: 1, 1913, pp. 1–10, in *Works*, Vol XII, p. 131.

27. Printed in *Die neue Zeit*, Stuttgart, XVI. II, 1897–8, pp. 486 and 488.

28. 'Un Voyage à Cythère'.

29. *Dernières Lettres Inédites a sa Mère*, ed. J. Crépet, Paris, 1826, p. 44.

30. 'À propos de Baudelaire' in *Chroniques*, Paris, 1927, p. 224.

31. Ibid., p. 217.

32. G. Benn, *Gesammelte Werke*, ed. D. Wellershof, Wiesbaden, 1968, Vol. 8, *Autobiographische Schriften*, p. 1884.

33. One of those concerts shimmering with brass with which the soldiers sometimes drench our public squares and which, on those golden evenings when we suddenly seem to come alive, upend a little heroism into our civilian hearts.

9. The Sheet of Glass

1. *John Buchan: A Memoir*, London, 1982, p. 61.

2. The teller at the Arms Bank in Glasgow was so skilled in obstruction, deliberately miscounting or accidentally dropping coins on the floor, that it once took him 34 working days to cash £2,893 into coin.

3. II, ii, 43.

4. 'The facility which it has afforded to the industrious and enterprising agriculturalist or manufacturer, as well as to the trustees of the public in executing national works, has converted Scotland, from a poor and miserable, and barren country, into one, where, if Nature has done less, Art and Industry have done more, than in perhaps any country in Europe, England herself not excepted.' Malachi Malagrowther, pseud., *Thoughts on the Proposed Change of Currency*

and other Late Alterations as they Affect, or are Intended to Affect, the Kingdom of Scotland, Edinburgh, 1826, pp. 21–2.

5. Alan Cameron, *Bank of Scotland 1695–1995*, Edinburgh and London, 1995, p. 11.

6. *PA*, September 29, 1883.

7. Reproduced in Cameron, op. cit., p. 139.

8. *PA*, October 26, 1878.

9. *Pamphlets: City of Glasgow Bank*, Edinburgh, 1879, frontispiece.

10. *PA*, October 26, 1878.

11. Anna Buchan (O. Douglas), *Unforgettable, Unforgotten*, London, 1945, p. 22.

12. *Pamphlets*, p. 226.

13. *PA*, February 8, 1879.

14. *Buchan* vs. *The City of Glasgow Bank and Liquidators*, Court of Session, 1st Division, January 23, 1879, in *Cases decided in the Court of Session etc, from July 20, 1878, to July 19, 1879*, Fourth Series, Vol. VI.

15. *Buchan*, etc, House of Lords, May 20, 1879, in *The Scottish Law Reporter*, Vol. XVI, pp. 512–16.

16. *Pamphlets*, p. 8.

17. *Unforgettable, Unforgotten*, p. 19.

18. 'Fountainblue,' *The Watcher by the Threshold*, 1902; also *The Power House*, 1916, where it is the central notion.

10. Mississippi Dreaming: Reprise

1. *The Education of Henry Adams: An Autobiography*, New York, 1918, p. 329.

2. La Farge reported later that Adams, on their return from Japan in 1886, had told Saint Gaudens in his studio in New York that the figure should symbolise 'the acceptance, intellectually, of the inevitable.' Adams mentioned as models a female Buddha he had been shown by Fenollosa in Japan and the Sistine Madonna in Rome. Saint Gaudens wrote in his notebook: 'Adams – Buhda – Mental Repose – Calm reflection in contrast with the violence or force in nature.' *Washington Evening Star*, January 17, 1910, and Burke Wilkinson, *The Life and Works of Augustus Saint Gaudens*, New York, 1985, pp. 235–6.

3. *The Letters of Mrs Henry Adams 1865–1883*, ed. Ward Thoron, Boston, 1936, p. 384.

4. *Education*, p. 330.

5. Ibid., p. 247.

6. Ibid., p. 328.

7. Theodore James, Jr., *The Empire State Building*, New York, 1975, p. 87.

8. Toni Morrison, *Jazz*, London, 1992, p. 34.

9. New York, 1987.

10. London, 1970, p. 152.

11. Op. cit., p. 228.

12. *The Wings of the Dove*, London, 1965, p. 228.

13. Ibid., p. 55.

14. Ibid., pp. 129–30. Of a simpler version of James' style, deployed in *The Portrait of a Lady*, Clover Adams commented: 'It's not that he "bites off more than he can chaw" . . . but he chaws more than he bites off.' *Letters*, ed. Thoron, p. 306.

15. A dollar promised a hundred years from now is worth much less than a dollar today, because it misses the interest today's dollar will earn during that century. At 10 per cent interest, the hundred-year dollar is worth only a fraction of a fraction of a cent today or, for most purposes, nothing. That is why a 99-year lease on a house, at present interest, is indistinguishable from a holding at freehold or fee simple.

16. On April 24, 1990, Milken confessed in federal court in Manhattan to six felonies, was sentenced that November to ten years in gaol, and served twenty-two months.

17. A zero bond pays no interest, but is issued at a discount to its face value and redeemed at that face value: the difference between the issue and redemption prices, projected back across the years, has the character of interest. Adjustable-rate debentures offered low interest at first but promised, as the issuer restored its ruined condition, a higher rate down the line.

18. F. W. Taussig, *Inventors and Money-Makers*, New York, 1915, pp. 16–17.

19. London, 1993, p. 125.

20. Andrew Carnegie, *Autobiography*, London, 1920, Chapter XIX.

21. 'In 1889, H. C. Frick became chairman of Carnegie Brothers and Company. As he had aroused the antagonism of the labour world

through his suppression of the strike in the coke region a few years before, the mill men feared that he would crush the Amalgamated Association. More keen, therefore, than their interest in the points at issue was the belief that if they failed in this strike, the power, if not the very existence of the union, would go. This fear accounts for the pertinacity with which the struggle was fought to the finish and for the deep-seated bitterness which followed the men's defeat. The strike began June 30 . . . Shortly after the trouble began, the company attempted to bring into the mill some 300 men in charge of Pinkerton detectives . . . The detectives started up the river in boats in the early morning of July 6, and a scout who had been stationed by the strikers came on horseback to warn the town . . . Men and women hurried to the mill, weapons were hunted up and barricades erected. Which side fired the first shot is still a debated question, but a miniature battle followed in which seven persons were killed and others wounded. The Pinkertons finally surrendered, were brought into the town and later were returned to Pittsburgh. There are conflicting stories as to the incidents of the day, stories of bloodshed and cruelty. The one clear fact is that the mob fury latent in most men was wakened by that first shot. It is hard to believe that the sober, self-contained workmen who told me the story fifteen years afterwards had been part of the frenzied crowd on the river bank.' Margaret F. Byington, *Homestead: The Households of a Mill Town*, Pittsburgh, 1910, pp. 8–9.

22. S. N. Behrman, *Duveen*, London, 1952, p. 116.
23. *Statements Submitted by Members of J. P. Morgan & Co to the Senate Committee on Banking and Currency at its Hearings in Washington, May 23 to June 9, 1933:* Testimony of June 9, 1933.
24. Quoted in W. Greider, *Secrets of the Temple: How the Federal Reserve Runs the Country*, New York, 1987, p. 300.
25. Savannah Unit, Georgia Writers Project, WPA, *Drums and Shadows: Survival Studies among the Georgia Coastal Negroes*, Athens, Georgia, 1940; reprinted, Athens, Georgia, and London, 1986, p. 58.

11. The Sinews of War

1. *Mémoires*, 1826, I, p. 129.
2. *Dans les pays ou il n'y a point de monnoie . . . rien ne peut être caché,*

parce que le ravisseur porte toujours avec lui des preuves de sa conviction; cela n'est pas de même dans les [pays ou il y a de la monnoie.] De l'Esprit des Lois, XVIII, 16.

3. Phil. V, 2.

4. perchè l'oro non e sufficiente a trovare i buoni soldati, ma i buoni soldati sono bene sufficienti a trovare l'oro. Machiavelli, Discorsi sopra la Prima Deca di Tito Livio, 1531, II, 10.

5. Considerazioni intorno ai Discorsi di Machiavelli sopra la prima deca di Tito Livio in Opere Inedite, Florence, 1857, Vol. 1, p. 62.

6. Political Arithmetick, 30, in The Economic Writings of Sir William Petty, ed. Hull, Vol. I, p. 266.

7. Mémoires, Vol. 1, pp. 205ff.

8. Oeuvres de J. Law, Paris, 1790, p. xvii.

9. The estimate of ten thousand is taken from conversations with reporters on the war, notably Patrick Cockburn of the London Independent.

10. Hamlet, Act IV, Scene iv, 17–27.

11. Shelby Foote, The Civil War: A Narrative, New York, 1958, Vol. 1, p. 339.

12. Quoted in Keynes, The Economic Consequences of the Peace, London, 1919, Chapter 5.

13. L'ultimo fallimento de' Bardi, che quasi assorbì tutte le ricchezze dei privati. . . . S. Ammirato, Istorie Fiorentine, Book 10, Turin, 1853, Vol. 3, p. 96.

14. 'How to Pay for the War' in The Times of November 1939, reprinted in the Collected Writings of John Maynard Keynes, London, 1971–89, Vol. XXII.

15. This account is taken from R. S. Sayers, Financial Policy 1939–1945, London, 1956, and D. E. Moggridge, Maynard Keynes: An Economist's Biography, London and New York, 1992.

16. Monetary Stability: Rhyme or Reason, Seventh Annual Lecture of the Economic and Social Research Council, October 17, 1996.

17. Della Moneta, Naples, 1750, pp. 262–3.

18. Mein Kampf, 129th edition, Munich, 1935, p. 234.

19. Hitler, op. cit., pp. 255–7.

20. W. Fischer, Deutsche Wirtschaftspolitik 1918–1945, Opladen, 1968, p. 102.

21. Brief des Präsidenten des Reichsbank-Direktoriums an den Führer und Reichskanzler vom 7. Januar 1939, Bundesarchiv, Az. R. 43 II/234,

partially reproduced in photostat in *Währung und Wirtschaft in Deutschland 1876–1975*, Frankfurt a.M., 1976, pp. 381–3.

22. *Statistiches Handbuch von Deutschland 1928–1944*, hrsg. vom Länderrat des Amerikanischen Besatzungsgebiet, München, 1949, p. 555.
23. *Februarbericht 1944*, MS quoted by Adler, op. cit., p. 443.
24. Ibid., p. 124.
25. *Erlebnisse einer deutschen Jüdin in Berlin, Theresienstadt und Deggendorf*, MS, London, quoted in Adler, ibid., p. 734.
26. Ibid., p. 168.
27. Ibid., p. 189.
28. *Besøg i Theresienstadt*, MS, Copenhagen, 1944. Translated from Adler's German translation, op. cit., p. 714.
29. *Bundesbankgesetz*, 26. Juli, 1957, Par III. '*Sie ist bei der Ausübung der Befugnisse . . . von Weisungen der Bundesregierung unabhängig.*'
30. Quoted in J. Schumpeter, *Ten Great Economists*, Oxford, 1952, p. 182.

12. Money: A Valediction

1. *Lezione delle Monete* before the Florence Academy, May 1, 1588; in P. Custodi, *Scrittori Classici Italiani di Economia Politica*, Milan, 1803–4, p. 33. Translation by John Toland, *A Discourse upon Coins*, London 1696, p. 15.
2. D. E. Moggridge, *Maynard Keynes: An Economist's Biography*, London and New York, 1992, p. 96.
3. Ibid., pp. 838–9.
4. Ibid., p. 798.
5. Op. cit., London, 1936, p. 293.
6. Ibid., p. 376.
7. Ibid., pp. 220–1 and 376.
8. *Tavallodi Digar*, Tehran, 1967.
9. *A Tract on Monetary Reform*, London, 1923, p. 8.
10. *Economic and Philosophic Manuscripts*, Moscow, 1959, p. 109.
11. *The Wealth of Nations*, II, ii, 86.
12. *Wenn sodann an die Stelle der Gegenstände der Lüste, für welche der Sinn abgestorben ist, der abstracte Repräsentant aller dieser Gegenstände, das Geld, tritt . . . dann hat sich . . . der Wille . . . in die letzte Festung*

geworfen, in welcher nur noch der Tod ihn belagert. Der Zweck des Daseins ist verfehlt. From *Die Welt als Wille und Vorstellung*, Chapter 49, in *Sämtliche Werke*, Darmstadt, 1968, II, 819.

13. *Hoch verursachte Schutzrede und antwwort wider das gaistlose Sanfft lebende fleysch zu Wittenberg*, 1524, in *Aus dem Kampf der Schwärmer gegen Luther: Drei Flugschriften*, ed. L. Enders, Halle, 1893, p. 25.

14. *Political Essays*, ed. K. Haakonssen, Cambridge, 1994, p. 171.

15. 'On the Want of Money' in *Selected Essays*, ed. G. Keynes, London, 1970, p. 311.

Index